THE
FIRST
SHOWMAN

CIRCUS CLOWN AT FAIR.

THE
FIRST
SHOWMAN

THE EXTRAORDINARY MR ASTLEY

THE ENGLISHMAN WHO INVENTED
THE MODERN CIRCUS

KARL SHAW

AMBERLEY

Page 1: 'Billy Buttons' in 1861: the knockabout equestrian act was still a huge crowd-puller nearly a hundred years after Astley created it.

Page 3: Trick riders in the early American circus. Library of Congress.

First published 2019

Amberley Publishing
The Hill, Stroud
Gloucestershire, GL5 4EP

www.amberley-books.com

Copyright © Karl Shaw, 2019

The right of Karl Shaw to be identified as the Author of this work has been asserted in accordance with the Copyrights, Designs and Patents Act 1988.

ISBN 978 1 4456 9549 5 (hardback)
ISBN 978 1 4456 9550 1 (ebook)

British Library Cataloguing in Publication Data. A catalogue record for this book is available from the British Library.

Typesetting by Aura Technology and Software Services, India. Printed in the UK.

CONTENTS

An Astley Family Tree

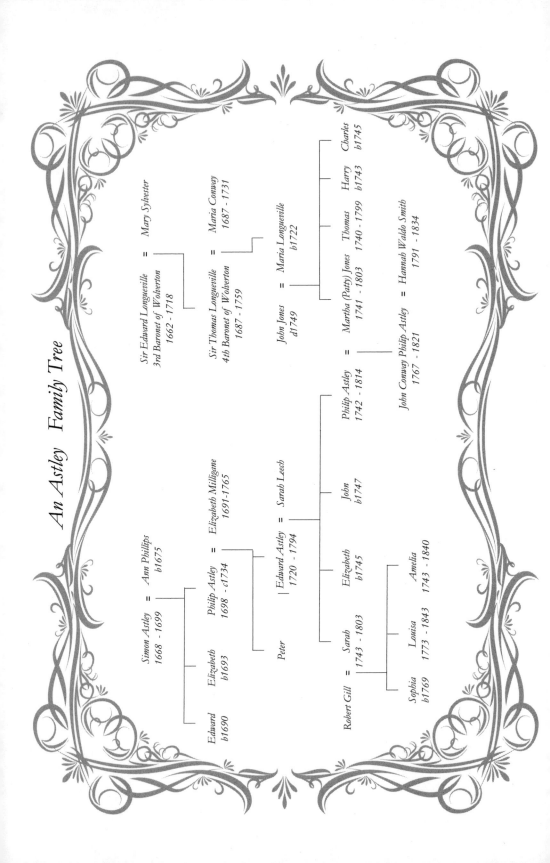

Sir Edward Longueville
3rd Baronet of Wolverton
1662 - 1718
= Mary Sylvester

Sir Thomas Longueville
4th Baronet of Wolverton
1687 - 1759
= Maria Conway
1687 - 1731

John Jones
d1749
= Maria Longueville
b1722

Thomas
1740 - 1799

Harry
b1743

Charles
b1745

Martha (Patty) Jones
1741 - 1803
= John Conway Philip Astley
1767 - 1821
= Hannah Waldo Smith
1791 - 1834

Simon Astley
1668 - 1699
= Ann Phillips
b1675

Edward
b1690

Elizabeth
b1693

Philip Astley
1698 - c1734
= Elizabeth Milligane
1691-1765

Peter

Edward Astley
1720 - 1794
= Sarah Leech

John
b1747

Philip Astley
1742 - 1814

Elizabeth
b1745

Robert Gill
= Sarah
1743 - 1803

Sophia
b1769

Louisa
1773 - 1843

Amelia
1743 - 1840

ACKNOWLEDGEMENTS

Many thanks to Beryl Carter, Andrew Van Buren and the Brampton Museum research team for sharing their work on Philip Astley's family history.

Thank you to the Garrick Club and the Van Buren Org for giving me permission to reproduce images from their private collections.

A special thanks to Andrew and his family for being generous with their time and sharing with me their remarkable journey.

INTRODUCTION

Easter Monday 1784. London is experiencing its coldest, wettest April for years. An Icelandic volcano has spewed a plume of toxic fumes over northern Europe, blocking out the sun and killing as it spreads. The chill is accompanied by a sulphurous, suffocating fog so thick that Londoners can barely see objects a few steps away and fit young men struggle for breath. A drunk has stumbled into the foul waters of the Fleet ditch and is found drowned, gripping his bottle of rotgut gin. The sick and gout-ridden Dr Johnson writes a letter to his friend Rev. Taylor praying for warmer weather. Despite the unseasonable conditions, the people of Lambeth Marsh are out and about in their holiday best and determined to make the best of it. At the foot of the Surrey side of Westminster Bridge, not far from the muddy foreshore of the Thames, next to a row of timber yards lying under the blanket of fine ash that fell with the hailstones the previous evening, shafts of orange light stream from gaps in a curious wooden structure, accompanied by bursts of thunderous applause. Outside the building are a dozen carriages waiting to take their owners home, their drivers dozing in their seats, or loitering in groups to share tobacco and curse the smog.

The two and a half thousand people packed inside Astley's Amphitheatre are oblivious to the conditions outside. It is 8.30pm and the ripe smell of horse manure, candles, sweat and orange peel hangs heavily in the air. Those who came early and paid the full price of two shillings have already sat through a two-hour bill featuring jugglers, strongmen, vaulters, a 'sagacious dog', a slack rope-walker who can spin on his line 'like a roasted pig', and a man who can play two flutes through his nose at the same time. In the centre, bathed in candlelight, is a sawdust-covered ring. The audience, sitting around the ring on their rickety benches, crunching on nuts, handing round oranges, flirting and heckling, falls silent. All eyes are on a tall, portly man who steps into this small opening amid the sea of enshrouding darkness. His military bearing disguises a slight limp, discernible only to those who know him well. He pauses to scan the pit, the boxes and the stalls, then allows himself a small smile, satisfied that despite the weather the late-arriving half-price customers have filled the house almost to capacity. 'My Lords, Ladies and Gentlemen! I give you Billy Buttons, or A Tailor Riding to Brentford!' His booming voice soars beyond the rafters and out into the night sky, then he bows and withdraws. Now everyone's attention is fixed on a solitary horse standing patiently in the ring. Billy appears and darts towards the horse. Billy is a clown, but he isn't wearing clown make-up or brightly coloured clothes. He has the look of a ragged, down-at-heel country yokel, his half-mast trousers flapping as he runs. He builds up speed then leaps onto the horse's saddle. Just as he is about to land, the horse takes a sideways step, leaving the clown sprawling. The audience laughs and applauds – they know that Billy's clumsiness requires split-second timing. He tries to mount again and fails. When he eventually succeeds, the horse refuses to budge at first, but then it bolts and Billy hits the ground hard. There are many more attempts, each funnier than the last, until the hapless rider is astride his horse but facing the wrong way. Finally, the animal ejects the tatterdemalion Billy from his saddle and chases him around the ring.

The audience rocks with laughter. Some of them have seen the routine many times before but it never grows old. The Tailor's

Ride has been a huge favourite since the proprietor of Astley's first performed it himself twelve years ago in a virtuoso comic performance that ran (and somewhere in the world is still running) for longer than any other clown act in history. The crowd claps and cheers and stamp their feet, then the hottest show in town moves on to the next act.

This is a circus, but not quite a circus as our parents and grandparents would have known it. They would be puzzled by the almost complete absence of children in the audience. There are no elephants or caged lions and tigers. The only beasts are domestic animals and a wire-walking monkey. Yet much of it would be reassuringly familiar. The ringmaster with his whip, the colour, the spectacle, the excitement, the stirring music, the clowns and acrobats, the forty-two-feet ring.

The big man in the top hat is Philip Astley. He is known by many names: Big Philip, Father Philip, Amphi-Philip, 'the most handsome man in England'. A showbiz writer today might describe him as 'larger than life', but this would be a massive understatement: colossal would be nearer the mark. Over six feet tall with a hot temper and a voice like a foghorn, he is impossible to ignore or forget. To some people he's a crude, ignorant, autocratic bully. Others are amazed by his stamina, or just amused by his bluntness and his simple devotion to king and country. By his customers, the paying public, he is universally adored. In an age that isn't yet obsessed with celebrity, his name is known not just in all four corners of the United Kingdom but in towns and cities right across Europe, where he erected a multitude of jerry-built amphitheatres, mad structures made from ships' spars and fir-poles that burned like matchwood. Everyone agrees that his most outstanding characteristic is courage. This he displays in all the crises of his life, in combat and in the ring and in the many adversities and financial reverses which have often threatened to overwhelm him.

If you look up the history of the circus the chances are you'll be told that it is a direct descendant of the circuses of Ancient Rome.

The most famous of its alleged forebears was Circus Maximus, a huge stadium rebuilt on the site of earlier models by Julius Caesar in the first century AD, capable of holding up to 150,000 spectators around an oval-shaped arena; *circus* is the Latin for circle or ring. It was where Romans went to watch chariots thunder around, or gladiators hack off each other's limbs, or slaughter exotic animals.

In truth, apart from sharing a name, the modern circus has nothing at all in common with the blood-drenched sands of the Circus Maximus. Most of the key elements we associate with the circus – clowning, acrobatics, juggling, strongmen, balancing acts – are probably as old as humankind itself and were evident in most civilisations through history. There are drawings of jugglers and acrobats on the walls of Egyptian tombs and Minoan frescoes of young acrobats jumping over charging bulls. They were mostly small groups of roving performers with special talents who wandered through Europe, Africa and Asia, entertaining people wherever they gathered, on street corners, marketplaces, fairs and communal celebrations. The staple of circus life – the clown – goes back even further, with roots in performances given during the Fifth Dynasty of Ancient Egypt. The modern idea of clowning grew out of the Italian tradition of *commedia dell 'arte* that began in the sixteenth century.

In Britain, most of these entertainments – tumbling, rope-dancing, juggling, animal tricks and trick-riding – were familiar sights in traditional fairs for centuries. Most towns and villages had their travelling players, jugglers and dancers who would arrive from somewhere or other and pitch up for a few days with booths and makeshift stages at harvest festivals. Some strung taut ropes high above the fair and walked from one side to the other, drawing curious folk hoping to see them lose their footing and fall. Others walked barefoot on coals, or devoured whole cats, or could balance several men on planks across their chests. Some brought animals along to perform tricks: monkeys in costumes climbed ropes, turkeys danced on hot plates, there were dogs that could read your mind. Others leaped, vaulted, somersaulted, tumbled and cartwheeled their way to earning a few coins dropped into a hat. Then they all moved on to who-knows-where.

The modern circus truly began two hundred and fifty years ago with Philip Astley. He was the first person to gather all of these acts together in one venue for a single admission price. By plundering the past, he created something completely new, something very familiar yet thrillingly strange and exciting. It was brazen, fleet-footed, agile-limbed, dangerous, magnificent and above all, ridiculously entertaining. It wouldn't be a stretch to regard the day of Astley's very first show as the birth date of modern popular culture.

Before the elephants and the freaks, before the big tops, a hundred years before P.T. Barnum ever sold a ticket to a show, Astley was the world's original circus mogul, an artist-cum-entrepreneur of astute judgement (mostly) and herculean work ethic. He was a natural born showman with an eye for every kind of popular entertainment. He understood that how you hooked the public was just as important as what you showed them. Unlike Barnum, he didn't foist spectacular frauds on gullible patrons. If Big Philip promised to show you a man (or woman) standing on their head in the saddle, riding around the ring while covered in bees, that's exactly what you got and then some.

For the best part of a hundred years Astley's Amphitheatre[1] (he never called it a circus) was a regular fixture on London tourist itineraries, a must-see destination for all classes. Long after his death and well into the late Victorian era, his brand was one of the best known and most successful in show business.

---

[1]   All through his career Astley was forever tinkering with the name of his venue: Astley's Riding School, The British Riding School, The British Riding Academy, Astley's Amphitheatre of the Arts, the Royal Grove and Amphitheatre, the Royal Saloon and Astley's Royal Amphitheatre and so on. Generally I've stuck to calling it his Amphitheatre because that's the name everyone remembered it by.

He left his mark, too, on the history and literature of the age: 'Going to Astley's' was a familiar storyline used by many writers including Charles Dickens, Jane Austen and William Thackeray, among others.

His life outside the ring was the stuff of *Boy's Own* comics. He ran away from home to join the army and became a war hero twice over. When he wasn't busy managing his business empire he was publishing hand-illustrated maps of the battlefields of Europe or writing books on horsemanship and magic tricks, or acting as unofficial chief of fireworks for the King or charging people to see some of Britain's first ever hot air balloon ascents. He rarely did anything that didn't make the newspapers. Anecdotes about 'Old Astley' were a staple of London legend and myths attached themselves to him as surely as the whiff of horse piss clung to his boots. Even allowing for exaggeration, he was a character as improbable as any invented by Dickens.

Philip Astley lived through extraordinary times. Born in the reign of King George II while Britain was at war with France, he died in the reign of George IV a few months short of Waterloo. In his early manhood, Britain lost her American colonies and Captain Cook circumnavigated Australasia – the Georgian equivalent of deep space – then was murdered in Hawaii. Britain locked away a mad king, France sent hers to the guillotine. At home there were violent confrontations between the government and the people, with London's worst ever riots taking place right on his doorstep.

For all Philip Astley's adventures and his achievements, he has been largely forgotten. If it wasn't for the efforts of a dedicated few who try to keep his memory alive, it is possible you may never have heard of him. His hopes of founding a personal circus dynasty died with his brilliant but flawed son, John. As the memory that the nation once held of the showman faded, so a semi-fictional version of him grew. He was caricatured by many circus historians as a grandiloquent buffoon; in mainstream theatre history he is little more than a footnote. The circus, too, has occupied an ever-diminishing role in popular culture, written off by some as a cruel entertainment from another age. In the late twentieth century, when people thought of the big top, instead of a glittering spectacle featuring incredible feats by human and animal, it was all too easy to conjure up images of chained elephants and big cats in cages. In a couple of decades, animal welfare activists turned a two-hundred-and-fifty-year-old art form into a cultural pariah.

But the circus is bouncing back. In a British circus you will no longer find big cats, dancing bears or sea lions balancing on balls. The last elephant paraded around the ring for the final time a decade ago. As animal acts have fallen out of favour, the entertainments have come full circle and many circuses are thriving with human-only performers celebrating individual artistry. Learning human circus skills has never been more popular. New and innovative shows are reclaiming the arena and pulling in the crowds with genre-bending acts. Some are offering equestrian acts alongside the clowns, the jugglers and the acrobats, just as Philip Astley intended it. Historians and cultural critics are also now paying more attention to the circus arts and a more balanced and sympathetic understanding is starting to emerge. It is time, too, to rediscover its creator's epic seventy-two years on this Earth.

This, then, is the story of a young trick-rider who staked out a ring, hired a clown and gave birth to the modern circus, and of how his struggle to stay one step ahead of his rivals in the greedy and cruel world of Georgian England gave rise to the greatest show on earth.

I

THE THREE HATS

Thomas Topham, celebrated Islington strongman and landlord of The Three Hats. Courtesy of the Wellcome Collection.

In the 1700s the airy suburb of Islington was a semi-rural hamlet north of London, a sort of dairy-farm for the metropolis, once as famous for its cheesecakes as Chelsea for its buns. It was a place where Londoners went to spend their summer evenings, relaxing in the local taverns and tea gardens. At the lower end of the hamlet was an inn called The Three Hats, a picture-postcard balconied hostelry on Upper Street near to the turnpike gate welcoming the Liverpool stage coach. It was once kept by Thomas Topham, the celebrated 'strong man of Islington'. With his fingers, the landlord of The Three Hats could roll up a pewter dish weighing seven pounds 'as a man rolls up a sheet of paper'. In anger he could twist a kitchen spit round the neck of a man, as he once did to a local shop owner who insulted him. Topham lifted the twenty-seven-stone vicar of All Saints with one hand while entertaining the crowd with a rendition of Mad Tom', although in a voice 'more terrible than sweet'. The landlord walked with a slight limp, having put his knee out while losing a tug-of-war with two horses. Towards the end of his life he took another public house in Hog Lane, Shoreditch. It was there, distressed by the infidelity of his wife, that the unhappy giant stabbed her to death, then killed himself. Buried in the church of St. Leonard's, Shoreditch, shortly afterwards he was spirited away by the resurrection men for surgical dissection.

By the 1750s The Three Hats was Islington's favourite Sunday resort. In a field at the back of the inn, the new landlord, a man with less brawn but more business brain, laid out a spacious green surrounded with a circle of boxes in which customers could drink tea while listening to music. The venue had various other attractions, including skittles and a manly diversion called Double Stick, where young men competed 'to brake (sic) the most heads' to win a prize.

In 1758 the landlord of The Three Hats engaged an ex-groom called Thomas Johnson and charged people a shilling to see him perform extraordinary, dare-devil feats on horseback.

The Irish Tartar, as Johnson was known, rode while standing on the saddle of one horse, and with feet astride on two, then three horses. He turned somersaults, rode backwards and mounted and dismounted at a full gallop. He could even ride a horse while standing on his head, a trick it took him eleven years to perfect.

The art of trick-riding goes back to the ancient Romans. At their games, acrobatic riders called *desultores* would race four or more horses abreast and leap from one to another. In the tenth century, a stable boy called Philoroeus entertained the Byzantine public by galloping around an arena standing on the back of a horse while juggling a razor-sharp sword. Renaissance court equestrians such as Louis XIII's riding-master Monsieur Pluvinel choreographed their horses for lavish exhibitions in a *grand ballette-dance*. In England, where riding had long been the popular pastime of the rich, nobles built riding schools for instruction in the finer arts of horsemanship.

Then the bottom fell out of the horse-trading market. Around the end of the seventeenth century, there was a flood of horses into the marketplace and their prices plummeted. For the first time in history, almost anyone could afford to own a horse. The English nobility, feeling the pinch of a downturn, closed their private ménages and suddenly the country had an abundance of unemployed riding-masters. Some became showmen, performing tricks in open fields near taverns and on village greens. They were a great novelty and drew such crowds that small fortunes could be made by passing round a hat to collect loose change, a practice known as 'doing a mob.'

The first-documented of these professional trick-riders was Jacob Bates from Newmarket. Bates entertained his audiences with extraordinary acts of horsemanship, often straddling up to four horses at a time. He was the first English equestrian to take his act abroad, travelling the length and breadth of Europe. In 1773 Bates went to America, performing in New York, Boston and other cities, towns and villages of New England and the mid-Atlantic. William Ellery[2] saw one of his electrifying performances:

> The famous Jacob Bates hath lately exhibited here his most surprising feats of horsemanship, in a circus or enclosure of about one hundred and twenty feet in diameter, erected at the east end of Mr Honyman's field. The number of spectators was from three to seven hundred. He exhibited four times, and took half a dollar for a ticket. I must confess, indeed, there is something manly and generous in the exhibitions of Mr Bates; for a well-formed man, and a well-shaped, well-limbed, well-sized horse, are fine figures, and in his manage are displayed amazing strength, resolution, and activity.

Bates stayed in America and established a riding school in Philadelphia. Back in England, meanwhile, there was a new the wave of trick-riders, many of them ex-cavalrymen recently returned from fighting abroad, offering thrilling displays of athleticism, strength, power and daring horsemanship of a type that, as one snooty continental visitor remarked, 'a certain type of Londoner cannot see too often'.

In the 1760s Islington was the epicentre of the trick-riding craze. The Irish Tartar, by common consent the greatest of them all, continued his dazzling exhibitions at The Three Hats and elsewhere for the next nine years. James Boswell enjoyed seeing him perform in Chelsea in 1763 – but was even more delighted later that day to meet a prostitute, one of the many from whom he contracted seventeen separate bouts of venereal disease. Thomas Johnson's performances drew all classes. In 1766 the Duke of York was among a crowd of around five hundred spectators who went to see him at Islington.

Even some of the Irish Tartar's spectacular feats were put in the shade by those performed by his successors. His residency at The

---

2   A signatory of the Declaration of Independence.

Three Hats was taken by a new equestrian superstar, a handsome, dashing ex-cavalryman, lately discharged from Lord Ancram's 11th Light Dragoons, known only as 'Old Sampson'. Sampson kept his customers in a state of constant amazement with 'the grandest feats of horsemanship that were ever attempted.' He stood in the saddle on one leg while his horse was at full pelt, hung so low that his hand brushed the ground, dismounted at full speed, fired his pistol then remounted.

Sampson had a rival. Just down the road from The Three Hats, Dobney's Tea Gardens and Bowling Green took its name from the widowed former owner. It had boxes with refreshments, painted with different scenes from Shakespeare's plays. When old Mrs Dobney died in 1760 the new proprietor, anxious to extend his business, converted the bowling green into a ménage and poached from The Three Hats their second-string, but no less flamboyant, equestrian performer Thomas Price to exhibit 'original feats of horsemanship'. At Dobney's, Price jumped over a three-foot bar while standing on two horses, picking up a whip from the ground at full speed, riding while simultaneously spinning plates on top of canes held in each hand.

Sampson was arguably the better equestrian, but Price was an astute showman and a formidable competitor. All through the summer of 1767 he and Sampson went head-to-head, winning customers and stealing hearts. For Price it became more than a business rivalry. While working at The Three Hats, Price became fixated on a beautiful young horsewoman. He was jealous of Sampson's success with ladies: insanely so, when he found out that object of his unrequited love only had eyes for his rival. Sampson seduced and married her, then employed her, billing his conquest as 'the First Equestrienne'. This advertisement appeared in the *Public Advertiser* later that year:

Mr Sampson begs to inform the public that besides the usual feats which he exhibits, Mrs Sampson, to diversify the entertainment and prove that the fair sex are by no means inferior to the male, either in courage or agility, will this and every evening during the summer season perform various exercises in the same act, in which she hopes to acquaint herself to the universal approbation of those ladies and gentlemen whose curiosity may induce them to honour her attempt with their company!

Price plotted revenge. Together they went to the tavern in Bagnigge Wells, where Price got his rival very drunk before introducing him to a local harlot. Sampson woke up the next morning in a strange bedroom without his trousers. The woman demanded fifty guineas for their return, threatening to inform his wife unless he paid up. When word got back to the distressed Mrs Sampson that her missing husband was not lying in a gutter somewhere with his throat cut by footpads, but had spent the night in the arms of a prostitute, she packed her bags and left. The beaten Sampson wallowed in drink and self-pity. The public deserted him too and went to Dobney's.

Poor Sampson was replaced by a rider called Coningham, who could vault over two horses while they jumped an obstacle, or play the flute as he stood on their backs. Sampson fell into debt and was forced to sell Coningham his entire stud and work for him as a rider. Price made a fortune and was able to retire. It was said he earned himself over £14,000 from his performances at home and abroad – about £3 million in today's values.[3] The wife of fallen hero Sampson returned eventually, but the couple was reduced to working for any showman who would take them. Meanwhile a new star had risen from the provinces. This young man would eclipse all of London's aspirants to equestrian glory, raising horsemanship to a level of excellence previously unknown.

---

3   His eldest son James settled in Scandinavia and founded a famous line of circus performers whose successors still perform in Copenhagen. While on horseback Price balanced on top of a ladder, shot bullets through previously selected cards thrown in the air by his wife and presented a fifteen-man pyramid, erected for reasons unknown 'in honour of Julius Caesar'.

Philip Astley opened his eyes on the world on 8 January 1742. It was a time when men were meant to know their place and, for Philip, that place was among the artisans and labourers of North Staffordshire. It was never the destination of choice for people looking to spend a weekend in picturesque surroundings. Arnold Bennett – perhaps the best and most successful novelist you've never heard of, unless you are from that part of the world or have eaten his eponymous omelette – was another, like young Astley, who left to make his mark elsewhere. An entry in his journal written forty years after the author departed says it all: 'I took the 12:05 back to London, which went through the Potteries. The sight of this district gave me a shudder.' In *The Road to Wigan Pier* George Orwell was hardly more flattering: 'The pottery towns are almost equally ugly in a pettier way.[4] Right in among the rows of tiny blackened houses, part of the street as it were, are the "pot banks" – conical brick chimneys like gigantic burgundy bottles buried in the soil and belching their smoke almost in your face.' H.G. Wells used it as a dystopian backdrop in *War of the Worlds*. Describing the carnage after the Martians had just zapped a train, he wrote: 'It was the strangest spectacle, that black expanse set with fire. It reminded me, more than anything else, of the Potteries at night.'

The features that Wells and others found so grotesque were a consequence of the region's unique geology. Beneath the undulating hills and valleys lies a vein of rust-red clay, contiguous to a subterranean seam of coal. Both of these natural resources are essential to the craft of the potter. Bricks, tiles and teapots were made there and delivered all around the world. At one time, more than two thousand great bottle-shaped kilns smoked against the sky, creating a permanent haze of pollution over the whole area. The clay-workers toiled in primitive conditions, men and women made old before their time and prone to a host of deadly

---

4   That is to say as ugly as Sheffield, in Orwell's estimation.

occupational diseases including the dreaded 'potter's rot'.[5] Today, the few kilns that remain exist as sanitised reminders of just how grim the working conditions were.

To the west of the grime and dust lies the market town of Newcastle-under-Lyme, cunningly disguised by Bennett in his books as Oldcastle. It takes its name from the ancient Forest of Lyme that once covered the area. The township has a reputation for producing feisty non-conformists. A local butcher's son, Tom Harrison, was one of the signatories to the death warrant for King Charles I. Come the Restoration, he was the first of the Regicides to be hanged, drawn and quartered by the House of Stuart. While his confederates fled for Europe and America, Tom Harrison sat at home, calmly waiting for his arrest. He took his punishment stoically. On the day of his execution at Charing Cross, Samuel Pepys reported him 'looking as cheerful as any man could do in that condition'. After being hanged for several minutes and cut open to reveal his entrails, the butcher's son leaned over and punched his executioner in the face. Much later, a local politician, Fanny Deakin, scourge of the right-wing press as 'Red Fanny', was a no-less fierce, indomitable campaigner for free milk for children and decent maternity care for their mothers, a sort of Maggie 'milk-snatcher' Thatcher in reverse. Fanny, like Tom Harrison, spoke a local dialect quite unlike anything used in the surrounding counties, so different from that spoken by people living just twenty miles south that it could have been a foreign language. It is an accent that has defied imitation on stage or screen despite the best efforts of fine actors who have tried. Even Bennett struggled to transcribe the speech patterns of his youth.

In the mid-1700s, Newcastle-under-Lyme was a decent-sized market town of around two thousand souls, a centre for dealing in grain, livestock and provisions. When Dr Richard Pococke

---

5   A form of silicosis caused by the inhalation of fine dust and lead poisoning from working with glazes.

visited it in 1750 he called it 'the capital of the Potteries'. Newcastle's relative prosperity arose from its position as a crucial road junction. The principal township straddled a well-worn coach road carrying travellers from London to Carlisle. Before the canals were built, the flint and clay used in pottery manufacture was also landed at Liverpool or Chester, then brought in via Newcastle and on to the other Pottery towns. The manufacturers were obliged to use the same roundabout route in the reverse direction with their finished crocks. Thanks to this transport monopoly, markets and fairs were held in Newcastle and it grew richer at the expense of the nearby 'six towns' – Burslem, Fenton, Hanley, Longton, Stoke and Tunstall.

The commercial backbone of the Newcastle township comprised dozens of small tradesmen. As well as clock makers, ironworkers and clay pipe-makers, the chief manufacture of the town was felt hats, which were prepared for London finishers, and nails, hammered into shape at the local iron market. There was also a small but thriving ceramics industry, with Joseph Wilson knocking out pots in Lower Street, but it was more of a place where the well-off pottery manufacturers and their families lived, away from the terrible pollution that their industry generated. The owner of the local drapery shop was the widowed Margaret, eldest sister of the master potter Josiah Wedgwood. The Reverend William Willet, the local Unitarian minister, was married to Josiah's younger sister Catherine.

When Dr Pococke passed through Newcastle, at least three generations of Astleys had lived in North Staffordshire. Philip's grandfather, another Philip, was a burgess of the town, a man of wealth and status. He married a local girl, Elizabeth Milligane. She, too, was from one of the town's most respectable families; her brother Richard was Newcastle's postmaster. Within a couple of years Elizabeth bore Philip two sons, first Edward then Peter. Their time together as a happy young family unit was all too brief. The younger boy died in infancy: with her eldest son barely in his teens Elizabeth was a widow, her husband dead before his thirty-fifth birthday. It was on the shoulders of young Edward that the future of the Astley family now rested.

When Edward was fourteen, his mother took him to London to be apprenticed as a joiner with one of the city's finest furniture makers, Giles Grendey. Apprenticeships were an attractive means of securing a child's future and an important part of leaving home and preparing for adulthood. For the teenage sons of well-to-do families, positions in London were the most sought after, but an apprenticeship in the city took considerable financial and organisational effort to arrange. It is likely the Astley family had good contacts there through the hat trade and that Edward's mother was calling in a favour.

Grendey was a cabinetmaker and timber merchant with workshops near St. Paul's. He enjoyed the patronage of the nobility and, unusually for an English cabinetmaker of his day, he also had a flourishing export business. Grendey was a difficult man when crossed. One of his apprentices petitioned for a discharge from his service on the grounds that his employer had beaten him 'in a very barbarous manner, sometimes with a great stick and at other times knocking him downe (sic) and then kicking him in the face and other parts'.[6] All the same, an indenture with a fashionable master craftsman in the metropolis was a golden opportunity and the potential rewards were great. But Edward was delinquent and he failed to complete his apprenticeship. When he was twenty-one years old, the prodigal returned home with a pregnant bride, having secretly married Sarah Leech. Edward set up in Newcastle as a veneer cutter, making decorative surfaces for fine cabinets. A son, Philip, was born the following year and three more children followed in fairly rapid order: Sarah in 1743, Elizabeth in 1745, John in 1747.

---

6   Giles Grendey was also one of the few cabinetmakers of his time to label his work. He retired a very wealthy man some years before his death in 1780.

It seems that from a very early age Edward's first-born Philip was mad about horses. He probably had his first exposure to the sight, sound and smell of them when the mail coach pulled in to disgorge its letters at his great-uncle Richard's post office at the Swan Inn, or when James Pickford's London to Manchester stagecoach stopped at one of the local taverns that lined the town's broad thoroughfare. Perhaps he watched as the older boys competed to earn themselves a few pennies by helping to harness, feed and groom the mounts or, if they were lucky, take turns riding them to the stable. Philip dreamed of the day when he too would be able to work with horses.

It should have been a good time for a craftsman like Edward Astley. Newcastle's population was growing, the local economy flourishing. There was ample work for furnishers and the windows of shops were crammed with goods. Edward also became a town burgess, a sign that the family was prospering. But when Philip was just five years old his world collapsed and his life changed forever.

His father's financial situation had gone rapidly downhill. Money passed through Edward's hands very easily and he fell into debt. Struggling to make ends meet, the family had to leave their home and share a tiny, cramped house in Lad Lane with a local shoemaker, his wife and six children. The situation was desperate, but it would soon become much worse. In 1847 Edward Astley was confined to the notorious Fleet Prison in London.

The Fleet was a debtors' prison, not just for those arrested in London, but for those imprisoned elsewhere in the country and transferred under a warrant from the high courts. Locking a man up for owing money seems illogical – how was he supposed to pay off his debts? – but it was a fact of Georgian life. The gaols were overflowing with people imprisoned for often quite trivial sums. With the wage-earner in prison, the consequences were often horrific. Assets were seized, too, so entire families often joined them in the Fleet rather than be left destitute and homeless.

Conditions in the prison were appalling. Penal institutions in London had been privatised by the crown centuries ago and there was no obligation on the owners to feed their occupants, so unless they had kind friends or a private charity to keep them from starving, inmates would be sent to the 'begging grate' and forced to seek alms from their cells overlooking the street to pay for their keep. The owners did not have to provide bedding, or keep the walls and floors clean, or help the inmates clean themselves or their clothes. Typhus flourished: a quarter of the inmates died there every year. Their gaolers, however, made a good living from the Fleet. They could make a prisoner's life uncomfortable by loading him with chains and manacles, unless the inmate paid his way out of them.

Edward Astley's release from debtor's prison was ultimately dependent on the charity and goodwill of his family. The public record shows that by 1751 his debt had been repaid and he was free. After his release, he started up again as a cabinet maker, this time in St. Mary le Strand in London, but the family's finances were ever-precarious. Philip was set to work in his father's workshop when he was nine years old. Living in the shadow of the Fleet, with a one-man business to run and a young family to feed, Edward was obliged to spend every waking hour at his workbench. Philip, for his part, was not a diligent apprentice and this was the cause of friction between them. He daydreamed about working with horses. When he heard the clatter of hooves on cobbles outside the carpentry shop he would abandon his work and run down to the street, testing the patience of his father. Even by the authoritarian parenting standards of the day, it seems Edward was a bully, given to towering rages. When the delinquent son returned, he felt the sting of his father's leather belt. Time and again the errant son clashed with his father, the latter imposing his will with brute force. But Philip was much bigger than his years and by the time he was seventeen he had grown into a formidable physical presence. One day, the story goes, in the middle of yet another ugly confrontation, he wrested the belt from his father's hand and threw it to the sawdust-covered floor. This day there would be no thrashing, no more welts on his back, nor would there ever again.

At least, that is according to circus lore. Perhaps the cash-strapped father had decided he had one more mouth than his struggling carpentry business could support. One way or another, Philip had to leave. The word was out, a cause of great public excitement, that the army was recruiting for a new regiment of Light Dragoons in Acton and Knightsbridge, the very first raised for permanent service, under the command of Colonel George Elliot. Philip picked up the small bundle that held his worldly belongings and left home to follow his calling.

2

THE ENGLISH HUSSAR

Philip Astley; silhouette from the frontispiece of his book The System
of Equestrian Education, *1802. A history of Lambeth published
just a few years after his death described him as 'an uneducated but
enterprising man'.*

The year that Philip ran away to join the army was one of the most victorious in his country's history. In 1759 Britain was half way through one of those violent eruptions that occurred from time to time between herself and the French, this time over colonial and trade rivalry, a struggle known to history as the Seven Years War. For the first time ever, all of the continental superpowers were involved, on one side Britain and Prussia, on the other France, Austria and Russia. It was a truly global conflict; beginning in America, it stretched across the Atlantic and spread over Europe, to the coast of Africa, the shores of the Caribbean and to the Indian subcontinent.

The year seemed one unbroken tale of success, full of foreign humiliations and British triumphs. She and her allies had just won a magnificent victory at the battle of Minden; in India, Robert Clive had driven the French down to the Coromandel Coast; in the Caribbean, British gains included the sugar-rich island of Guadeloupe; at sea the French fleet were vanquished and the British controlled the Mediterranean. In North America, Wolfe's daring but fatal attack on Quebec secured the conquest of French Canada. Horace Walpole thought the church bells must be worn threadbare with ringing for victories. 'These are days', noted the diplomat, 'when one has to be careful o' mornings lest one miss a British victory.' The effort of fighting such a far-flung battle, however, had stretched King George's army to the limit. Despite the great triumphs, in Europe the French still posed a clear and present danger to Britain's island empire.

The army's appetite for new manpower was insatiable. It had little trouble recruiting new officers because it was a career choice for younger sons of the aristocracy and gentry. The way into – and up – the officer class was money. One junior officer, John Floyd, received his commission in the 15th Light Dragoons when he was only twelve years old, having inherited it from his dead father two years before. For the rank and file of the British army, recruitment was a more haphazard affair.[7] Most were seduced by the rattle of the drum and the call of the recruiting sergeant. Like travelling players, announcing their arrival with a parade, regiments sent out a small band, usually a captain, a sergeant and a corporal, plus a drummer and a couple of private soldiers. Swaggering, scarlet-coated and sword in hand, they would make their way to the town centre, then when they had planted their flag, the drummer would take up his batons. As a crowd gathered, the captain would jump onto a bench or a cart and invite likely lads to join up, with tales of the glories of military life and the promise of bounty and the prospect of booty ahead. A potential recruit would be given the king's shilling as a reward for his commitment and was then subjected to a medical. About a third failed even this perfunctory examination. Young men who had taken the king's shilling in drink, then sobered up and fled, were pursued and recaptured.

The very poor and the very desperate were the first to be tempted, regular pay being the principal draw. Countless boys and young men like Philip enlisted to get away from the bleak conditions of life at home, or for a chance to travel the world. Others were dispossessed tenants, farmers and farm labourers, victims of enclosure and other agricultural 'improvements'. There were also criminals in the ranks, sent by magistrates to an often-ungrateful army as though it was some kind of penal institution.

---

7   Sergeant William Roberts served for twenty-one years with the 15th Light Dragoons (or Light Horse), having enlisted in 1779 at the age of fourteen. Sergeant Roberts was born Elizabeth Roberts, the daughter of a Manchester bricklayer. During her service she was wounded in action twice, by a sabre cut to the head and a musket ball in the leg. After transferring to the 37th Foot in the West Indies she had an attack of yellow fever and on her deathbed disclosed her secret to a sergeant's wife. Soon after her unexpected recovery in 1801 she married another sergeant in the 37th and they had three children. Quite what the 15th Light Dragoons (or for that matter the 37th Foot) made of this bombshell when it burst can only be guessed at, but the story is telling of the rigour of the British army recruitment process.

There were those who joined up for the prospect of a scrap with the French, England's natural enemy. Fighting with a regiment also had a certain romantic attraction. Some signed up to wear the scarlet uniform for its legendary pulling-power. Bribery, coercion, an alternative to imprisonment, sex – these were all as much a feature of recruiting as any patriotic impulse.

Army service was unlimited: once in, you were in for life. That life might be very short, because disease was just as likely to cut you down as battle. For the common soldier, service in the Georgian military was relentlessly grim, certainly a very long way from the romantic ideal of soldiering and more like the eighteenth-century labourer's world of drudgery and exhaustion. A good regiment required tough sergeants and pitiless officers prepared to lay down unforgiving discipline. Punishments were harsh, ranging from a flogging to a death sentence. Camp life was dirty and cramped. Packed into insanitary barracks without basic plumbing, soldiers ate, slept, defecated and cleaned their kit in the same shared space. It was worse in the cavalry because the barracks were usually shared with manure-saturated stables. Desertions were a fact of life. Most fled in the first year of service because they couldn't cope with the exhausting daily grind of military life.

In Germany, reinforcements were needed to replace the casualties sustained by Britain's ally, Frederick the Great. Six new regiments of light dragoons were raised, of which the first was the Fifteenth, known as 'Elliot's Light Horse' after their colonel, George Augustus Elliot, a tough, battle-hardened cavalry officer who had fought and been wounded at Dettingen and Fontenoy. He was famous for his Spartan diet in the field, living on nothing but vegetables and water. Elliot's regiment was the unwitting beneficiary of an industrial dispute. A large number of the new recruits were striking journeyman tailors who were marching on Parliament to present a petition about poor working conditions. The enlistment of so many tailors in the 15th Light Horse gave the regiment the nicknames Elliot's Tailors or The Tabs.

One of the first volunteers to join the 15th Light Dragoons was seventeen-year-old Philip Astley, described by the regimental historian Colonel Whylly as 'the son of a respectable tradesman at Newcastle-under-Lyne (sic).' The 15th was delighted to have him: the average private stood five feet seven but young Astley towered above them all at well over six feet tall, with 'an oaken chest' and 'the proportions of a Hercules.' The shock of induction into military life could have been immense for a teenage runaway but for Astley it was tempered by the opportunity to do something he loved - working with horses. He was assigned to a group of horse breakers – 'rough riders'. Of all the equestrian employments, this was the most dangerous. The military broke large numbers of mounts in times of war and it was hard, risky work with many casualties. The chances of a horse throwing itself down and crushing a rider, or trapping a stirupped foot and dragging him to death, were great.

The army took kindly to the large, loud, generous lad from North Staffordshire and within a matter of days he was impressing everyone with what Whylly called his 'peculiar power' over animals, especially his extraordinary gift for training and subduing difficult horses. His speciality was caring for and training the horses to be 'bomb-proof', that is, not to bolt at the sound of gunshot. His enthusiasm soon got him fast-tracked for promotion and he was sent for special equestrian instruction at the Earl of Pembroke's estate at Wilton, under the tutelage of the great fencing and riding-master Domenico Angelo Tremamondo.

Angelo, as he was most often known, was one of the most flamboyant, most talked about characters of the age. He was adventurous, charismatic and a lady-killer. Born in Italy in 1717 into a wealthy merchant family, he enjoyed a classic gentleman's education, studying riding and fencing under Europe's finest. He was expected to join the family business and so was sent to France to study international trade. Angelo spent ten years in Paris, breaking hearts and overspending badly. His father, despairing of his son's lifestyle, withdrew his financial support. From then on Angelo had to get by on his wits, especially his talents with the sword. In the early 1750s he fell in love with the celebrated Irish actress Peg Woffington, who was on tour in France. Angelo followed her back to London. The affair cooled, but Angelo stayed in London and in Soho he established a fashionable fencing and riding school. It was the best in England, teaching the likes of David Garrick, Joshua Reynolds, Richard Sheridan and Johann Christian Bach. Although chiefly remembered as a great swordsman, Angelo was also a superb equestrian, according to King George II 'the most elegant horseman of his day'. Angelo's equestrian skills soon gained him entry into the homes of the great and the good, including Henry Herbert, 10th Earl of Pembroke.

The Earl was only nineteen years old and just back from the Grand Tour. He, too, was a horse-lover and already one of those Georgian hard-core rakes that appear in romantic fiction. He was married to the beautiful Lady Elizabeth, daughter of the Duke of Marlborough. Pembroke made himself unpopular with his father-in-law by disguising himself as a sailor and eloping in a packet boat to France with his young mistress Kitty Hunter: he covered his tracks by threatening to murder any servant who made any mention of it to his wife. Marlborough despatched a man to find them and bring them back. Pembroke returned briefly, inviting his wife to join himself and Kitty in a threesome: when she declined his generous offer he skipped off to the Low Countries with his mistress. Horace Walpole punned; 'As Pembroke as horseman by most is accounted / Tis not strange that his Lordship a Hunter has mounted'. Kitty returned to England at the end of a six-month affair, pregnant with Pembroke's child. Just in case anyone had any doubts about the parentage of her baby she named it Augustus Retnuh Reebkomp – the last two names an anagram of Hunter Pembroke. In philandery terms this was just Pembroke's warm-up act. In Italy, he caused a bigger scandal by running off with a young woman on her wedding day to some poor, unfortunate groom in Venice.

When he wasn't too busy deflowering Europe's womanhood, Pembroke found time to establish two private riding schools at his London home in Whitehall and his ancestral home at Wilton. He had taken it upon himself to try to improve the British cavalry – specifically the newly-formed 15th Light Dragoons, of which Pembroke was also lieutenant-colonel – by modernising old army training methods. His plan was to introduce a new and superior method of riding that would make British horsemanship the envy of the world. In 1758, he invited Domenico Angelo to become his riding-master at Wilton House where he would train the star pupils of this regiment. Through his patron, Angelo was now unofficial riding-master to the British army and the experimental principles he introduced of riding, breaking and training horses would eventually be adopted by the whole of the British cavalry.[8]

In young Philip Astley, Angelo discovered a precocious talent. He was soon soaking up everything his riding-master could teach him and more. He learned how to pluck a pistol from the ground while riding at full gallop and how to slip out of his saddle to avoid an enemy bullet by lowering himself against the horse's haunch. He could leap off his horse travelling at full speed and then remount without breaking pace. Less usefully, you would imagine, Astley learned how to perform a headstand on a moving horse: it seems this sort of exhibitionism already came very naturally to him. His tutor was impressed, if not a little astonished, by the young protégé's confidence in handling horses. So, too, were the workers around the Wilton estate who dubbed Corporal Astley, as he now was, 'the devil in disguise'.

For most new recruits in the 15th Light Dragoons the training process didn't go quite as smoothly. The cavalry must have

---

8   Angelo was almost certainly the ghost writer behind the Earl of Pembroke's book *Method* of *Breaking Horses* published in 1761.

seemed an attractive option for any conscript, especially if he knew nothing about horses or the hard work involved in looking after them. Many of Astley's colleagues were tailors who had never ridden a horse before. For the first few weeks they weren't allowed saddles or stirrups, the chief aim of the instructor being not to give his pupil confidence, but to get him used to the idea of hitting the ground hard.

Elliot's regiment of light cavalry was to be raised after the Prussian and Austrian hussars model and it was a fairly new concept in the British army[9]. The word hussar conjures up images of charismatic types with too much facial hair; romantic rascals, in popular fiction rough, hard-drinking rogues who looted everything that wasn't nailed down and bedded anything in a skirt. As Arthur Conan Doyle's hero Brigadier Gerard put it, the hussar 'always had the whole population running; the women towards us, and the men away'. As far as Astley's unit was concerned, however, this stereotype was far in the future.[10]. Ironically his unit – the 'Tailor's regiment' – was known for flashy uniforms. Scarlet was for the army as a rule and blue for the dragoons, but the 15th Light Horse was one of the exceptions. They wore scarlet coats with blue facings, white breeches and waistcoats and knee-length black boots. 'There was much smartness in these light dragoons', noted the British Army chronicler Sir John Fortescue.

The Fifteenth were a 'light' brigade' because they were more lightly armed than 'heavy' cavalry and so cast in a supporting role with scouting and reconnaissance duties. Astley's unit were armed with straight-bladed sabres which could be used to cut and thrust in close combat, and a carbine – a shortened flintlock musket

---

9   The word *hussar* derives from the Hungarian *husz*, 'twenty', because at one time in Hungary one cavalry soldier was levied from every twenty families.

10   The Georgian cavalry were clean-shaven – the whiskers didn't come until the following century.

with a bayonet. The carbine was notoriously difficult to load and operate and highly temperamental. In wet or windy weather, the priming powder might not ignite. If a musket failed to function, it was easy to make the mistake of thinking, in the din of battle, that it gone off and you might set about reloading, in which case the next ignition would most likely blow the weapon to pieces in your hands. It was much more difficult to handle on the back of a fast-moving horse. The gun couldn't be relied on to hit a target more than fifty yards away, so you pointed it in the general direction of the enemy and hoped for the best. At close range, however, a heavy lead musket ball could do egregious damage to flesh and bone and could easily take the top off a man's skull. Eighteenth-century battlefields were terrible scenes of carnage with men running around with eyes, noses or other extremities that had been taken clean off by a musket ball.

On 10 June 1760, barely a year after its formation, the 15th Light Dragoons were sent to war. They embarked at Gravesend on flat-bottomed troopships crammed with horses and men and crossed the North Sea to join the Allied army in Germany. Promotion for Corporal Astley came unusually swiftly. When the horses were being landed at Bremen on the Weser River, one or possibly several of the animals panicked and jumped overboard, and were rapidly carried by the tide. Astley dived in and brought them safely back to shore. For his bravery and quick-thinking he was rewarded with an extra stripe.

He didn't have to wait very long for his first taste of proper action. After a short period in quarters his regiment was ordered to march with all speed to join the Allied army at Zewesten under Duke Ferdinand of Brunswick. The Duke didn't look the part of a great general – a middle-aged man of undistinguished appearance, five-feet six inches tall and with a heavily pock-marked complexion – but he was an able commander and had the respect of his men. Reassuringly ever-visible in his greatcoat covered in medals, he impressed his new troops by joining them around the fireside on their first evening in camp, then every evening thereafter, regardless of the weather.

Just two days later, on 16 July, Brunswick's forces came face to face with the enemy. Five French battalions and a regiment of hussars were encamped in the woods near the village of Emsdorf.[11] Their packs were off and they were settling down to eat their midday meal. It was too good an opportunity to miss. After silently overpowering an enemy guard, Brunswick's infantry crept round to the north of the woods and advanced on them, catching them completely unawares. The French foot soldiers fled directly into the path of the novice 15th Light Dragoons.

It was a murderously hot day and the horses of Astley's unit were already so exhausted by the long march they could barely charge, but charge they did, galloping headlong into the massed ranks of a French infantry bristling with loaded muskets. The French held their fire until the horses were within about thirty yards, then released a lethal volley of lead, but Astley's regiment pressed on. The two squadrons in the centre suffered the heaviest casualties but they continued, crashing into the French ranks. The 15th Light Dragoons astonished the veterans by charging another three times against formed infantry, cutting them down in their scores. They were shaping up for yet another charge when the enemy commander, Glaubitz, signaled that he had had enough. As well as the 1,655 men that surrendered to the 15th, they also took six French guns and captured nine colours.

Astley's regiment suffered the lion's share of the Allied casualties that day. The 'Fighting Fifteenth' lost a hundred and twenty-five men, including six who died of heat stroke, and a hundred and sixty-eight horses, about a quarter of their strength, but they had achieved a famous victory. The news of this success was greeted with widespread amazement and admiration. The regiment had

---

11   In actuality, they were mostly German troops serving under a French flag.

only been in existence a few months and at the front a matter of days. If Emsdorf was a sensation in Germany and Britain it was the source of undying shame in France. Losing one colour was embarrassing; the loss of nine a massive humiliation. Emsdorf has unique significance in the history of the British armed forces because it was the first time a single action was recognised as a battle honour: the word Emsdorff was to be engraved on the helmets of all ranks.[12]

The next day, the tired but triumphant force, complete with its prisoners, headed back to camp. That evening, anecdotes about the battle lost nothing in the telling: the French wounded, officers on their knees, begging for mercy, infantrymen being massacred, the flight of the French hussars, these are stories they would one day tell their grandchildren. Their twelve-year-old officer John Floyd had his horse shot under him and was saved from certain death at the hands of a French dragoon by the timely intervention of Captain Ainslie. One of the most heroic tales involved Astley himself. At Emsdorf he, too, had his horse shot from under him and he was wounded in the thigh but he cut his way to safety, still carrying an enemy standard.

The casualties of the 15th were heavy and were sent back to Hanover to reorganise, but after just a few days rest Astley was back in the saddle. After the glories of Emsdorf, the weeks that followed seemed flat and dull, but they were far from idle. There was patrolling, scouting, not to mention foraging for food. There was a general shortage of rations, the cause of considerable resentment towards the Commissariat. Sickness was on the increase, too. That summer there were flies everywhere and widespread dysentery was the result. This threw an even bigger burden on Astley and his fellow regimental officers who, as always, were responsible for the maintenance of discipline and morale. The mood darkened in the autumn of 1760 when news filtered

---

12   The second 'f' in Emsdorff was later dropped.

through to Astley's camp of the death of King George II. According to reports, his demise was hastened by news of the recent defeat at Kloster Kampen.[13] Astley's regiment wore improvised mourning clothes, officers covering their sword knots with black crepe and wearing black hat bands and armbands. Morale among the rank and file was also damaged by the number of officers allowed home on leave that winter. The Duke of Newcastle complained to the Marquis of Granby, head of the British armed forces serving in Germany: 'There seems to be so many (on leave) that I should think there were not enough left to command their corps'.

The following winter, although quiet on the battlefront, proved to be just as unhealthy for his regiment as fever swept the camp. Colonel Pierson wrote home; 'It is very melancholy to see how fast our men die here; there is a contagious fever that carries the stoutest men off in two or three days.' In early 1761 Astley's regiment tramped through heavy snow to Gudersberg, Zeigenhahn, Kirchain, Marpurg and Paderborn. In March, a thaw set in and the roads turned into quagmires. Horses and guns were stuck in the mud and had to be abandoned. The troops became so scattered by terrible travelling conditions that the supply lines failed. If not for the magazines and stores captured from the French, Astley's unit would have starved. Over the twelve months from January to December 1761 they lost eight privates killed in action, one officer and sixty-seven men died of disease, twelve died of wounds, eighteen deserted, six had been discharged owing to wounds and thirty-five 'from other causes' – a total of a hundred and forty-seven dead.

On 30 August 1762 Astley was in the thick of the action again. The 15th Light Dragoons were at Friedberg where the

---

13   More likely he had a stroke, causing him to fall off his toilet seat, smashing his head as he fell. According to the king's German valet de chambre there was a roar from the palace privy 'louder than the usual royal wind' and he broke in to find George slumped dead on the floor.

Allied infantry was attempting to drive a wedge between two advancing French armies.[14] The Allies were forced to fall back across the Wetter. The Duke of Brunswick's twenty-six-year-old nephew, Prince Karl Wilhelm Ferdinand, who was at the rear of the retiring troops, was felled by a musket ball and marooned behind enemy lines. With three dragoons at his rear, Astley rallied to rescue him. He charged the enemy and, after a desperate skirmish, brought the Prince back under heavy fire. For his extraordinary act of valour, Astley received the usual plaudits of his commanding officer Sir William Erskine.

The Seven Years War, as far as the English soldiers who served in it were concerned, lasted no more than six. On 7 January 1763 Astley was promoted to the rank of Sergeant Major, just in time for the Treaty of Paris, marking the end of hostilities between Britain and France and the end of the war in Europe. His regiment continued to serve in Germany until Spring. They returned to England and, on the 5th April, marched over the new Westminster Bridge 'with every man a sprig of box in his hat in token of victory, having been in almost every engagement in Germany, and always beat the enemy.'[15] On 25 July the colours captured at Emsdorf were presented in Hyde Park to the new King George III who expressed his thanks for the gallantry of 'the Fighting Fifteenth'.

Britain emerged from the Seven Years War in better shape than ever. With a swathe of new territories gained at the Treaty of Paris, she was now the world's leading colonial power and the foremost naval power, heralding the birth of the British Empire. The peace of 1763, however, did not bode well for Britain's returning heroes. The lanes and turnpikes were clogged with around 75,000 demobilised veterans, still wearing their old

---

14 This campaign is known to scholars of the Seven Years War as the Battle of Nauheim.

15 *Gentleman's Magazine.*

regimentals and with nothing but a fortnight's subsistence money to take back to their homes. Men discharged with one leg or none, or one eye or none, could be seen begging on every street corner. Newspapers reported an upsurge of robberies and appeals were made to patriotic landowners to save returning servicemen from a life of crime. The Marquis of Rockingham and Sir George Saville promised a five-pound bounty to men who had served at Minden, Emsdorf and elsewhere in the hope that the cash would help veterans readjust to the 'honest industry' of civilian life. Sir Ludovick Grant, who had encouraged his own tenants to enlist in the ranks of Montgomery's Highlanders, was another benevolent landlord who did the right thing, inviting 'reduced soldiers' to settle on new estates on favourable terms.

In 1765 Astley took leave to tie the knot with his girlfriend Martha Mary Jones, known to everyone as Patty. At twenty-four she was a year older than Philip, the second of five children and only daughter of John and Maria Jones from the English-Welsh border town of Whitchurch. Patty had royal blood. Her maternal family, the Longuevilles of the baronetcy of Wolverton in Buckinghamshire, could trace their distinguished line back to the Plantagenets. Patty's notorious ancestor Sir Everard Digby, a wealthy landowner sympathetic to the plight of Britain's oppressed Catholics, had given his backing to Robert Catesby's Gunpowder Plot. Digby was convicted of high treason and hanged, drawn and quartered. The Longueville family fortunes had seen a tragic collapse owing to their commitment to the losing side in the Civil War.

We can only speculate how she and Philip met, but it is reasonable to assume there was an equestrian connection because Patty was already an accomplished horsewoman. Perhaps she was a pupil at Domenico Angelo's private fencing and riding school in Soho, where mixed riding lessons were available to men and women. On 8 July, Philip and Patty were married at St. George's in Hanover Square, London, a church which specialised in cheap, expeditious marriages at a guinea a time without the inconvenience of banns or licences.

With a new wife and career prospects on civvy street so dismal, the obvious course for Astley would have been to stay on the army payroll. The huge, handsome Sergeant-Major with his 'perfectly stentorian' voice and his dare-devil courage was the regiment celebrity, a natural-born soldier, a leader of men and a patriot through and through. According to one commentator, 'had he been born into a higher sphere he might have been a field marshal.'[16] If he had simply elected to spend the rest of his life serving his king and country it would have been one of the easiest decisions he would ever make. On his regiment's return to England, however, he found something even more alluring than the whiff of grapeshot.

One day while off duty in London, Astley came across an ex-cavalry man offering riding lessons and trick-riding for loose change in a makeshift arena in a field. He was impressed by the performer's riding skills: they were the kind of tricks he had been performing to entertain his army colleagues for years. What really grabbed his attention was the size of the crowd and the amount of money the man was making just by passing around a hat. Astley was seized with an idea. He had seen Domenico Angelo make himself rich as the master of a fashionable riding school in Soho, teaching equestrian skills to the nobility. If he had enough money to buy horses and build a school he might be able to do the same. Perhaps trick-riding was a way to raising all the cash he needed to turn his passion into a career? There was only one way to find out.

Astley returned from London to his billets at Derby and went directly to his commanding officer, Lieutenant-Colonel William Erskine, to ask for a discharge. Acceptance was by no means a given: he had enlisted for life, which in practice meant until he

---

16   *A Biographical Dictionary of Actors*, Volume 7.

was too old or infirm for combat. Astley was only twenty-five and had served just six years. On account of his valiant service and 'general proper demeanour' however, discharge was granted. As a parting personal gift, Erskine, on learning that the young soldier intended to better himself by opening a riding school, presented him with a dark bay stallion. This gift was a singular act of generosity and a true measure of the unit's huge respect for Astley's valiant service.

On 21 June 1766, the ex-hussar bade an emotional farewell to his army colleagues, packed away his regimentals and certificate of loyal service and rode off to start his risky new life in civvy street. He was heading into the unknown but he was young and possessed two characteristics that would serve him well throughout his life, courage and resilience.

3

HALFPENNY HATCH

Southwark Fair, *print by William Hogarth. Despite the fun and the variety of entertainments to be had, the festivities went hand in hand with danger, vice and riots. The fair was finally banned in 1763, five years before Astley's first entertainments at Halfpenny Hatch. Public domain Wikimedia Commons.*

To a foreigner visiting London for the first time in the late 1760s, the most striking thing may have been just how incredibly prosperous the city appeared to be. It was the biggest in Europe and the industrial revolution and the strength of the British naval fleet had made it the centre of commerce and industry, not just for the nation, but for the world. It was getting wealthier at a rate that was quite dizzying. Our visitor would no doubt look in astonishment at the spacious houses of aristocrats and wealthy merchants, the royal parks, the well-stocked shops of Piccadilly and the Strand and the pleasure gardens of Vauxhall and Ranelagh. London was expanding and improving in every direction. Gone were most of the unlit, dung-ridden, pot-hole filled streets that people had to pick their way through. There were numbered houses, proper pavements and new street lamps. It could truly be said that 'London is the best paved and best lighted city in Europe'.[17] There was fine new architecture too. In the city, the Bank of England and Somerset House had been rebuilt on a grand scale and a new Corn Exchange was being erected. Newgate prison was demolished and rebuilt, Buckingham House was remodelled as a new palace, the last of the old houses were cleared from ancient London Bridge and a new bridge was being built at Blackfriars.

As people, gold and goods poured into the capital, for the city's richest it was a time of conspicuous consumption. In 1768 the potter Josiah Wedgwood, born in Burslem just a couple of miles from Astley's childhood home, was opening his new showroom in Great Newport Street, beguiling fashionable Londoners with his wares and receiving orders from the highest levels of the British nobility. It was a time of great advances, too, in the arts and sciences. In 1768, King George III opened the Royal Academy of Arts on Piccadilly. In the same year James Cook was commissioned to view the transit of Venus from the South Pacific and set sail on his first voyage around the world.

---

17   *A Tour to London, Or, New Observations on England and Its Inhabitants,*
     Volume 1 published 1772.

If our foreign visitor had stayed around in London a little longer he may have found a different place, for this was a city of great extremes. Vast wealth and immense luxury lived cheek by jowl with obscene poverty, squalor and deprivation. In 1768 a founding member of the Royal Academy, William Hogarth, published his grim depiction of a city in the grip of an addiction to gin which, for many people, offered the only quick release from the grinding misery of everyday life. The London sex trade dwarfed that of any other European city. Sex tourists could invest in a guide book, *Harris's List of Covent Garden Ladies*, to help them find company to suit their particular tastes and income. The trade fostered the runaway growth of venereal disease. In 1768 one in five women in London were prostitutes and many would be dead by the age of thirty. The disappearance of symptoms of sexually transmitted disease were taken as proof of cure, so the poxed went on poxing others: the widespread belief that deflowering a virgin cured syphilis really didn't help either.

London's population had doubled over the century and the pressure of numbers made living conditions intolerable for the vast majority. With so many people arriving from the provinces and from abroad to find work, slum areas grew rapidly. Large families lived in single rooms in ramshackle tenements or in damp cellars with no sanitation or fresh air. Drinking water was often contaminated and rubbish left to rot in the street. The Thames under the new Blackfriars Bridge was black with raw sewage. Adding to the stench and decay were London's dead, filling graveyards to capacity, coffins left partially uncovered in 'poor holes' close to local houses and businesses. With overpopulation and appalling sanitation came the spread of disease. Epidemics, infections and occasional food shortages contributed to the high mortality rate. Medicine was primitive and the connection between personal hygiene and good health not yet understood. In one year, more than eight hundred deaths in London were attributed simply to 'teeth.' Even the smallest wound could lead to death by infection. Surgery was available, anaesthetic was not. Male patients could go under the knife drunk and insensible, but a lady such as the diarist Fanny Burney had to endure her mastectomy while fully conscious. She was lucky by Georgian standards because the operation was successful, prolonging her life.

The Grim Reaper harvested London's poor children in their thousands. If a baby survived childbirth it faced the twin evils of malnourishment and ongoing abuse.[18] The children of the poor were dispatched to crowded, backbreaking workhouses or were apprenticed to tradesmen who used them as unpaid labourers. In 1768 only seven in one hundred workhouse infants survived for three years. Workhouse children swept London's chimneys, hawked milk and fruit round its streets or laboured unpaid in tailoring, shoemaking, stocking making, baking, river work and domestic service.

Pickpockets were everywhere, operating in swarms or working alone, some relatively clean and well-dressed so they could mingle easily. The lowest and most despised class of London criminal were the footpads – armed street robbers. The London newspapers carried daily stories of murders committed for the sake of a few shillings. At dusk, gangs armed with knives assaulted people as they left the theatres in Covent Garden. In an age without police, the machinery of law was uncompromising and brutal. In 1768, two-hundred and forty offences were punishable by death, with hanging also prescribed for accomplices. Punishments for lesser offences ranged from the pillory to branding and whipping to burning. In July the previous year, Henry Ludlow, aged eleven years and

---

18 In London, one in five children died before their second birthday. In some districts the infant mortality rate reached 75% of all births (Dr Matthew White, Research Fellow in History at the University of Hertfordshire).

eight months, was sentenced to seven years transportation for stealing a silver spoon.

If you managed to steer clear of alcoholism, the footpads, the venereal disease, the sewage-tainted water and survive the vagaries of eighteenth-century medicine, you could still fall victim to apparently innocent foodstuffs: bread adulterated with ash and ground bones, milk thickened with minced snails, or sweets coloured with red lead. Dying penniless, you could be buried in one of the dreadful poor pits, a mass grave heaped with coffins before being earthed in. At least the putrid stench of the pit might repel the resurrection men who stole cadavers for dissection.

Little wonder there was an explosion in the number of entertainments available to people seeking diversion from the horrors of their everyday lives. For the very poorest, the punishment of criminals was the cheapest and most popular form of mass entertainment. Public executions at Tyburn were set aside as public holidays. Huge crowds of rowdy, jeering onlookers would arrive in the morning to follow the prisoner to the hanging platform. Men, women, children, paupers and gentry alike looked forward to these days in the hope of witnessing a dramatic declaration, a last-minute reprieve or a courageous, applause-worthy farewell from the condemned. When the authorities banned public executions at Tyburn because they were upsetting the posh residents of nearby Mayfair, even London's wisest, Dr Samuel Johnson, was indignant: 'Executions are supposed to draw spectators,' he complained. 'If they do not draw spectators, they do not answer their purpose.'

Londoners took their entertainment wherever they found it. A French visitor struggled to differentiate local sport from riot, noting local amusements 'such as throwing dead dogs and cats and mud at passers-by on certain festival days'. Bethlehem Hospital, aka Bedlam, the home for 'lunatics' and the insane, exerted a fascination on the Georgian public like no other. It was a human zoo: people paid a few pence to stare at the inmates for as long as they cared to. Visitors were thought to be beneficial because they brought 'jollity and merriment'.

Thousands of sightseers came each year, wandering through the wards, teasing the patients to heighten the fun. On public holidays the hospital took on the appearance of a fair, with food and drink salesmen plying their trades in the galleries and mixing with visitors and patients. Eventually, concerns about Bedlam being used as a public show led to male visitors being excluded from the women's quarters and admittance restricted by ticket, visitors to be accompanied by keepers. Bedlam's pull extended to all classes. Dr Johnson and his friend James Boswell went to see the inmates in May 1775, noting that the general contemplation of insanity was very affecting'. Tourists came from far and wide to see London's top attraction. A Russian traveller reported; 'Many of the men made us laugh. One imagines that he is a cannon and keeps firing charges through his mouth. Another grunts like a bear and walks on all fours.'

Freaks of nature were great attractions. An English giant seven feet four and a half inches tall was shown at a public house in Cheapside. 'The Tall Black' or 'Indian King' was to be found at the Golden Lyon, Smithfield. An Essex giantess 'near seven feet high... though not nineteen' was displayed at the Three King Court in Fleet Street. Dwarfs, too, were big crowd-pullers. The tiny, talented German, Matthew Buchinger, performed at the Two Blackamoors' Heads, Holborn, playing the violin and flute despite having neither arms nor legs. Twenty-nine inches tall, Buchinger married four times and fathered fourteen children. Female dwarfs were generally called 'fairies' or 'fairy women': a German fairy, thirty-two inches tall, danced and sang at the Brandy Shop in the old Stocks Market. A married couple, Judith and Robert Skinner, Judith being the taller at twenty-six inches, were displayed in Westminster and in two years made enough money to retire.

The entertainments were often sordid and disappointing. Monsters drew crowds, meanwhile stretching credulity, such as the 'sea-monster or white bear with wool and webbed feet' exhibited in Leicester Fields, or the 'Syren or Mermaid with breasts fair and full, but without nipples, and in all respects like the cod-fish from the waist down'. Spectators who had paid to see a 'pig-faced woman' in 1750 felt cheated: 'The lady was nothing but a bear, its face and neck carefully shaved, while the back and top of its head was covered by a wig, ringlets, cap and artificial flowers in the latest fashion.'[19]

Ethnically diverse or 'exotic' people excited huge attention, including former slaves with special talents. The arrival of American Indians caused great interest. Three Cherokee chiefs and their wives were a profitable exhibit at Marylebone Gardens, eating their suppers and smoking their pipes every evening in front of admiring crowds. According to gossip, the three ladies were 'with Child before they left Marylebone by little Bob the waiter, to whom they took a fancy'. There were curiosities of every kind on commercial display from hermaphrodites to singing cats and hairy women. Hand-to-hand combat, puppet shows, conjurers, strange inventions, quack doctors and cock fighting all had their place as popular amusements.

When the real thing was not available, waxworks took their place. Mrs Salmon's exhibition of 'historical tableaux and horrific scenes in wax' opened in Fleet Street in 1711 and prospered for more than a century until it was outclassed by Madame Tussaud's new display in Baker Street. Mechanical shows were also a huge draw, astonishing all with their ingenuity. In 1772, James Cox's

---

19 Wilson and Caulfield's *The Book of Wonderful Characters*. James Caulfield (1764–1826) spent his career publishing illustrated books about 'remarkable persons'. His vignettes, accompanied by engravings of each individual, describe a wide-ranging group from the man who died aged 152 to a 'remarkable glutton' and a woman who lived on the smell of flowers, their only common factor being that they were in some way 'wonderful'.

Museum at Charing Cross displayed jewel- and gold-encrusted mechanical animals including a screeching peacock and a crowing cock: part of this collection was later acquired for Catherine the Great's Hermitage. Puppet shows by the Italian, Fantoccini, were a hit in Panton Street, while Loutherbourg's Eidophusikon, in Lisle Street in Soho, displayed views of London or Italy or the Niagara Falls, delighting audiences well into the next century with a primitive form of movie-making.

Talking automata, trick-riders, jugglers and rope dancers, boxers and wrestlers, quack doctors and tooth drawers, card sharpers and dice rollers rubbed shoulders at the various fairs held annually around London. The biggest, Bartholomew Fair, drew thousands to Smithfield every summer for profit or entertainment. At this fair could be seen a six-legged ram, Miss Biffin who painted miniatures without arms, and 'A Surprising Large Fish, THE NONDESCRIPT'. Southwark Fair, shown in a famous print by Hogarth, opened in September and ran for two weeks until it was shut down by the city authorities in 1763 on the grounds that it was a hotbed of vice and an obstruction to trade. May Fair, held from May Day in that part of London which eventually took its name, was also suppressed by the Westminster authorities in 1708, illegally revived until brought finally to an end by a show of arms in 1764.

The banning of public fairs had closed off one avenue of entertainment for London's poorer inhabitants but the quality of public pleasures for the better-off was improving. For the wealthy, eighteenth-century London was a greedy, rumbustious place in which men and women placed few constraints on their appetites, whether it was for food, drink, sex or gambling, but there was also a curiosity for more cerebral entertainment. For a hefty five shillings you could see Sir Ashton Lever's collections of natural history and ethnographic items, the Holophusikon, at Leicester House. In 1768, at the British Museum, enjoying its fifteenth successful year in Great Russell Street, access was free but strictly limited to ticket-holders who applied in writing, plus 'persons of distinction for rank or learning'.

London's parks were the recreation grounds and meeting places for all classes and frequented by King and commoner alike: foreigners were astonished to find in St James's Park the cream of English society walking side by side with the poorest of the poor. It also came as a shock for the country's German-born Queen Caroline. When she asked her prime minister Sir Robert Walpole what it would cost to enclose the park for the sole use of the court, he replied, 'only a crown, madam.' Over time, Caroline would appreciate and become a great benefactor of Kensington Gardens and Hyde Park, lavishing improvements, including a spectacular forty-acre recreational lake, The Serpentine. From seven to ten o'clock on a summer evening, the London parks were so full of people 'that you cannot help touching your neighbour'.[20]

Then as now, London's sheer size exercised a gravitational pull on the rest of the country. Mass migration from the provinces was a fact of life – around eight thousand people a year. London's appetite for labour of all types was unquenchable, but most of all it was the place where talented people went. It was the seat of sophistication, drawing in its wake craftsmen, musicians, writers and actors, such as Staffordshire's Samuel Johnson and the greatest theatrical celebrity of the age, David Garrick.

Getting there wasn't easy. The roads into London were generally in terrible shape despite the efforts of turnpike trusts to improve them. A provincial town such as Derby was more than twenty-four hours away and the travel was uncomfortable and dangerous. Highwaymen with colourful names such as Galloping Dick, Gentleman Foster and Seven Stringed Jack were bold and vexatious, and London-bound travellers were easy prey.

---

20 According to the Swiss travel writer Césare de Saussure.

It was to leafy Islington in north London that Philip and Patty Astley went to start their new life together. The army had given Philip a great deal of practical experience in horsemanship, but no training at all in how to run a business. He corrected that deficiency by taking a job at the Jubilee Gardens, working for one of London's original equestrian superstars, Old Sampson, not as a performer, but as groom and horse breaker. Trick-riding was hugely popular but financially unpredictable. In the mornings, Sampson offered riding lessons to aspiring horsemen and women and occasionally the children of the aristocracy, before making his daily appearance at five o'clock playing the flute while standing on the backs of two horses. In addition to his equestrian chores, Philip was expected to parade the neighbouring streets with a cracked trumpet to advertise his employer's evening show.

Sampson at this point was in bitter rivalry with his neighbour Thomas Price and their success spawned several more competitors. At nearby Pentonville, in the Belvedere Tea Gardens, Zucker's Little Learned Horse had become a great equestrian attraction of a different variety. This horse performed amazing tricks by word of command. It would lie down and get up again, pick up a handkerchief in its mouth, answer questions by nodding or shaking its head or perform mathematical computations by striking the ground with a hoof. It was even trained to climb stairs and look out of a second-storey window to greet newly arriving customers.

Astley's business plan was to perform trick-riding as a means to establishing his own riding school, but when he saw the fortunes that his employer and his rivals were making from equestrian shows his strategy changed. He spent hours studying and practicing Price and Sampson's tricks and added a few specialities of his own, meanwhile picking up the basics of running a business and drawing a crowd.

In May 1767 Patty gave birth to a boy, whom they named John. Now that he had a young family to feed, Philip's plans took on a new urgency. He decided the time was right to strike out on his own. But there was no room in Islington for yet another equestrian show. He needed to launch somewhere less fashionable, free of rivals.

Across the river, on the Surrey side of Westminster Bridge in the northwest corner of a large loop of the Thames from Lambeth to Blackfriars Bridges, is the area then known as Lambeth Marsh and now called Waterloo. The Thames was wider and shallower than it is today. When the tide was in it was dotted with wherries, fishing boats and sailing ships, but at low tide it became a murky ribbon running through a wide channel of grey silt where small, ragged figures could be seen moving around the riverbed, picking their way through the useful objects left exposed. If you stood with your back to the river you could still imagine you were in the countryside, with open fields beyond. The area was mostly scrubland full of ponds, ditches and rivulets, where children played and hopeful sportsmen shot at birds. Lambeth also had its own more savage local amusements, such as cock-throwing – stoning or throwing bottles at a cockerel tied to a stake – and dog-on-dog or dog-versus-rat fights. In Lambeth, Bandogs, the even-more-ferocious relative of the pitbull, were bred for baiting larger animals. The few roads in the area were punctuated by turnpikes that, despite the extortionate fees paid to their keepers, still 'constituted an intolerable grievance'.[21]

Even on a sunny day the sky above Lambeth was thick and yellow with smoke from the manufactures that sprang up along the riverbank. The bones used in the local soap factories gave the stench of rotten meat to the whole area, competing with the stink of human urine and dogs' excrement used in the local tanneries. In short, few people were in a hurry to live there. Many of the houses that did exist were so old and

---

21 Survey of London 1830.

rotten that a strong wind could blow them down. Many of those who lived in the area did so involuntarily, as inmates of the prisons that studded the area; the King's Bench, the Marchalsea and the Clink.

Mid-way between the bridges of Blackfriars and Westminster, Astley found a field known as Glover's Halfpenny Hatch.[22] Running along the length of this field was a path providing a shortcut between the two bridges. At the eastern end was a tollbooth where hurrying pedestrians could pay their halfpenny at the 'hatch'. The field was enclosed partly by sheds and partly by rough palings. In the middle stood a pigeon house, which would later serve as a bandstand. Astley hired the field for the summer, then pegged out a circular arena and erected a flimsy fence around it, just high enough to keep it out of sight from passers-by. The ring, or 'ride' as Astley called it, made it much easier for spectators to follow the action, watching horses moving round in a circle rather than charging forwards and backwards up and down a field. Most importantly, he found that if he galloped in a tight circle, the centrifugal force struck exactly the right balance to allow him to perform seemingly impossible feats on a horse's back without falling off.

He had saved enough money to buy a couple of horses for five pounds apiece from Smithfield market. His first purchase was a scruffy-looking but lively little brown pony he called Billy. The second was much bigger and more useful for riding lessons, but it was the smarter, smaller horse that intrigued him most. In time, he found that little Billy was a born actor and could be taught to perform all of Zucker's tricks and more. Billy's new owner could not have guessed at this stage that his fiver had just bought him one of the most famous animals in circus history.

---

22 Astley's original circus ring roughly corresponds to the site of the current White Hart public house in Cornwall Road, Lambeth.

On 4 April 1768 four lines of text appeared in a London newspaper under a very small headline, 'Activity on Horseback'. It urged readers to make their way to a 'Riding School' in Lambeth Marsh at Halfpenny Hatch where they would see a performance by 'Mr Astley, former Sergeant-Major in his Majesty's Royal Regiment of Light Dragoons.' No-one would have guessed from this very modest, low-key introduction that it was the first step towards what would become the most hyperbolic of entertainments. The advert also cautioned, 'NOT THE DOG and DUCK' in St George's Fields, Southwark. Despite his best efforts to find somewhere that wouldn't provide competition, Astley was alarmed by the discovery, a month or so before his premiere, that the trick-rider James Wolton and his wife were already staging equestrian spectacles combined with 'feats of activity' at the nearby Dog and Duck inn, a tavern whose gardens were once renowned for duck-baiting, but were now more usually associated with whores and highwaymen.

To Philip and Patty's huge relief the Woltons performed for just a few weeks, then vanished. The location of the Astleys' new venture, however, was still a challenge. Unlike Islington, there were no pleasure grounds or tea gardens next door to bring in respectable passing traffic. He was relying entirely on his own ability to draw a crowd with his only attractions – himself, his wife and three horses. His performances were in the open air and an April shower could wash away his fortunes in an instant. Adjoining the ring were a couple of open-fronted wooden sheds which for the price of two shillings functioned as seating if it started to pour, but the performing area was still hostage to the weather. Admission was just sixpence, about the same price as a glass of wine, or wealthier patrons could book a seat for a shilling. In the unlikely event that those who Astley termed 'nobility and gentry' might pass by, they could enjoy a private matinée, ambitiously priced at ten guineas.

In the hours before his first show the huge ex-hussar, resplendent in his full regimentals, sat astride his horse, prowling the streets of Lambeth, bellowing news of the forthcoming entertainments, while Patty trotted behind distributing handbills. As soon as the pre-show publicity had done its job and the curious had made their way inside, the entertainments were ready to begin. In the centre of the circle a small boy had scrambled on to the roof of the pigeon house and was beating a drum to try to whip up some atmosphere. Astley stepped into the centre of the ring and made a speech in his most resounding tones, describing the amazing feats he and his wife would perform.

They didn't disappoint. Astley's size alone made him a spectacle on horseback – six feet plus was hardly the ideal size for an equestrian. The public watched in something like stupefaction as he executed a series of jaw-dropping manoeuvres. He rode with one foot on the saddle and the other touching his head. He mounted and dismounted his horse at full gallop, vaulted over two or three horses, stood on one leg on horseback as the 'Flying Mercury,' picked up coins or handkerchiefs from the ground at full gallop, or performed a headstand in the saddle as the horse cantered around the ring. From his time studying Old Sampson he had learned exactly how to engage an audience: how to build up to a climax by doing the less technically demanding tricks first, then raising the bar slowly until he was galloping around the ring at full tilt, performing something thrillingly dangerous. In all there were twenty daring stunts on horseback with the odd sword and pistol trick thrown in for good measure; or as his handbills promised, 'displayed with the greatest warlike appearance'.

The show continued in this way with various eye-popping equestrian stunts being performed by Astley, then he introduced his trump card, Billy the Little Learned Military Horse. Little Billy could fire a pistol, dance, jump through hoops, remove his own saddle, wash his feet in a pail of water, sit up and beg like a dog, play hide and seek, compute, perform mind-reading tricks, spell ASTLEY by marking his hoof in the tanbark, set a table, lift a kettle of boiling water off the fire and make a cup of tea. If the handbills are to be believed, Billy could do everything except take your admission fee on the door and give you the correct change.

Then Billy provided a touch of drama with a sketch titled 'A prologue on the Death of a Horse'. In this routine, Billy lay limp and motionless while Astley bellowed a short self-penned monologue:

My horse lies dead, apparent at your sight
But I'm a man can set this thing to right
But first pray give me leave to move his foot...
That he is dead is quite beyond dispute...

At this, Astley picked up Billy's limp foreleg and let it fall:

This shows how brutes by heaven were designed
To be in full subjection to mankind
Rise, young Bill, and be a little handy
To serve that warlike Hero, Granby.[23]

To general astonishment, Billy rose obligingly from the dead and was led off to thunderous applause.

Now it was Patty Astley's turn, entering the arena on horseback with a display of her own. With her long skirt flying around her ankles and her long, flaxen hair trailing behind her, she fired a pistol while straddling two horses, then performed a headstand on her saddle. Female equestrian performances were a huge novelty: this was remarkable if only because at the

---

23   The Marquis of Granby, British war hero. In recognition of his service there are more British pubs named after him than anyone else.

time she was the young mother of an eleven-month-old child. Finally, husband and wife rode around the ring astride two horses together, before Patty dismounted at full gallop 'with elegance and ease'.

To begin with, the business was based on Old Sampson's riding school, with riding lessons in the morning and shows in the afternoon, but it quickly became clear that the afternoon entertainments were the real bread-winner. Word got around, first south of the river, then in the city, that a big man with a thunderous voice and a physics-defying way with horses was doing something very special. He wasn't the only person giving trick-riding demonstrations in the metropolis but his natural showmanship easily set him apart. Within a few weeks a trickle of spectators had turned into a large crowd of people, thrilled by his seemingly superhuman stunts, some no doubt in morbid anticipation that Astley might break his neck. On show days, the thoroughfare through Halfpenny Hatch was blocked by a throng of children trying to get a peep at the show through gaps in the fence.

By the end of his first summer season at Halfpenny Hatch, Astley had filled out his programme to two hours in length with the help of a new act. It was inspired by an actual event, a sharp reminder that he was living in very dangerous times:

This was a period of great economic distress and political strife, the likes of which had not been seen by Londoners for generations. In 1768 a series of long, hard frosts had pushed up the price of everything except beef; the farmers in the surrounding area would rather drive their cattle into London for slaughter than see them starve in the field. The misery was made worse by flooding on both banks of the Thames. Rising food and coal prices sparked protests and a wave of disputes swept London over wages and working conditions. The labour market was already overstocked with demobilised servicemen returning home from the Seven Years War. Desperate silk weavers rioted in the streets in their thousands to protest against low wages, attacking their masters' houses and destroying looms. This was the year that the word 'strike' entered the English language through the actions of a handful of East End dockers. The first event to bear the name was violent and seven coal-heavers from Wapping were hanged for taking part in it.

St. George's Fields was a ramshackle neighbourhood on the western boundary of Lambeth Marsh, just a few hundred yards from Astley's Riding School. It was too swampy to grow food on, but close enough to the centre of London to make it the ideal spot for public gatherings of all kinds, including the famous Southwark Fair, a riot of stalls, strolling players, dancers, puppet shows and all kinds of entertainments that arrived every September. By the mid 1700s century, the fields had become something more like an unofficial civic park. It was also a handy gathering place for political demonstrations, the consequences of which were occasionally dire.

Just a couple of weeks before the opening of Astley's new venture, London was in turmoil. The government's bête noire that year was John Wilkes, political journalist, rakish wit and 'the ugliest man in England' (he was cross-eyed and missing most of his teeth). Wilkes was a rabblerousing champion for reform and a lightning rod for popular discontent. He had spent the early 1760s mocking King George III and his government in the press. He pushed his luck too far when he said that Lord Bute got to be Prime Minister by sleeping with the king's mother. The king sued for seditious libel: Wilkes fled to France. In 1768, he returned to stand as MP for Middlesex and was promptly arrested and sent to King's Bench Prison, a stone's throw from St. George's Fields.

On 10 May, fifteen thousand Wilkes supporters gathered in the fields to protest. A magistrate reading the Riot Act was struck on the head with a brick. Soldiers fired two volleys of musket balls into the crowd. Seven civilians died, including a woman orange seller and a passer-by driving a hay cart. William Allen, the son of a farmer at work in his father's stables nearby, was mistaken for a ringleader and shot dead in cold blood. The 'St. George's Fields Massacre', as it become known, was deeply shocking and led to riots all over London. The American statesman Benjamin Franklin, who was in the city at the time, wrote of 'sawyers destroying saw-mills, sailors unrigging all the outward-bound ships... watermen destroying private boats and threatening bridges.'

A few weeks later, Astley introduced a new comic routine to his programme called The Taylor's (sic) Ride to Brentford.[24] It followed the horseback-riding misadventures of a hapless tailor called Billy Buttons, played by Astley himself. It involved a good deal of knockabout fun, as the inept rider is outwitted and outmanoeuvred by his clever mount and tumbles off again and again. He went on to develop more sophisticated versions of this simple routine (in some, Billy Buttons is assisted by a 'stooge' placed in the audience) but the basic formula was roughly the same, the act always ending with the tailor being chased around the ring by his horse.

The Taylor's Ride is sacramental in circus history. It marks the appearance of the first ever circus clown/acrobat – Astley himself – and, arguably, the birth of slapstick. The formula may still be familiar to circus-goers today, like the clown-car routine. Whether the audience were aware of its origins or not, it was a piece of surreal social commentary, indirectly inspired by the riots in nearby St. George's Fields. The story about a tailor galloping to Brentford in time to vote for the radical Whig leader John Wilkes in the controversial Middlesex election had made its way into folklore and various books and prints. Why a tailor? They were always good value for a cheap laugh because tailors were

---

24 The act often also bore the intriguing subtitle, The Unaccountable Sagacity of the Taylor's Horse.

supposed to be foppish, effete types, inept at manly pursuits such as horsemanship. Depicting a Wilkesite as a comic fool being give the run-around by a clever horse was a satirical attack on radicals.

This was ground-breaking stuff: trick-riding, clowning, slapstick and politics rolled into one. The Taylor's Ride became a beloved staple of the venue and helped make its creator famous, putting Astley's Riding School on the London entertainment map. The act proved so popular that every Victorian circus company was re-staging exactly the same routine a hundred years later and versions of it are still being staged all over the world. [25] You can't help wondering what Astley's old army colleagues, former tailors who rode and fought with courage at Emsdorf, felt about being made the butt of this long-running joke.

That autumn, Philip took his horses to New Spring Gardens in Chelsea, then on a small tour of northern England, joining the regular trail of itinerant players travelling the fairs. This was his most difficult test as a showman yet, competing for attention with dozens of noisy rivals in booths and sideshows. At Carlisle his ring, pitched on the bank of a river, was flooded and he had to watch as a whole week's takings were lost in the water. But lessons had been learned and he had picked up a few new ideas along the way. Astley was back at Halfpenny Hatch in time for a Christmas performance with two new acts; a wire-walking, horse-riding monkey called Colonel Jackoo (or Jacko) and a young gentleman tumbler from Germany – his very first paid act from outside his immediate family.

In the meantime, he had kept up his old trade as a cabinetmaker. This was his safety net, just in case his new career didn't work out. He needn't have worried. On a good day in the ring he was taking more than forty guineas – about £2,500

---

25 America was first introduced to The Taylor in 1773 when Jacob Bates took it to New York. Charles Dickens refers to it in *Hard Times* as the 'highly novel and laughable hippocomedietta of The Tailor's Journey to Brentford'.

in today's values. His faith in his own abilities was more than justified and his first season had exceeded his wildest expectations, but he was already dreaming of expansion. He had seen at first-hand just how tough and transitory the life of a travelling performer could be and it impressed upon him the importance of owning his own permanent site. It was also clear that he was fast outgrowing Halfpenny Hatch. He needed somewhere bigger and better to showcase his and wife's talents.

4

AN ASSEMBLAGE OF STRANGE THINGS

OLD WINDMILLS AT LAMBETH, ABOUT 1750.

Lambeth Marsh viewed from the Thames in around 1750.
Public domain.

Even as Philip and Patty Astley arrived there, Lambeth Marsh was
changing rapidly. Two new bridges had opened up the once-green
oasis to traffic from the City and Westminster, and new roads were
being built, transforming the surrounding area into a hub for light
industry. It was turning into a centre for timber yards, brewers,

wire-makers, glass-makers and anchor-smithies. There was a stone manufacturer and a wine factory, a pottery works and a dye-works. There were 'tenter-grounds' for the bleaching and drying of clothes and factories where rags were turned into paper or sold to clothe the poor. There was also a candle works, an offshoot of a less respectable Lambeth business; the local press reported that 'a society of persons did exist at Lambeth... who made a trade of digging up the bodies of the dead; they made candles of the fat, extracted volatile alkali from the bones, and sold the flesh for dog's meat'. There was also the famous 'Lactarium', established by a lady who called herself Lactaria. She sold milk and would 'accommodate no disorderly people'. Very soon, Lambeth Marsh would also have the world's first permanent circus.

Philip didn't need to look very far for his new site. Less than ten minutes' walk from Halfpenny Hatch, at the Surrey end of Westminster Bridge, they found a vacant plot of land, a corner site at the junction with Stangate Street[26] with a frontage overlooking the Thames, close enough to the bridge to be seen by everyone passing along the busy road, but far enough back from the river to be safe from flooding. It had once been home to one of the many timber yards that lined the half mile of riverbank downstream from the Lambeth end of Westminster Bridge. Lately it was used by an old man who had tried to make a living by raising pheasants. Astley had heard on the grapevine that this business had failed and the owner was anxious to raise some cash so he could travel abroad. The showman approached the owner and made an offer. After a reasonable amount of haggling, he was able to secure a five-year mortgage on the plot for £200. He reckoned his money was well spent because he could earn it back in a matter of weeks.

---

26 Coincidentally, the legendary clown Joseph 'Joey' Grimaldi had lodgings very nearby. Although he and Astley were contemporaries, the greatest ever clown and the inventor of the circus never worked together. Grimaldi appeared for a season at Astley's former Dublin Amphitheatre in 1803, but by that time the venue had been sold to a rival company.

Astley had a site for his new venue. He also had access to a large quantity of timber, conveniently left behind by the owner. But he was still desperately short of funds to complete his project. Fate intervened, or so the story goes. According to Astley, he was crossing Westminster Bridge one day when he found a diamond ring lying in the road. The ring's loss was never advertised by the owner, so he sold it for seventy guineas. This mysterious find is most likely Astley's invention. He was a natural story-teller and this is probably one of those occasions when he allowed his imagination to run away with him. The public records show that, around the same time, his deceased great uncle, Newcastle-under-Lyme's postmaster, Richard Milligane, left him fifty pounds in his will.[27] One way or another, he was the recipient of good fortune and had enough funds to build his new venue. For the next few months the Surrey end of Westminster Bridge was a whirlwind of activity as he worked to transform the derelict timber yard into something like a theatre for entertainment.

In the days leading up to the opening of their new season in May 1769, Patty paraded around the West End of London banging a drum to announce the forthcoming high jinks, accompanied by two pipers, together with Little Billy and an assistant distributing handbills. In effect, it was the precursor of the first ever pre-show circus parade, where performers would arrive in a town and walk the streets drumming up support for their show while people gathered along the route to see if the circus was worth going to. Meanwhile, Patty's husband, an imposing figure in full military rig astride his stallion, stood at the foot of Westminster Bridge, brandishing his sword and inviting all to see the wonders they would perform.

The pre-show publicity was a huge success. On the opening day there was a much bigger crowd than before and the roads around the new Astley's Riding House were blocked with people

---

27   About £8,500 in 2019 values.

flocking to the show. Extra constables were laid on to deal with the traffic and control the large crowd who had been left outside. The opening programme was much the same as before. There were dazzling displays of horsemanship from Astley and his wife; these feats displayed 'without any happaratus whatsoever from the saddle'. Little Billy, 'three feet high from the deserts of Arabia', now a firm favourite, performed all his usual tricks and there was comedy with The Taylor's Ride. To this he added a few new acts: his German tumbler, his wire-walking monkey Colonel Jackoo and, for the first time, Astley performed card tricks on horseback. He also experimented with a couple of audience participation events. There was a 'bloodless' broadsword fight in which the contestants were invited to hit each other with soot-blackened sticks while wearing white jackets to show the marks, and a sack race in which competitors wore sacks over their heads as well as around their legs.

The building work was finished in time for the 1770 season. The new venue was basically still an open-air arena in the middle of a field but the addition of high wooden fences gave the impression of a substantial purpose-built structure for equestrian displays. The outside walls were whitewashed and decorated with painted canvas depicting some of spectacles to be enjoyed within, mostly pictures of horses and riders striking various poses. Above the main covered entrance was a large cut-out of a figure with raised whip on horseback. Inside, the ring was about sixty-five feet in diameter and covered with a mixture of topsoil and sawdust to make it easier on the horses' feet.[28] The arena was surrounded by a gallery of two or three rows of covered seating. The back of the building, facing the riding circle, served as a grandstand, with stables for the horses below and boxes for

---

28 Still the standard surface for travelling circuses the world over. Some permanent circus venues today use coconut matting instead, but it is more slippery and limits the speed at which the horses can work.

spectators above. Outside there was an area containing apparatus 'for breaking and training vicious horses.' It was all very crude and makeshift compared to other theatrical venues but it was a huge improvement on Halfpenny Hatch.

Although his show was bringing in plenty of paying customers, the capital improvements were still a big drain on Astley's pocket. He also knew that displays of horsemanship with the odd sideshow wouldn't keep the public's interest forever. With each passing year there were also more and more trick-riders setting up shop across London. There was another consideration – his health. Remarkably, given his shows of great athleticism, Astley spent the whole of his career as a performer to date under the handicap of a war wound in his leg. Although he was in his prime, the scar from his German campaign was troubling him more and more. He needed something that would give him a break from the punishing, exhausting trick-riding routines. At the same time his riding school business was growing and he was working hard to establish himself as a fashionable riding-master.[29] Every morning from six o'clock onwards he was up and ready to receive new pupils or to take in new young horses to break and train, meanwhile buying and breaking in new horses of his own for his riding school and his evening performances. It needed phenomenal drive and stamina to keep all of these plates

---

29 As promoted in this advertisement:

The True and Perfect Seat on Horseback. – There is no creature yields so much profit as the horse; and if he is made obedient to the hand and spur, it is the chief thing that is aimed at. Mr Astley undertakes to break in the most vicious horse in the kingdom, for the road or field, to stand fire, drums, &c.; and those intended for ladies to canter easy. His method, between the jockey and the *ménage*, is peculiar to himself; no gentleman need despair of being a complete horseman that follows his directions, having eight years' experience in General Elliot's regiment. For half-a-guinea he makes known his method of learning (teaching) any horse to lay (*sic*) down at the word of command, and defies any one to equal it for safety and ease.

spinning. If he was to survive, he had to diversify, so Astley started to look around for new acts. His timing couldn't have been better.

The actor-manager David Garrick, talented and haughty purist of Drury Lane, was London theatre's most outspoken advocate. He enjoyed his reputation as an epic intellectual snob. Garrick was contemptuous of all forms of 'popular' stage entertainment and, for that matter, anything else that didn't meet his own high standards; he once claimed he walked out of a Punch and Judy show because it made him physically sick. He especially resented the idea of rope-dancers and clowns on the stage; 'Nothing but downright starving would induce me to bring such defilement to the home of William Shakespeare,' he said. Eventually the popularity of clowns and the like grew to the extent that Garrick was forced to eat his words: 'If you won't come for Lear or Hamlet, then I must give you Harlequin.' For the meantime, however, he was purging the London stage of anything that didn't look like serious acting. The London authorities had also recently closed some of the city's fairgrounds, citing a lack of sanitation. Happily for Astley, there were now lots of unemployed clowns, jugglers and other sideshow workers desperate for work.

In 1770 he took on a fourteen-year-old equestrian, Master Griffiths, who was joined shortly after by Astley's very first hired clown, a gentleman referred to in the handbills only as Porter. Then came the Ferzis, a family of Italian rope-dancers poached from the Sadler's Wells theatre. In the following months he introduced Fortunelle the clown and rope-dancer, then the first ever circus strongman act, Signor Colpi and his family. This Italian performer lay on his back while balancing up to four of his children on his feet in various postures and combinations. Patty also continued to pitch in, riding two or three horses. Meanwhile her husband dominated the ring, presiding over this curious mixture of spectacle, amusement and skill as master of entertainments.

Every month, new names were being added to the handbill, including another strongman called Mr Hawtin with 'heavy and light balances' and Signor Rossignol the bird imitator. Rossignol could produce the birdcalls of the finch, goldfinch, canary, skylark, woodlark, blackbird, linnet, robin, thrush and nightingale. He could also imitate the sound of a violin, although his reputation suffered when it was discovered that he was concealing an actual violin under his cloak.[30]

Equestrianism was still the backbone of the show. The Astleys opened the 1771 season at the end of March with Philip performing on one, two, three and four horses 'in a manner far superior than ever exhibited.' In May, he rode two horses at a gallop 'while carrying a young lady on his head', enacted a 'Grand Deception with the Cards' and picked up a shilling from the ground at full gallop while blindfolded.

His old war wound was an ever-present reminder that he also needed another trick-rider to do some of the heavy lifting. In March, Astley made an addition to his equestrian troupe, a brilliant young horseman called Charles Hughes. Astley must have thought very highly of his new recruit because he allowed him to develop the now famous 'Taylor's Ride' theme by introducing a new slapstick character, based on a comical drunken sailor riding to the hustings from Portsmouth. Astley was so impressed with Hughes' horsemanship that he invited him to take over the entire programme for a week in June while the proprietor took a break.

There were improvements to the infrastructure, too. Astley was now making enough money to build a new hundred-and-twenty-foot-long covered gallery. He was always at pains to inform his customers that a light shower wouldn't lead to the cancellation of a show, but there were still too many performances lost to heavy downpours. At least now most of his audience could stay

---

30 Rossignol probably warbled his last at Astley's Amphitheatre at Westminster Bridge in the summer of 1778. Confusingly, there was also a Rossignol imitator performing around this time while the real Rossignol was chirping in Norwich.

dry while they watched Astley and his wife risking their necks on slippery saddles.

Apart from his pre-show parades and the distribution of handbills, for the most part he relied on word-of-mouth and local neighbourhood trade to drum up publicity for his entertainments. He received little newspaper publicity other than paid advertisements in the local press. One of these promised:

> Horsemanship by Mr Astley, Mr Taylor, Signor Markutchy, Miss Vangable, and other transcendent performers, a minuet by two horses, in a most extraordinary manner, a comical musical interlude, called The Awkward Recruit.

There was a new animal act too: all the way from Naples, Signor and Signora Malizia and their menagerie of dancing dogs.[31]

Philip was never shy about trading on his military credentials, promoting himself in his handbills and advertisements as the 'English Hussar'. Most of the other equestrian performers dressed as jockeys when they were performing, but Philip deliberately set himself apart by wearing his military uniform, cannily marketing himself as a patriot who had fought for king and country. Meanwhile his programme was evolving with new novelty acts, a bewildering medley of theatre, acrobatics, comedy, trick-riding – in fact anything that he thought might pull an audience – and it was changing almost on a weekly basis. A typical show at Astley's could last up to five hours and was described in one of his very first press reviews as 'a hodge-podge':

> For here you have rope-dancing, singing, pantomime, wire-dancing, the warbling of birds, horsemanship, women vaulting on the slack

---

31 In July 1786 the Malizias fell foul of Georgian theatre licensing laws that treated travelling players as criminals. They were arrested as vagrants while parading their mutts through Bristol and were flogged.

rope, imitations of hounds, organs, and dying wild boars, stage-dancing, buffoonery, mimicry, and agility of all kinds; in short, the eye and the ear are amused by an incessant variety, and we wonder how, in the name of Fortune, Astley contrives to procure such an assemblage of strange things.

Astley's apparent knack for being in the right place at the right time hadn't deserted him. King George III was making his way over Westminster Bridge one day when his horse suddenly bolted, panicked by the mass of people crowding to see him pass. Astley, among the crowd clamouring to catch a glimpse of the monarch, stepped forward and calmed the horse. To show his gratitude, King George invited the showman and his company to give a command performance before the royal household in Richmond Park. The French Ambassador, who was present at the Royal Court on the day of the show, was so impressed that he invited Astley and his troupe, Little Military Learned Horse and all, to stage a repeat performance for the King and Queen of France at Fontainebleau. Lady luck was smiling on Astley again.

Astley's London season ended in the early autumn, then he and his company toured through the winter. He spent the early winter months of 1772 performing in Dublin, then in April they set sail from Greenwich for France, leaving behind a smaller unit in Lambeth to prepare for the new season due to open on Easter Monday. The royal chateau at Fontainebleau was a day's ride south of Paris. There, Philip, Patty and their ensemble performed before the ageing King Louis XV, accompanied by a phalanx of royal couriers including his *maitress-en-titre,* the young Madame Dubarry, whose job it was to ward off the king's periodic bouts of depression by keeping him entertained. There is no record of Astley's private performance at Fontainebleau, but it is likely that he would have been unable to resist showing off with some of the finer points of dressage and *haute école* that his royal audience would have been very familiar with, before getting down to the crowd-pleasing showmanship that he was more famous for. In any event it is reasonable to assume that his audience was appreciative of his artistry in the saddle because it was the beginning of a long and very fruitful working relationship in France.[32] The performance had also greatly enhanced his reputation, for now he could claim with some legitimacy that his acts were 'as performed before the crowned heads of Europe'.

Astley raced home in time for the opening day of his season, Easter Monday. The day was special in the lives of all ordinary men and women in eighteenth-century London. Their working hours were long, from five in the morning till seven at night for six days a week. Apart from the eight 'hanging days' a year when they went to see the execution at Tyburn, the only official holidays were Christmas Day, Easter Monday and Whitsun. No wonder, then, that they let rip on their days off. Astley anticipated that the opening of the new season would see holiday crowds descend on his venue in greater numbers than ever.

Back in London, however, he received news that made him turn the air blue. Lambeth had not just one circus, it had two.

---

32 Although there are some reports that Philip Astley first performed at the Paris fairs and showgrounds as early as 1770.

5

THE WAR OF THE CIRCUSES: PART 1

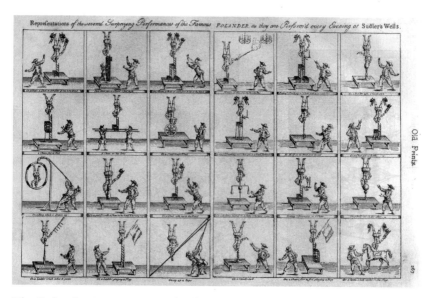

The Polander in action. He displayed his sensational balancing tricks at Astley's in 1870. Public domain.

Charles Hughes was Astley's best horseman. Some thought he was an even better trick-rider than Big Philip himself. He was twenty-three when he first joined Astley's troupe, four years younger than his employer but already a veteran performer in London and elsewhere. The circus comedian Jacob DeCastro, who worked with Hughes and knew him well, described him as 'a man whom nature had not been niggardly to in her favours': Hughes was charming, handsome, dashing and muscular, 'strong enough to carry an ox across his shoulders then take it home and eat it'. He also had a fierce temper and was prone to black moods. An early circus historian described Hughes as 'a dark, envious man'.

In Hughes, it is likely that Astley saw something of himself, a fellow grafter who had come up the hard way, a born horseman possessed of a riding talent almost equal to his own. If he thought Hughes was going to be a grateful protégé he was sorely mistaken. Beneath the surface charm, Hughes had a depth of ambition that almost matched his own. He was in Astley's company that day at Richmond Gardens, performing for King George, already plotting to set up on his own. While Astley was away in France, Hughes made his move. He leased a plot of land in St. George's Fields, less than a mile from Astley's new Riding School at Westminster Bridge.

Hughes's set-up was all too familiar. It was almost an identical copy of Astley's original venue at Halfpenny Hatch, an open-air ring surrounded by rickety wooden benches, the whole fenced-off with a wooden palisade. Outside, a large sign proclaimed 'Hughes's Riding School' – another direct imitation of his former employer. Later that season it became the more grandly-titled British Horse Academy.

Hughes opened on Easter Monday 1772, charging one shilling admittance or two shillings for 'a commodious room for the nobility (80 feet long)'. The company comprised its proprietor and three female riders: Mrs Hughes, a lady billed as Sobieska Clementina,[33] but who was in fact Hughes's sister and an un-named eight-year-old girl. A few weeks later the company was joined by 'the famous Miss Huntly from Sadler's Wells' and a young male equestrian, Master Jones.

The programme was also more or less a direct copy of Astley's show, including the Taylor's Ride slapstick routine and card-tricks

---

33   The name was a play on Clementina Sobieska, consort of the Jacobite claimant James Edward Stuart.

on horseback. Mrs Hughes could accurately fire a pistol from the saddle while leaping over a bar and she rode full tilt while standing on pint pots – a feat Hughes' advertisements claimed would instill 'terror' in spectators. His sister rode while standing upright in the saddle and the young girl did the same. The only entirely original act was Hughes in the role of puppet-master, standing on his saddle and riding around the ring while operating a marionette.

Mostly it was a vehicle to showcase Hughes' skills as horseman and athlete. He could do everything Astley did and more: vault backwards and forwards over three horses, or over a single horse forty times without pausing; stand facing backwards on the saddle while his horse jumped a bar; balance on his head on a broad-bottomed bottle placed on the saddle of a cantering horse; and so on.

When Astley saw that Hughes' show was almost a replica of his own he was angry beyond forbearance. He had trusted him and treated him as a top performer, and even let him run the show while he took a break. All along Hughes had been using him for his own ends. As far as Astley was concerned this was the vilest treachery, a diabolical deception – which was a bit rich, considering he had taken up employment in Islington with Old Sampson with the express intention of doing pretty much the same.

Astley went public with his grievance. Putting on his old army uniform, he jumped on his stallion and, accompanied by trumpeters and various members of his company, crossed the bridge to Westminster. Startled Londoners going about their daily business were treated to a verbal broadside directed against Hughes and 'these here pretenders to horsemanship', expressed in characteristically forceful and salty terms. His own forthcoming attractions, he pointed out to anyone within earshot – quite possibly most of the population of Westminster – were 'too tedious to mention' and featured a company of performers 'upwards of fifty, all different'.

It probably hadn't occurred to Astley that this was all free publicity for Hughes. A lot of people wanted to see for themselves what this 'pretender' could do and they flocked to his new Riding School in their thousands. Hughes' equestrian assault took London by storm. For Astley, almost literally sharing the field with a competitor was bad enough. When his spies reported that even more aspects of Hughes' growing programme were carbon copies of his own, he was livid.

The battle lines were drawn, each man attempting to outclass and vilify the other. Down the road, Hughes kept an anxious eye on Astley activities, while Astley's spies kept a beady eye on Hughes. As soon as Hughes developed a new trick, Astley immediately worked up a better version of it. If Hughes could jump over a five-bar gate standing on a horse's back, Astley would do it blindfold. If Astley promised to ride with one foot on his head, Hughes would do it with his left toe in his mouth. Astley rode around the ring balancing a nine-year old girl on his head. Mrs Hughes countered by riding around the ring with her head balanced on a pint pot. To rival Astley's Little Military Learned Horse, in July, Hughes introduced his own Horse of Knowledge, 'the wisest animal in the Metropolis'. This horse could fire a cannon and a pistol and was 'the only horse at present in the kingdom that will fetch and carry'.

Like many parents in the theatre, Astley saw little point in allowing his offspring to be idle when they could be learning a skill and earning a wage. On 17 August 1772, his five-year-old son John made his equestrian debut. According to the handbills, while on horseback the youngster could dance, vault, play on the violin and 'display a flag in attitudes which have never been exhibited or even thought of by any horseman in Europe'. Within a matter of weeks Hughes offered further provocation with his own infant performer, who 'will exhibit at Blackfriars-road more Extraordinary things than ever yet witnessed, such as leaping over a Horse forty times without stopping between the springs –Leap the Bar standing on the saddle with his right foot on the Saddle, and his left Toe in his Mouth.' Never missing an opportunity to make it personal, whereas John Astley was merely a 'Young Gentleman', Hughes's juvenile equestrian was billed a 'Young Gentleman, son of a Person of Quality'.

This faintly absurd equestrian rivalry, with each owner straining to outdo the other with original performances on horseback, reached its apotheosis when Astley hired the astonishing Daniel Wildman[34], equestrian performer and bee-wrangler. Wildman was a trick-rider who could stand on the back of a horse as it galloped around the ring, with one foot on the horse's saddle and the other on the animal's neck. He could also stand on the saddle with the bridle in his mouth while firing a pistol. This was unexceptional by the standards of his peers. Wildman's unique competitive advantage was that he performed these equestrian stunts with a swarm of live bees covering his entire face and head. Wildman could command his bees to do more or less anything. He could make one column of bees march over a table while another column swarmed in the air then returned to their hive. The trick, apparently, is simply a matter of getting the queen bee under your control, after which the rest of the colony will follow your every command. Wildman also made sure his bees were thoroughly sated with syrup: a full bee is a happy bee. Wildman had other talents besides. For instance, audience members were invited to participate by cutting off the head of a chicken, then watch in

---

34 Daniel Wildman was also the author of *A Complete Guide for the Management of Bees Throughout the Year*, practical advice for putative bee tamers and a plug for his Bee and Honey Warehouse in Holborn. Available from all good bookshops and the foyer at Astley's.

amazement as Wildman reconnected the parts and restored the bisected poultry to full health.

Wildman taught – or accidentally disclosed – his bee-taming secret to Patty Astley, thereby ensuring his own redundancy because, before the season ended, she too was riding around the ring engulfed in a 'muff' of bees and was still astonishing all-comers with her apian partners three years later.

Astley and Hughes also competed on literary terms. Hughes published an equestrian manual, *The Compleat Horseman; or, the Art of Riding Made Easy*, in which the newly self-proclaimed Professor of Horsemanship offered riding tips such as, 'Your loins should be lax and pliable, like the coachman on his box' and, 'Ladies should wear Italian shoes with very long quarters, and the heel of the shoe coming forward to the middle of the foot'. Astley (now self-titled 'Professor of Equitation') countered with his book, *The Modern Riding-master, or, a key to the Knowledge of the Horse, and Horsemanship*, dedicated in groveling prose to King George III.

The feud between Astley and Hughes was very public. Astley, with some justification, accused his rival of using his promotional literature to copy his performances. Mysterious, unattributed handbills were distributed around the city, blasting Astley's reputation. Astley returned fire with some self-penned doggerel denouncing Hughes. The press advertisements in which they trash-talked each other made entertaining reading. When, in July, Astley announced that he and his wife intended to set off for Normandy the following Tuesday for their usual season in Paris, his rival scoffed:

Hughes has the honour to inform the Nobility, etc., that he has no intention of setting out every day to France for three following seasons, his Ambition being fully satisfied by the applause he has received from Foreign Gentlemen who come over the Sea to see him.

The sparring continued when Astley returned to London. Wittily, he published an advertisement promoting his new playbill entirely in French.

Across the river, the equestrian stalwart Old Sampson was watching the rivalry unfold and no doubt appreciating the irony of his former employee's vexation. In May, however, he tried to bring the two rival circus owners together to broker some kind of deal. He offered to ride alternate evenings at each venue. His attempt at arbitration failed and the two parties were soon at each other's throats again. From now on, as long as both men were alive they would remain bitter rivals, each seeking to disparage and outdo the other at every turn.

As Hughes continued to draw crowds away from his business, for the first time in his professional life Astley was on the back foot. An exceptionally wet September had also washed away a large part of his programme, forcing him to lay off his performers, to close his season much earlier than usual and take a break in newly-fashionable Bath. His consolation was that the bad weather was wrecking Hughes's season as well. Even so, his rival continued to mock him in his handbills:

Hughes humbly thanks the Nobility etc. for the Honour of their Support, and also acquaints them his Antagonist has catched a cold so near to Westminster Bridge, and for his recovery is gone to a warmer Climate, which is Bath in Somersetshire. He boasts, poor fellow, no more of activity... Therefore Hughes is unrivalled.

As a businessman, Astley knew these defamations were to his advantage because they created curiosity. Their public rivalry was good for both venues. As well as the artisans who worked at the local docks and wood yards, Astley's and Hughes' entertainments were now being visited by the well-to-do from Westminster and they were picking up footfall from Vauxhall

Gardens about a mile down-river. The patent theatres were only open during the autumn and winter, so there were more than enough customers to go round to keep both venues full throughout their summer season.

The competition also spurred Astley on to create more ambitious entertainments. For the 1773 season he was back with fire in his belly, opening on Easter Monday with a bigger and more varied programme than ever before. As well as the usual astonishing displays of horsemanship and slapstick, there was a Sagacious Dog who could answer questions such as, 'Does Beauty or Virtue in the Fair Sex more attract our Affections?' There was also a family of acrobats from Verona performing 'La Force d' Hercule', building a human pyramid by standing on each other's shoulders. A 'Polander' performed balancing feats on ladders and chairs[35] and a Spaniard vaulted over a ribbon suspended eight feet above the ground, somersaulted off a board sixteen feet high, firing a pair of pistols before landing, leaped over fourteen grenadiers (including one who had a boy standing on his shoulders) then jumped through a flaming hogshead suspended eight feet from the ground. Astley was also overjoyed to add to his troupe another family member, his sister Elizabeth, performing on horseback. When Philip's family first moved to London, Elizabeth had stayed in Newcastle to live with their great-uncle Richard Milligane.

In reply to Hughes's increasing variety of spectacular equestrian tricks, there was also a new military-based spectacular, a reconstruction of the battle of Emsdorf, with his own 15th Light Dragoons heroically charging the French infantry and taking their

---

35   In the circus, a polander was someone who performed a balancing act usually on top of a pole, nowadays known as a 'perch act' performed by perchists. It may have been named after the 'Little Polander' who performed in from the mid-1700s.

colours. His establishment also had a new name – The British Riding School.

Charles Hughes, having completed a winter tour of Hungary and France with his wife and sister, opened his 1773 season with three new acts, the first an Italian violinist who played the instrument in 'five different attitudes' and bird impressions,[36] the second an enigmatic performance called the 'Potius of Italy' – 'the particulars of which are inexpressible'. If the first two new acts were unlikely to give Astley sleepless nights, the third certainly did. Philip Breslaw was a brilliant German conjuror who travelled extensively in England from the 1750s. In Cockspur Street in Westminster he opened the first ever purpose-built theatre for magic acts, Breslaw's Exhibition Rooms, where for three night a week he performed sleight-of-hand tricks with cards, watches, rings and other paraphernalia. He was chiefly famous for what was probably the world's first mind-reading act. His show bills promised:

> First, to tell any lady or gentleman the card that they fix on, without asking any questions. Second, to make a remarkable piece of money to fly out of any gentleman's hand into a lady's pocket-handkerchief, at two yards distance. Third, to change four or five cards in any lady's or gentleman's hand several times into different cards. Fourth, to make a fresh egg fly out of any person's pocket into a box on the table, and immediately to fly back again into the pocket.

Breslaw was triumph at Hughes' establishment and became a popular fixture, to the great annoyance of Astley who, despite his best efforts, failed to secure a rival illusionist of equal standing. Having bitterly denounced imitations of his own performances, Astley simply decided to do all the magic acts himself.

---

36 Most likely one of Astley's original acts, Signor Rossignol.

In fact he had already performed as a slight-of-hand artist. In 1770 he rented a room in Soho where he produced a show called 'The Invisible Agent: or Proteus of Sieur Comus'.[37] He performed all the illusions himself, charging an entrance fee of two shillings and sixpence, undercutting the real Comus, who was performing nearby, by fifty per cent. He threw himself into his new career with his usual gusto, performing an astonishing exhibition of bullet-catching, as advertised in this handbill:

On Monday next (besides the usual diversions of this place) Mr Astley will perform the grand Experience with a LOADED PISTOL. He will suffer any man in the company to Fire at him, when he will receive the Ball at the Point of a Knife, on a principle never attempted by anyone before (Sieur Comus of Paris excepted).

For the audience, it must have been an extraordinary sight to see the popular war hero Astley facing a loaded pistol.

Breslaw saw this incursion into his territory as a personal affront and publicly attacked Astley as a 'hobby-horse rider'. Astley responded by promoting his 'little learned military horse' as being as good as any conjurer – 'Breslaw not excepted'. More bitter recriminations followed, Astley publishing an article in a local newspaper claiming that the German had performed in Cambridge and had been 'tossed in a blanket' by three university students because of alleged lewd behaviour towards some female spectators. Breslaw replied with a sly reference to Astley's well-documented public feud with Hughes, noting that, as there were 'already several Actions against Astley for quarrelling with and abusing different persons', he would not fight a Paper War.[38]

---

37 The stage name of the French magician, fortune-teller and 'Physician to the King' Nicolas-Phillipe Ledru.

38 The death of the enigmatic Herr Breslaw was reported in the press three times: in 1783, 1794 and correctly, in Liverpool, in 1803.

The summer wore on, with the only two circus owners in the world going almost eyeball-to-eyeball, operating just a few hundred yards apart, deadlocked in an increasingly venomous rivalry, offering competing, but often entirely similar programmes. There was no reason to suspect that this state of affairs would not continue *ad infinitum*, but then fate intervened, bringing their seasons to a sudden, dramatic close.

6

BRIDEWELL

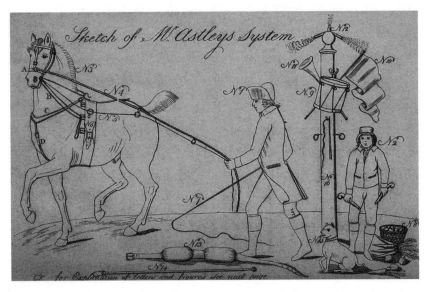

Illustration from Astley's book A System of Equestrian Education *published in 1801.*

The eighteenth century was a boom time for London theatre. It was the place where everyone went to be entertained, from aristocrats to apprentices. In terms of reach it had something like the combined power of the TV, cinema and internet today. But putting on any sort of entertainment in Georgian Britain was legally risky and the laws governing public performances opaque and confusing, to put it mildly. For the likes of Philip Astley and Charles Hughes, operating on the margins of respectability, they were a minefield.

Oliver Cromwell rang the death knell for theatre in Britain when he had them all shut down in 1642. When the theatres reopened eighteen years later King Charles II issued just two Royal Patents, to Drury Lane and Covent Garden, giving them the right to put on theatrical entertainments, at the same time banning anyone else from doing the same. Effectively, the two theatres royal, situated within yards of each other in Covent Garden, enjoyed a duopoly over London theatre. The West End audience, however, was rapidly growing. The two patent establishments couldn't satisfy demand and new theatres were springing up all over town. At first, the authorities turned a blind eye, until these new illegal patent-less theatres and their playwrights and actors started saying very rude things indeed about their betters and rulers. In 1728 The Little Theatre in the Haymarket produced John Gay's hugely popular anti-government satire *The Beggar's Opera*, which lampooned government ministers in barely disguised terms. It was followed by Henry Fielding's *Grub Street Opera* which openly mocked the prime minister, Robert Walpole, to the considerable amusement of the nation. A production of *The Golden Rump* pushed the envelope too far when it scandalously suggested that the Queen administered enemas to her husband.[39]

The paranoid prime minister began to find sedition everywhere and in the patent-less theatres especially. In April 1737 he drove through his infamous Licensing Act. From now on, anyone performing a play without a royal warrant or a special licence issued by a magistrate could be thrown into prison. All new work had to be submitted to the Lord Chamberlain for vetting. Anyone failing to comply could be heavily fined or 'silenced'. At a stroke, apart from the two patented theatres, every playhouse in London was put out of business. West End theatre was effectively muzzled, a situation which persisted, to some degree, until the 1960s.

---

39 Henry Fielding and others suspected that this play was engineered by Walpole himself.

Walpole's legislation was rightly condemned as one of the most heavy-handed acts of state censorship in British history, but it had some unintended benefits. The first was a sudden boost for the career of William Shakespeare, whose works had lain largely forgotten up to now but, because they were existing work, were not subject to the scrutiny of the Lord Chamberlain's office. Another was that most of the London theatre was effectively driven underground with increasingly creative efforts to circumnavigate the law. For example, plays were taken off the main theatre stage and performed at 'events', billed as 'an evening of music' or 'a cup of tea' with a sideshow. The Lord Chamberlain wasn't entirely successful at censoring plays, of course, and quite a few jokes at the expense of the authorities were smuggled past him and his officials, to the amusement of the rather more streetwise Georgian audiences. If anything, it created something of a boom in the satire industry. Further scrutiny of the 1737 Act also revealed that only complete plays had to be submitted for approval. Non-patent theatres could still produce melodrama, ballad opera and burlesque which incorporated music between short scenes and were not classed as plays. This gave birth to the form of entertainment which would become variety theatre, featuring singers, acrobats, jugglers and dancers with the satirical or otherwise subversive sketches sandwiched between the other acts and therefore safely away from the Lord Chamberlain's desk.

The legal status of the non-patent theatres, however, was still very complicated. The Disorderly Houses of 1751 stated that places of entertainment within twenty miles of London had to get a licence from a magistrate in order to carry on staging entertainment for audiences. These licenses were not a forgone conclusion. You could be refused one or have it withdrawn as a result of a local complaint about rowdy behaviour, for example. Theatre managers who invited trouble could find themselves hauled before a magistrate at the Quarter Sessions. Travelling actors meanwhile had the same legal status as 'rogues and vagabonds'. Anyone acting in a play, or involved in its performance in any way, who didn't have either a letter patent or a Lord Chamberlain's licence and who was wasn't legally settled in the place of the performance, was subject to fines or imprisonment. Repression, suppression and confusion followed as legislators, magistrates and theatre proprietors alike tried to negotiate and make sense of the complexities of absurd and unworkable legislation.

Not that any of this bothered Philip Astley. He had little time for the forces of law and order or, for that matter, the 'legitimate' theatrical establishment in Westminster. He was from the wrong side of the tracks or, in this case, the river, among the so-called transpontine[40] establishments. Ever since his performance before the king's household at Richmond Gardens he liked to let on that he too had a royal licence but in truth he didn't have a licence of any kind. Partly because he was taking advantage of lax theatre law enforcement on the south bank of the river, but mostly because of his reckless disregard for authority, he had never bothered to apply for one. To be fair, there were good reasons to believe that he might have been wasting his time even if he had. Apart from the two royal patent theatres, in the whole of London only three other performing licences had been granted: Sadler's Wells, Vauxhall Gardens and Ranalegh.

In Lambeth, anything went, without censorship and without licence. When it was just Philip, Patty and their three-horse show at Halfpenny Hatch, they were under the radar of the local magistrates. The appearance of Hughes in the vicinity and their very public spat, however, made both operations quite impossible to ignore. When the proprietor of Vauxhall Gardens lodged an official complaint, Surrey magistrates decided it was time they got involved. On 13 July 1773 Astley and Hughes were arrested and thrown into Bridewell prison. Astley was bailed. With an appeal

---

40   Literally, on or from the other side of the bridge.

pending but still no licence to perform legally in London, he took his company on an extended tour of the British Isles. In December 1773 he opened in Dublin and stayed there for a whole six months. In 1774 he travelled to France and performed his 'feats of horsemanship' at the Manège de Razade, rue des Vieilles Tuileries. In the years to come, Paris would become his second home.

Astley wasn't going to be bullied by the authorities. He liked to think of himself as more than a match than any magistrate; legal restrictions were minor annoyances to be overcome. In 1775 he returned to London and at the Surrey Assizes successfully argued that there was nothing in theatre law that banned displays of horsemanship. He also threatened to sue the Surrey magistrate Sir Joseph Mawbey for £10,000 for damaging his livelihood. This was a huge amount – around £1.4million in today's values – and an indication of just how profitable Astley's circus venture had become even at this early stage of his career. Charles Hughes, however, had no appetite for a fight. Released from Bridewell as a 'nuisance' he took his company on a long tour of Europe. His British Riding Academy would never open its doors again. For now, at least, Astley had the field all to himself once more.

He also had arguably his greatest stroke of good fortune. Almost five years had passed since he first took out his £200 mortgage on the land at Westminster Bridge and he was expecting his landlord's imminent return, but the owner never showed up. As far as anyone could tell, he had simply disappeared, thereby defaulting and surrendering the site. Astley was able to foreclose and take out a lease on the land until 1839.

Philip Astley's star was once again on the ascendancy. He had seen off his rival, beaten the system and his showground was his for at least his lifetime. On Easter Monday 1775 he opened on an even grander scale to great acclaim, with old favourites including 'The Taylor' and his wife's perplexing performance with her 'bee muff'. He added to his programme 'a variety of amusements from the Boulevards of Paris' including 'the roasted pig on the slack rope', whereby an acrobat lay on a twisted rope and was spun round as if he was on a spit.

Philip Astley was now a household name, commemorated in song and in popular dance tunes, *Astley's Ride*, *Astley's Flag* and *Astley's Hornpipe* – ironically, as dancing isn't high on the list of activities you associate with a man his size. Even Dr Samuel Johnson paid him a compliment: 'Were Astley to preach a sermon standing on a horse's back he would collect a multitude to hear him'. His prices had gone up, too. In 1769, Astley was charging a modest six pence for standing admission but now the charge was two shillings.

He was still testing the patience of the authorities. Having failed to nail him under the Theatre Licensing Act, in October 1777 Astley was summonsed to appear at Kingston assizes under the Disorderly Houses Act for 'performing contrary to Act 25 Geo. II, various feats of horsemanship accompanied with music'. Georgian trial procedures would be startling to a modern lawyer. The accused would approach the prosecuting counsel before the trial and offer them money to abandon the case. Bribery was endemic on both sides. Informers were routinely paid rewards for bringing criminal prosecutions: it was considered the most cost-effective way of catching law-breakers. When Casanova, who had some experience of legal procedure abroad, came to London he was shocked by the ease with which witnesses were bought or paid off. He once came across premises with the word EVIDENCE written in large characters in a window, advertising the fact that false witnesses could be bought within. Magistrates were easily corrupted: in London, Horace Walpole believed that 'the greatest criminals of this town are the officers of justice'. At Kingston, Astley was acquitted after a three-hour hearing, having allegedly bribed several witnesses. Contemporary press reports show that when he went on tour there were several more charges brought against him by magistrates up and down the country during this period, but he just paid a fine and moved on.

If there was one thing he loved more than anything it was a bargain. In February 1772 the unlamented Augusta, Dowager Princess of Wales and mother of King George III, died at Carlton House of throat cancer, aged fifty-two. Her funeral procession achieved two unwanted distinctions. The first was when the royal deceased was heckled and jeered all the way to the grave by a rowdy mob. The second was when the timber used to construct the covered way leading from the Painted Chamber to Westminster Abbey found its way into Astley's new roof.

Although the seats at his venue were now mostly covered, his ring was still at the mercy of the weather. In late 1778 he embarked on his most ambitious building plan to date. Using the timber he had cheekily acquired at a knockdown price from the royal funeral, he began work on covering his entire venue. Through the winter a gang of workmen was busy lashing and nailing wooden crossbars in place to form the framework, over which huge tarred canvasses were stretched to shelter performers and spectators alike. While the roofing work went on, Astley hired the Large Room at 22 Piccadilly for a temporary exhibition of 'Fire-Side Amusements' featuring *ombres chinoises* (silhouettes of cut-out Chinese figures against a screen) plus Little Billy, a 'learned dog', and Signor Rossignol was back with his bird calls. By all accounts the stint in Mayfair under Astley's management was a resounding success, but by the following Easter his new roof was finished and he was ready to return to Lambeth.

His showground had another new name, 'The Amphitheatre Riding-House... the most complete building of its kind in Europe.' It was the first time he called his venue an amphitheatre, the name he would be most associated with. It had classical Roman associations but Astley's use of the term was most likely inspired by somewhere much nearer home – Stoke's Amphitheatre in the Islington Road, famous for unregulated cudgel fights and pugilism from the 1730s and 1740s.

Significantly, the ring size had also shrunk from about sixty-five feet in diameter to forty-two feet. He found that this was the smallest area that still worked within the confines of the building, both for good horsemanship and good audience sight lines, a perfect blend of physics and sound management. This was the size he adopted for the rest of his career. The forty-two feet diameter circus ring, now internationally expressed at thirteen metres is, today, with very minor variations, the same the world over.

Thanks to the new roof his venue could remain open all year round. He knew full well that only the patent theatres were allowed to open through the winter but Astley wasn't the type to be bound by legal technicalities. He was soon thumbing his nose at the authorities once again by promoting 'Winter's Evening Amusements by Candlelight' which combined 'horsemanship, the pyramids, vaulting, balancing and all manner of feats on ladders, slack rope and springboard or 'trampoline.'[41] In November 1780, John Astley was being described on the handbills as 'the greatest performer that ever appeared in any age, and as a horseman, stands unparalleled by all nations'. The advertisements show him standing on his head on the saddle, or on one foot, all at full gallop. A speech bubble issuing from the mouth of young Astley announces, 'I'm only five years old!', although by that time he was about thirteen. The busy programme also promised:

Mrs Taylor, a young lady from Vienna, (who had the honour to perform many times by command of the Emperor of Germany, and other Royal Personages at different courts in Europe)

---

41   In circus folklore, the trampoline was named after an artiste named du Trampoline, who saw the possibility of using the trapeze safety net as a form of propulsion and landing device. According to the circus historian Disher the word trampoline was simply Astley's misspelling of the French *tremplin*, meaning springboard. While the etymology of trampoline may still be open to debate, the trapeze and his eponymous costume were invented by Jules Leotard in the mid-1800s.

performing several feats of horsemanship on a single horse; Tricks of STRENGTH and AGILITY, by the celebrated Mr Richer, equilibrist; Master and Miss Richer; Miss Hudson, and Miss Vangable. (Clown to the little family) Sieur Baptista Duboi, and Sieur Paulo and The POLANDER's TRICKS on chairs, tables, pedestals, ladders, &c.

It also featured a novelty never previously seen before at Astley's:

A BEAUTIFUL ZEBRA will walk round the Riding-School for the inspection of the nobility, gentry, and others. To describe the beauties of the Zebra would be much too large for a newspaper; and as many ladies and gentlemen have visited him in the Haymarket, a description of him would be superfluous.

Exhibitions of wild animals provided a great source of wonder and education in Georgian Britain, as well as opportunities to demonstrate their terrifying ignorance of animal welfare. The public fascination for 'exotics', as the beasts their colonialists sent home were called, was seemingly endless. Exotic animals had been around in London for a long time but the trade really took off after 1749 when an intrepid Dutch sea captain packed Europe's first rhinoceros into his hull. An advertisement boasted breathlessly: 'It runs with astonishing lightness! It knows how to swim and likes to dive in the water like a duck!' Entrepreneurs made small fortunes from acquiring and displaying extraordinary animals. In London, the roaring of wild animals being held in pitifully small cages was one of the sounds of the city. The writer Charles Lamb could hear the familiar cries of big cats as he walked home most evenings to his lodgings in Temple Lane. Eighteenth-century animal fanciers could get much closer to wild beasts than we ever do. A menagerie in Tottenham Court Road offered exotic birds alongside antelopes, lions, monkeys and porcupines. You could visit Richard Heppanstall's camels at the Talbot Inn on the Strand, or pick up a kangaroo from Pidcock's at Exeter Exchange, or be allowed to pat and stroke his rhinoceros. No self-respecting aristocrat with a scientific bent was without a private menagerie. The Duke of Richmond's private zoo at Goodwood housed five wolves, two tigers, a lion, two leopards, three bears, monkeys, eagles and 'a woman Tyger' plus 'a new animal he is very fond of which he calls a mangoose'. The Duchess of Portland collected so many exotics that friends suspected she was anticipating another Biblical deluge. The Earl of Shelburne kept an orangutan and a 'tame leopard' in his orangery at Bowood House. Sir Robert Walpole's pet flamingo warmed itself by his kitchen fire, while Sir Hans Sloane was followed round his Chelsea home by a tame, one-eyed wolverine; it was company for his opossum and his porcupine. The 4th Duke of Marlborough kept a tigress in his grounds in a cage, fed by regular orders made to the local butcher's shop. Records show that the tigress cost the same as three servants to feed.

The Georgians were most fascinated by really dangerous animals, with occasionally horrific ramifications. A Wiltshire maidservant was the first human victim of a tiger in Britain when she was mauled to death in a tavern yard. A panther was the star attraction at the Tower of London menagerie because she had 'recently torn the arm off a woman in a terrible manner'. Wallace the lion, who went on a national tour with Wombwell's Menagerie in the 1820s, chewed hands and limbs off three people, including his handler. When Wallace escaped in Derbyshire and killed a man he was returned to captivity, too valuable to put down.

Zebras were highly fashionable because the Queen herself once owned one. Charlotte of Mecklenburg-Strelitz was said to be extremely fond of her zebra, a wedding present from the governor of the Cape of South Africa on the occasion of her marriage to King George III on 8 September 1761. It was one of a pair, but a male companion didn't survive the journey on board

HMS Terpsichore. The 'Queen's Ass',[42] as she was called from the outset, was the first zebra ever seen in Great Britain and a firm favourite among the royal menagerie, drawing a constant stream of visitors from home and abroad, obliging her keeper to warn them to expect a hoof in the groin if they got too close.[43] Astley's own zebra was booty, plundered on the high seas. *The Ranger* was one of Bristol's most successful privateers, a two-hundred-ton American frigate carrying eighteen six-pounder guns and a hundred and ten men. On 24 August 1779 she and her partner *The Amazon* took a valuable prize, the rich Spanish ship *Santa Inez*, as it was sailing from Manila to Cadiz. It was captured after two hours' action, in which the two British ships took just one casualty: the unlucky master's mate on board *The Amazon* had his arm shot off by an eighteen-pounder. The cargo of the *Santa Inez*, sold in Bristol in February 1780, was valued at about £250,000 and comprised two hundred chests of sugar, nine tons of black pepper, ninety tons of dyewood and a quantity of beeswax. There was also an unexpected bonus on board, described in the newspapers as, 'a beautiful zebra, remarkably tame and quite young.' The article continued:

Of all the exhibitions that ever were exhibited in this city the Zebra or Wild Ass, taken by the Ranger and Amazon on its passage to Spain has the pre-eminence; this most beautiful animal is visited daily by the first families in Bristol. The Zebra continues in this city this day and absolutely no longer as she will be removed to Bath on Monday next for the inspection of the curious.

---

42 Satirically, her eldest son George was strongly associated with the 'Queen's Ass', other rump-related jokes also available.

43 The Queen was keen to breed from her zebra, so in the absence of a male of the species she bought a donkey and had white stripes painted on it. The ploy worked: the zebra became pregnant and gave birth to a 'zebroid'. The zebra's fearsome temper eventually persuaded the Queen to part with her pet. When the animal died it was stuffed and displayed at the Blue Boar Inn, York.

The auction of the zebra took place on 17 January 1780 at the Exchange. Three days later the *Bristol Gazette* reported that the zebra was 'sold to Mr Astley of London'. As it turned out, his zebra wasn't quite the star attraction that he had hoped for and after one or two showings he put it up for sale again. As far as we know the display of wild animals at Astley's amphitheatre was an experiment never repeated under his management and it wasn't until the following century that wild-animal acts became a circus institution.

Astley's was now so famous that its owner no longer felt the need to parade around London before a show announcing the forthcoming attractions,[44] but during actual performances he liked to prowl around the ring, holding a pair of lit candles, giving a running commentary on the exhibits, amusing the crowd and no doubt provoking many rude imitators and hecklers – although you imagine that one look from the huge ringmaster would silence the rowdiest catcall. Patty often walked alongside her husband, her luxuriant hair now so long that it trailed along the ground behind her. One evening there was a mishap when a candle was held too close and set her hair alight. After this incident she took the precaution of keeping it tucked under a massive wig. The unfortunate effect of this was that her head now appeared several times too big for her body.

Another regular feature Astley developed was his banter with a clown known as Mr Merryman. Clowning was born in the seventeenth century but it took another hundred years before it found its natural home in Astley's circus. This clown was a foil for the proprietor's self-scripted wisecracks: for instance, 'Ladies and gentleman, Mr Merryman has a great deal of wit'. The banter was

---

44 In 1773 he announced to the London press that he was too busy to parade the streets and 'never more intends that abominable practice'.

simple, almost childlike, and existed to underscore the talents of his main acts.[45]

That summer, the smooth running of Astley's Amphitheatre was rudely interrupted by the worst urban violence in modern British history. Radicalism was stirring again in nearby St. George's Fields. A couple of years earlier the government had started to relax the strict laws that denied Catholics the right to vote, buy land or even inherit property. Many people were unhappy about this, notably Lord George Gordon, a twenty-nine-year-old member of parliament and third son of a Duke. He was widely suspected to be mad: he was certainly unhinged in matters of religion. Gordon was a well-known agitator in the House of Commons where his anti-Catholic rhetoric was dismissed as the ravings of a crank, but he knew how to whip up a crowd. On Friday 2 June 1780, he organised a demonstration to petition parliament for the repeal of the Catholic Relief Act. The weather that day was oppressively hot and thundery but still some sixty thousand people, sporting blue cockades and No Popery banners, turned out in St. George's Fields to march on the House of Commons.

Astley and his company watched nervously as a large section of the crowd made its way past his amphitheatre across Westminster Bridge. The protest quickly turned into a violent, out of control mob, burning and destroying anything it came across. For the next week, London was submerged in the throes of civil war as the mob rampaged across the capital. Gangs armed with clubs and iron bars roamed the streets by day and night, knocking door to door and demanding money 'for the true religion' or 'the poor mob'. Damaged or destroyed buildings were systematically looted. Fifteen thousand troops poured into London to quell the disturbances and two hundred and ten rioters were shot

---

45 This banter doesn't seem to have changed much for the next hundred years or so: In the middle of the next century a London newspaper complained; 'there is a sad lack of originality in the sayings of circus clowns generally.'

dead. Another seventy-five or so died in the hospitals, unknown others died from drinking neat looted liquor or at home from their wounds. The mob laid siege to 10 Downing Street and were only driven off by Astley's old regiment of mounted dragoons. Although his business was spared any damage, for the next week his customers stayed at home, fearful that they would be attacked or taken as looters and shot dead on the spot. By the seventh day, London looked like a city recovering from the ravages of invasion and remained under military occupation for much of the summer to come. Besides the great loss of life, one shocking statistic stood out: ten times more property was destroyed in London than in Paris during the entire French Revolution.

Everyone in London was rattled by the violence but within a couple of weeks it was business as usual at Astley's Amphitheatre. One evening, while he was performing his signature 'Mercury flying' routine, Astley dismounted by springing from the horse's back and as he landed, a familiar but much more vicious pain shot up his thigh, causing him to double up in pain. The crowd gasped as an ostler stepped forward to help him to his feet. After laying up for a week he found that his leg was so stiff he could still barely stand. At thirty-eight years old his body was paying the price of hard, physical work and exposure to all weathers. In truth, his old tricks including the Mercury routine were not only now extremely painful for him to perform, they were also starting to look dated: his son John could dance a minuet on horseback while playing a hornpipe. Reluctantly, Philip Astley decided that it was time to retire from trick-riding. From now on he would only perform occasional clowning tricks in his burlesque The Taylor's Ride. Very soon, however, he had much more to vex him than the botheration of old battle injuries. His nemesis Charles Hughes had parked his artillery on Astley's lawn again and this time he had brought reinforcements.

7

THE WAR OF THE CIRCUSES: PART 2

Astley's on tour: Manchester playbills from 1773. Reproduced with kind permission of Chetham's Library.

If it hadn't been for a fumble with a guardsman in Hyde Park, the story of the circus could have turned out rather differently:

Charles Dibdin was typical of those jack-of-all-trades that the Georgian theatre world throw up from time to time. He wore many hats over his long career; actor, musician, playwright, songwriter, theatrical entrepreneur, newspaper publisher and theatre historian. At one point he had a one-man show in which he played a modified piano with percussion instruments attached and special keys to make animal noises. He was most famous for writing massively popular seafaring songs; this despite having only been to sea once, briefly, in his entire life. His patriotic shanties about jolly Jack Tars with faithful sweethearts and wives, who often died bravely in the cause of their country, were so successful that Napoleon complained they were the real inspiration for Britain's naval victories.[46] Jane Austen was one of Dibdin's biggest fans.

He was the youngest of eighteen children fathered by a silversmith from Southampton. Blessed with a 'remarkable good voice', at the age of sixteen he was performing minor acting parts at Covent Garden. He quickly graduated to more prominent roles thanks to his willingness to take on parts turned down by more established performers. Not all of his early notices were positive. When he played the character of Hawthorn in *Love in a Village* a critic noted, 'Mr Dibdin is no more like Hawthorne [sic] than I am like Hercules: his lank belly, lanthorn jaws, lounging figure, and unmanly gait, but ill bespeak the robust country Farmer... some of the songs he sung tolerably well, and some of them very indifferently.' Critiquing *The Busy-Body*, the same reviewer noted that, while the Prompter read, 'Dibdin gesticulated; but whether or not his gesticulations corresponded with what the Prompter did read, is a question infinitely too difficult for me to determine.'

---

46   One of these, Tom Bowling, is still a staple of the BBC's Last Night of the Proms.

By 1770 Dibdin had found a lucrative niche co-writing musical productions for Covent Garden and Drury Lane. His chief musical collaborator was an Irish dramatist called Isaac Bickerstaffe. Although not quite Gilbert and Sullivan, Dibdin and Bickerstaffe made a very comfortable living knocking out popular comic operas. One of their best-known efforts was a hugely successful musical called *The Padlock* in which Dibdin also appeared in a starring role as a drunken West Indian servant called Mungo. With his catchphrase 'Mungo here, Mungo dere' it is thought to be the first ever blackface comic role and the forerunner of similarly racist stage stereotyping.

Beyond their professional relationship, Dibdin and Bickerstaffe didn't have a great deal in common. Dibdin was a vain, touchy and quarrelsome character with an appalling record of seducing and abandoning women. He was almost permanently in debt. Bickerstaffe was openly but discreetly gay – a fact presumably known to his writing partner and the wider London stage fraternity. All the same, it came as a complete shock to Dibdin when Bickerstaffe suddenly fled to France to avoid prosecution for allegedly sodomising a member of his Majesty's armed forces in a royal park. From then on, Dibdin's career was steadily on the wane. He also got himself into even more debt when he decided to sue the publisher of *The Observer* and others for insinuating that he had plagiarised Bickerstaffe's songs and that their association went beyond songwriting. He won, but with the derisory award of one shilling damages.

Dibdin took a position at Covent Garden as house dramatist and composer but he scandalously seduced then abandoned a chorus girl, fell out with the actor-manager David Garrick and lost his job. Now he had a pile of unproduced plays and was desperate for a source of income to pay off his mounting debts. That is when Dibdin met Charles Hughes.

After his discharge from Bridewell, Hughes and his wife took their equestrian show on a leisurely, extended tour of Europe, performing in France, Sardinia, Naples, Portugal, Germany, Spain and Morocco. At one point they were licensed to play in Valencia at the Plaza de San Domingo on condition they donate twenty-four pounds from their takings to the local hospital. They concluded their tour with a show for the Sultan of Morocco at his summer residence. In the summer of 1781, after almost nine years on the road, Hughes returned to England.

Dibdin saw in Hughes a great commercial opportunity. In truth, he had very little regard for the type of entertainments laid on by Hughes and Astley. In private he thought that equestrian performers were vulgar, uneducated 'blackguards' and that their audiences weren't much better, but he was intrigued by the amount of money being made. Dibdin's idea was to present horsemanship in a more 'classical and elegant' form by laying on worthy equestrian dramas and musical pantomimes, but make them much more commercially viable by combining them with Hughes' crowd-pleasing equestrian stunts with a few clowns and rope dancers thrown in for good measure. Dibdin found four financial backers from the world of horse-racing, including the fabulously eccentric Sir John Lade, heir to an enormous brewing fortune.[47] They were joined by a fifth, Colonel Temple West of the Grenadier Guards, second cousin of William Pitt and owner of a large tract of land in St George's Fields, near to Hughes' old Riding School. When Hughes' cooperation was invited he, too, was eager to accept.

It was clear from the outset that this was a marriage of convenience. Dibdin and Hughes came from very different backgrounds and from opposite ends of the entertainment spectrum. Hughes, like Astley, was a first-rate trick-rider turned

---

47 For reasons not entirely clear, Sir John liked to dress up as a mail coachman, even in formal social settings. He went so far as to have his front teeth filed, as many coachmen did, so he could mimic the special loud whistle they could make through the spaces in their teeth.

showman, a grafter with a nose for a profit. He wanted nothing more than to take on his circus rival and beat him at his own game – and for that he needed Dibdin's stagecraft and wealthy connections. Dibdin was assured of a quarter of the profits for putting up the scheme and finding the backers. He would act as stage manager and write the plays as well, while Hughes would also take a quarter for managing the company and providing the horses. Colonel West would provide the land and the speculators would put up the cash to build the venue.

In the spring of 1782 work began on the new Royal Circus and Equestrian Philharmonic Academy.[48] The high-minded Dibdin chose the Latin word 'circus' for his new venue because it had romantic, classical connotations. This was the very first time the word was used in its modern sense. Philip Astley may have been 'the father of the modern circus' but it was Charles Dibdin who christened it. Astley stuck to calling his venues 'amphitheatres' all his life. The new building was finished by September, to the considerable annoyance of Reverend Rowland Hill, whose own new Surrey Chapel – an octagonal building 'to prevent the devil hiding in any of the corners' – was being erected just across the road. For Reverend Hill, any place of entertainment was a 'temple of sin' and he suspected that local builders had completed this one on time at the expense of his own project.

Hughes' new venue had the benefit of a much better location than his old Riding Academy. It was situated next to a five-way intersection of new roads at the centre of which there stands to this day an obelisk providing a focal point and signpost for the radiating roads leading to various parts of the city from Southwark. From the outside the new establishment looked very much like Astley's amphitheatre, right down to the winged Pegasus on the roof – a blatant imitation of Astley's

---

48 Too much of a mouthful for anyone to remember, it was known simply as The Royal Circus.

horseman figure. There were obvious similarities inside, too, including a ring surrounded by benches and a circle of boxes above. There was, however, one important innovation. Next to the ring, hidden behind a curtain and flanked by stage doors, there was a small stage. Above the stage, the roof opened so that fireworks could be let off more safely without burning the house down. This was Dibdin's idea – a dual-purpose venue that could lay on a mixed show of pantomimes on stage and feats of horsemanship and acrobatics in the ring. He and Hughes could now produce an uninterrupted programme of burlesque, pantomime, acrobatic displays and equestrian performances while the scenes were changed in the stage area. Hughes moved into a house next to the theatre, which eventually became the Circus Coffee House managed by his brother-in-law.

Astley, meanwhile, having conquered Britain, was reaching out to the wide shores beyond, building and performing in semi-permanent amphitheatres in Brussels, Belgrade, Budapest and Vienna, making useful contacts everywhere he went. In Vienna the British envoy to the Austrian court, Sir Robert Murray Keith, introduced Philip to the Emperor Joseph, who requested a private performance. Despite his leg injury and the fact that he was riding a horse provided by the court that he had never set eyes on before, Astley persuaded it to execute a series of dressage movements with perfect precision, to everyone's amazement. The meeting concluded with the showman and the Emperor chatting about the relative merits of feeding carrots or apples to horses. Vienna wasn't the only royal court honouring the Astleys. Back home, King George III granted him a fourteen-year monopoly on the training of horses 'to stand the noise of drums, trumpets, music, explosion of ordnance and small arms'. All in all, 1782 had been a fantastic year for Astley, but there was a shock waiting for him when he got back to Westminster Bridge in October. Less than a mile away, the new venue had sprung up and, from the outside, it looked suspiciously like his own.

When Hughes and Dibdin's Royal Circus opened its doors for the first time on 4 November 1782 it seemed as if all of London was curious to see what was inside. The new venue was besieged by an enormous crowd and more than half had to be turned away. The combination of stage and circus ring was a sensation. An enthusiastic reviewer predicted that the Royal Circus would be 'one of the most frequented public places in this kingdom'. On the opening night Astley didn't send his usual spies; he wanted to see what was going on for himself. To his horror he found that it was even bigger and better than his own recently-updated amphitheatre. When he saw the combined use of ring and a stage, according to one report, he literally shook with envy. For now, the Royal Circus had the initiative. Astley resisted the temptation to open his amphitheatre out of season, perhaps to avoid losing money on what would inevitably have been a split audience. This was clearly a much more serious challenge to his monopoly than Hughes' earlier venture. Even the press noted that he would have to up his game. In what may well have been a 'puff' placed by Hughes, the *Morning Post and Daily Advertiser* reported: 'Upon the whole, we must declare, that it will be necessary for Mr Astley to make some improvements in his exhibition, unless he will allow his Amphitheatre to be totally eclipsed by the Royal Circus.'

Astley retired to plan his counter-offensive. He had seen off Hughes once and he would do it again, with new riders, new tricks, new acrobats. More furious, near-libellous exchanges followed in the newspapers. Three of Hughes's best horses died in mysterious circumstances, apparently poisoned. A local reporter, briefed by Hughes, pointed the finger of suspicion at Astley. Although he wasn't named directly, Astley felt sufficiently slighted to issue an angry denial.

Then the row became even more personal. Earlier that year, Astley decided it was time for a reconciliation with his father. It would have been impossible for Edward Astley to ignore the career of his now internationally famous son, but the two hadn't spoken since the day Philip ran away from home when he was seventeen. The only public record of his father's activities since that time shows that he was again incarcerated in the Fleet prison for debt in 1762. Whether Philip reached out to him through pity, or duty, or remorse, it is hard to know, but in the summer of 1782 Edward accepted his son's invitation to move into his family home in Bridge Row, Lambeth.

The truce between father and son lasted only a few months. On Christmas Eve, Edward swore on oath before the Lord Mayor that his son had assaulted him and kicked him out of the house having 'used him with such unbecoming abuse and scurrilous language that the deponent cannot, without impropriety, state the same in a public paper'. The old man also made a cheeky public appeal for charity, asking for donations to be left at his new lodgings at Reeve's Mews or at the nearby inn, the Punch House on Ludgate Hill. What caused this new rift? Philip was shocked by the discovery that his father was secretly working as a doorman and bill-sticker for Hughes at the Royal Circus for half a guinea a week. For the first time since Philip was a teenager the two men squared up to each other. This time it was the older Astley who left the house, never to return.

Naturally Hughes, having manipulated Edward Astley to embarrass his professional rival, leapt on the opportunity to besmirch Astley's character in the press for turning out his own father, 'A man near 80 Years of Age, into the streets to starve'. Twisting the knife, Hughes offered a benefit for 'Mr Astley, senior and a distressed Family'. Following this final split, Edward Astley was employed as Hughes' full-time ostler, to Philip's eternal disgust. Christmas 1782 was a desperately unhappy time in the Astley household, but there was even more trouble to come. Hughes and Dibdin's wonderful new neoclassical venue with its lavishly appointed auditorium and large stage hadn't gone unnoticed by the patent theatre managers in the West End of London. As far as they were concerned it all looked suspiciously like a regular theatre which, of course, the proprietors of the Royal Circus were not licensed to operate. In fact, they didn't have any sort of licence at all. Colonel West assured his business partners that he had simply to smooth things out with his friend, the Lord Chamberlain. His lordship, however, had no jurisdiction to licence public entertainments: the application should have been made to Surrey magistrates. It was probably an early sign of their dysfunctional working relationship that neither Hughes nor Dibdin, as managers, had bothered to follow up on West's promise. Moreover, the Royal Circus was also openly defying the law by offering winter entertainments, also expressly forbidden by the Theatre Licensing Act. At the eleventh hour, the proprietors applied for a performing licence to Surrey magistrates but it was rejected. Despite Dibdin's serious misgivings, the proprietors of the Royal Circus voted to open without one.

Just nine days after it opened a complaint was lodged against the Royal Circus. A petition signed by several local parishioners alleged that Hughes and Dibdin were running a 'disorderly house' without a licence. The Disorderly Houses Act was aimed at the owners of 'bawdy houses' but was loosely defined and could be used as a punitive weapon against any place of public entertainment. It carried heavy fines for defaulters and generous rewards for informers. Surrey magistrates swung into action. Justice William Hyde, accompanied by two officers, marched into the Royal Circus mid-show, pushed their way to the front of the stage and demanded that the performance be stopped. A near riot ensued and one of the justices ran away. The rough and ready Southwark crowd was cleared only after the military were called in. The two remaining law enforcers found Hughes hiding in his dressing room and marched him off to Bridewell. Hughes was convinced that Astley had informed on him. He was wrong; all the same, Astley was enjoying every moment of his rival's discomfort until, on 27 December, the very same officers went round to Astley's and arrested him as well under the summary powers of the Vagrancy Act. Prosecution under the Vagrancy Act was no laughing matter. Since 1744 the law had lumped together a whole range of undesirable occupations that were prosecutable under the law, including anyone performing or hiring to perform for the stage without a licence. The convicted could either be publicly whipped, branded or sentenced to six months of hard labour.

Fortunately for Astley, he had made a chance connection with one of the most powerful men in the country. In Edward Thurlow, 1st Baron Thurlow, the British legal system had a Lord Chancellor worthy of its eccentricities. His official portrait shows him in his ceremonial robes, heavy-set, jowly and beetle-browed under a huge powdered wig covering his shoulders and reaching down to his chest. The son of a Norfolk clergyman, Thurlow was by all accounts a mediocre lawyer but he landed his plum job by good fortune and a good deal of boot-licking, most notably those of King George III. Thereafter, he distinguished himself by hanging on to his post for a very long time (fourteen years and under four Prime Ministers) and with his stubborn opposition to reform of any kind: he was a particularly staunch supporter of the slave trade. In his private life, Thurlow was much more liberal-minded. Although unmarried he fathered four children, a son by the daughter of the Dean of Canterbury and three daughters by his mistress Polly Hervey. As luck would have it, two of these daughters, Caroline and Maria, were taking lessons at Astley's riding school. On Thurlow's intervention, Astley was bailed. Hughes offered to pay a fifty-pound fine to secure his own release but was refused and so had to sit out the next three weeks in prison awaiting his trial.

The two circus proprietors were brought before the Surrey Quarter Sessions on 17th January. Hughes was up first and his hearing took the best part of the day. Justice Hyde, who was almost certainly acting for one of the patent theatres in Westminster, had offered three men a shilling each to attend the

Royal Circus and make a record of Hughes' activities, with the further promise of a ten-shilling reward on his conviction. The trial descended into a famous farce. One of the witnesses failed to identify Hughes, pointing instead to John Astley. Two other witnesses could pick out Hughes from seeing him in a local tavern but couldn't swear that they had ever seen him in the Royal Circus. After a great deal of legal wrangling, point by point, the bench narrowly voted to acquit, once again on the grounds that there was nothing in the law that prohibited equestrian displays. Amid the cheers of a reported fifteen hundred supporters, Hughes was carried from the court house back to Southwark in triumph. Meanwhile Astley was kept waiting, pacing up and down in silent fury. By the time his case was heard it was so late in the day that there was only just enough time for him to argue that, as local householders, neither he nor any of his performers could ever be considered 'vagabonds'. The charges against Astley were dropped and he and Hughes were granted performing licences under the Disorderly Houses Act for the duration of spring and summer, with the provision that no alcohol was served.

This was a very odd state of affairs: there was nothing in the Disorderly Houses Act that gave magistrates the right to award performing licences. Suffice to say at this point possibly no-one, least of all the officials paid to interpret and uphold the law, really knew what was going on. All that mattered for the time being, however, is that the Royal Circus and Astley's Amphitheatre were back in business. Astley celebrated his release with an indoor fireworks display, employing the pyrotechnical expert, Mr Hengler, a new name in the world of circus but whose family would one day be very famous.

After their lawsuits were settled, the public bickering continued much as before. Astley's mood lightened when the Reverend Hill weighed in with his regular thunderous attack on the Royal Circus from his pulpit every Sunday morning, at one point accusing the owners of sending children to steal the lead from the roof of his chapel across the road. Astley had his local critics, too. Despite his best efforts to present his business as a highly respectable venture, there were unintended consequences. As his and Hughes' circuses grew in size and popularity there were benefits for local businesses such as farriers and saddlers but not all the economic growth was desirable. The pleasure-seekers who headed south of the river for their entertainment also provided rich pickings for the prostitutes and pickpockets who targeted the area. A local churchwarden complained to a Commons Committee that the borough now had hundreds of brothels which would not have existed without Astley's and the Royal Circus. Lambeth Marsh was acquiring a reputation as one of London's sleaziest neighbourhoods.

One rather curious feature of The Royal Circus that was not repeated at Astley's was the widespread use of children as performers. Astley was happy to feature the occasional talented juvenile on his bill – his own son was performing from the age of five – but Hughes and Dibdin's establishment was specifically set up to operate under the guise of a theatrical academy for children. It was Colonel West's idea and possibly a condition of him becoming a business partner that The Royal Circus should be a kind of nursery for actors. Up to fifty children from the age of five to fourteen years of age were to be trained in the circus arts of pantomime, equestrian feats and acrobatics. Much of this training would be accomplished under the tutelage of the Royal Circus 'Dancing Master' Guisseppi Grimaldi, father of the famous circus clown Joseph Grimaldi.

This was indeed a curious and dangerous appointment. As the younger Grimaldi's memoirs attest, 'Old Grim' or 'the Signor', as the elder Grimaldi was known, was a violent, sadistic man, given to picking up his own children by their hair and flinging them across the room. This erratic behaviour may have been explained by the onset of tertiary syphilis. He also had a taste for very young girls who had barely achieved puberty. The Signor worked the children at the Royal Circus long and hard and subjected them to beatings and other cruel punishments. This harsh treatment included placing them in stocks, or in a cage hoisted high above the stage. After a series of complaints from concerned parents, local magistrates ordered an investigation into the management of the Royal Circus. When the children were choreographed for a comic dance called 'The Quakers', it was deemed libellous and potentially obscene by the Society of Friends, who obtained a court injunction and had it stopped. Following this furore, after just one season, the children were replaced with adult performers in the entertainments, although Hughes continued to use very young apprentices for his equestrian stunts.[49]

The exploitation of children in the Georgian theatre ran much deeper than the odd beating. There was a strong suspicion that children were being served up for the sexual titillation of men. At the time there was a short-lived and disturbing craze for showcasing very young children on the stage, specifically in roles written for adults.[50] Perhaps it was driven by an innocent desire for novelty, but there were heavy hints in the press that a more sinister motive was behind Hughes and Dibdin's attempt to found

---

49 Theatrical progeny often made their stage debuts as young as three or four years old. It wasn't until 1879 that law came into force in the UK banning 'places of public amusement from using children under 14 in performances that might be dangerous to life and limb.

50 This craze peaked with the career of the child prodigy William Betty, one of the most peculiar episodes in the history of British theatre. Master Betty trod the boards from the age of nine. He was a sensation in theatres everywhere and appeared at Covent Garden and Drury Lane for massive fees, the highest yet paid to any actor. His performances were compared favourably with the theatrical greats. Everywhere he went he was mobbed and the armed forces were called out to quell rioters trying to get hold of tickets. The first doubts about Master Betty's acting abilities were raised when he attempted to play Richard III at the ripe old age of fourteen. His performance was greeted with catcalls and was never repeated. An attempted comeback was ignored by the public and Master Betty was washed up at eighteen.

a company at the Royal Circus where most of the performers were under fourteen and, as the *London Chronicle* noted ominously, where horsemanship 'was only intended to be served up as a dessert'.

Astley and Hughes remained in bitter competition in London, each copying the other's ideas and attempting to better them, but in the provinces Astley was unopposed as a circus performer. Every city, town and village had its fairs and itinerant players but he realised that there was scope to supply his new circus format to a growing urban audience. Every year Astley toured the provinces or the continent through the autumn and winter months, returning to London for the traditional opening of the summer season on Easter Monday. This was his standard routine for the best part of forty years and made him the most familiar theatrical figure in the whole of the British Isles. For people in the north, London seemed as far away and unfamiliar as a foreign city, so a visit by Astley's troupe, bringing with him the smash-hit shows which had played to full houses in the metropolis, would have been a truly exotic experience. The sight of Astley's caravan making its way through the countryside excited as much attention as a royal visit and sightseers would gather along the way to watch the cavalcade pass by. Toll gates at turnpike roads were a favourite spot for spectators to gather as there would be delays and a good opportunity to scrutinise the visitors at close quarters.

These tours around Georgian England were physically testing for the performers. Most of the roads were slow and badly maintained. In summer they were dusty and difficult but when the weather was bad they became sticky, impassable swamps. Journeys between the principal cities took several days. The men rode the show horses while the women occupied the baggage wagons with the props and the costumes, although Astley's wife Patty and some of his highest paid actresses often preferred to travel at their own expense by mail coach. On tour, Astley generally paid his performers three guineas a week, retaining a guinea in return for paying all their living expenses and keeping them, in his own words, like 'sons of kings'. He stayed for weeks at the larger cities such as Liverpool, Birmingham, Manchester and Edinburgh, using existing venues that lent themselves easily to displays of horsemanship, including the riding schools at Inns Quay in Dublin, Monmouth Street in Bath and Christian Street, Liverpool, or he threw together semi-permanent venues made of wood. The ubiquitous showman was known in the provinces as 'amphi-Philip' because of the number of amphitheatres he built – as many as twenty across the country over his lifetime.

His pre-publicity was always carefully prepared but, like that of other traveling shows, rarely committed to a set length of time for any specific visit. The duration was open-ended so he could take advantage of a bigger than average turnout and was never embarrassed by dwindling audience numbers. Although the touring was difficult, with treacherous travel, long hours away from home and incessant hard work, in many ways they were among the high points of his career. He always drew crowds with his seemingly inexhaustible supply of wonders, bringing for a few days or weeks colour, vibrancy, spectacle and novelty to communities starved of the types of entertainment that were in such rich supply in the capital. It shows just how popular his shows in the provinces were that, on his first recorded visit to Liverpool in February 1773, his troupe performed to more than 20,000 people in a large field in Mount Pleasant.

Following the same wheel ruts as Astley's wagons there were various other entertainments whose proprietors were also keen to puff up the credentials of their exhibits. One of the most successful rival commercial entertainments was George Wombwell's Travelling Menagerie. He boasted that his collection had as great a variety as Noah's ark and he maintained a punishing touring schedule around the country, much to the disadvantage of his giraffes, gorillas, leopards and kangaroos, many of which died in the British climate. Wombwell had the showman's knack of turning adversity into opportunity. When his elephant died, prompting a rival menagerie to puff their elephant as 'The Only Living Elephant in London', Wombwell's immediate response was to print posters offering the public the chance to see 'The Only Dead Elephant in London'.

It might seem surprising to us today that 'the father of the modern circus' didn't tour in a circus tent. It seems fairly obvious that a travelling show would work best in a light, spacious, airy fabric structure rather than in an enclosed wooden fire trap. The 'big top' was probably first used in America in 1825 by J. Purdy Brown, who found that canvas tents made it easier for him to travel around Virginia.[51] Astley did in fact take a circus tent with him on a tour of the UK in 1788, in January pitching a 'Royal Tent' off Dale Street, Liverpool. As far as anyone knows he never repeated his experiment under canvas again.[52]

On a typical UK tour Astley cleared up to £2,000 after expenses; around £300,000 in today's values. London, however, was still his main bastion and chief source of revenue – until, one day, he received an unexpected letter bearing the Royal Seal of France, heralding the start of exciting new business venture.

---

51 George Speaight *A History Of The Circus*.

52 He also occasionally performed in the open air behind a 'wall of canvas' to prevent non-paying spectators seeing his show. In 1794 two men were badly injured when they fell from a tree while trying to watch Astley's show for free at Oxford.

AMPHITHEATRE ANGLAIS

Astley's Amphitheatre Anglais in Paris, France's first permanent circus building. Public domain.

On 12 September 1783, Horace Walpole, the raffish youngest son of the British Prime Minister, wrote a letter from his gothic pile, Strawberry Hill House, to his good friend Lord Strafford:

> I could find nothing at all to do, and so went to Astley's, which, indeed, was much beyond my expectation. I do not wonder any longer that Darius was chosen king by the instructions he gave to his horse: nor that Caligula made his consul. Astley can make *his* dance minuets and hornpipes. But I shall not even have Astley now: her Majesty the Queen of France, who has as much taste as Caligula, has sent for the whole *dramatis personae* to Paris.

Astley's ambitions always extended far beyond his own country. It had been eleven years since he performed for the French royal family at Fontainebleau and every year after he returned to Paris during the off season to exhibit in the open air. As an ex-soldier and a sturdy patriot he might have been understandably equivocal about working among and performing for the people that he and his countrymen had been at war with for what must have seemed like most of his adult life, but he relished the opportunity to take his brand of entertainment to new audiences in unfamiliar and challenging surroundings. Astley's showmanship was received as warmly and with just as much enthusiasm in France as it had been at home. He was remembered widely and well, and acknowledged as a star from Normandy to Provence, but especially in Paris, which would become his second home.

Britain's row with France over American Independence prevented the Astleys from working in France in 1778 and for the next three years but, on 27 February 1782, the British government voted to end the war. Philip was back and, having lost his monopoly in London, more determined than ever to establish a permanent base in Paris. Anglomania was on the rise again and all of fashionable France wanted to know about the English style of riding. The Astleys were on their way to a command performance for Queen Marie Antoinette at Versailles. Patty Astley was laid low by her usual bout of sea-sickness from the Channel crossing, but the troupe was otherwise in fine fettle. The road from Paris to Versailles was busy with foreign diplomats hurrying to complete treaties and with courtiers trundling back to their homes after completing their day's duties. As the Astley's caravan approached the town's western edge they caught a glimpse of the palace for the first time, the original modest stone and faux-brick building enveloped on three sides by vast, yellow marble wings. At the rear and sides, manicured gardens sloped away in a series of groves. As they got nearer, they could make out figures dispersed all around the gardens, which on closer inspection became bronze and marble figures from classical mythology.

Versailles no longer gleamed quite as it did under the Sun King Louis XIV, but it was still the most lucrative font of patronage in France and possibly in the whole of Europe. It accommodated around twenty thousand people, a vast colony of worker bees employed to supply and service the needs of the King and his immediate family, hived off in the palace; among the thousands of servants there was a man whose sole duty was to wind the king's watch every day. Philip was no doubt amazed to learn that the palace stables held 12,000 horses. Although this was where the business of government was transacted, all around was evidence of boredom; daily hunts, fortunes lost in card games, and endless balls. It was a carefree oasis of excess, its inhabitants oblivious to the rising tide of discontent beyond its gates. But for the Astleys this was the rarest of privileges. Usually only the families with the oldest, most impeccable lineage were entitled to be presented to the Queen of France at Versailles. Nothing ever fazed Philip but he could have been forgiven for pinching himself in disbelief at just how far his brilliant career had taken him.

When the Astleys first came to perform for the French court, the ageing Louis XV was in the final decade of his long reign. The King's popularity had plummeted from the early years when his people called him 'the well-beloved' but he still commanded huge respect. His son was less impressive. The new King Louis XVI was a pot-bellied, lethargic-looking twenty-seven-year-old, his slack, podgy features dominated by a huge nose, unmistakably the great eagle's beak of the Bourbons; disloyal courtiers referred to him as 'the fat pig'. He walked with a waddle and was dressed very plainly in a grey coat. He had a permanent squint, the result of extreme short-sightedness. Astley's encounter with Louis supposedly prompted one of the showman's most-often quoted malapropisms, 'that their King can't be the father of the Dolphin. Why, he's omnipotent.'[53]

The king's wife, however, was all charm and elegance. Queen Marie Antoinette was ash-blonde, a head taller than all her ladies with big, blue eyes, a long slender neck and a high pale forehead, her hair built up as dictated by the fashion of the day in a tower with countless feathers and ribbons. Her protruding lower lip, a relic of her Habsburg ancestry, made her at first appear sullen and surly, but she surprised everyone who met her for the first time with her affability and spontaneous generosity. She was in charge of laying on the court entertainments and her choices were eclectic. Among the performers she invited to Versailles were the rope dancer Henry Hengler (son of Astley's fireworks expert Johannes); the astonishing Jean Richer, equestrian, clown, acrobat and strongman, who could lie on his back with a 200lb anvil on his chest while men beat on it with hammers; Placido Bussart, a gymnast who somersaulted over eighteen grenadiers with upright bayonets, and a family of comic actors, the Grammants. Ironically, the latter would become officers in the revolutionary army, weeding out traitors for the guillotine.

The Astleys' command performance in the courtyard of Versailles was a triumph. With Philip no longer performing on horseback, but still in control, taking on his recognisable role as original ringmaster, the spotlight fell on his star equestrian asset, sixteen-year-old John. Dressed in a short, white, Greek-style tunic and wearing gold sandals, John performed a fine display of vaulting and balancing, then finished by dancing a minuet on the backs of three horses. The Queen pronounced herself delighted by 'his manly agility, symmetry of figure, elegance of attitude and gentlemanly deportment'[54]. As a souvenir of the occasion, she was said to have presented him with a gift, a gold medal encrusted

53   Maurice Willson Disher
54   *Memoirs of Jacob DeCastro.*

with diamonds, and called him her 'English Rose'. This was high praise indeed, an allusion to the famous French ballet dancer Auguste Vestris, considered the greatest dancer of his generation and styled the 'French Rose'. After performing seven times over a two-week stay, the Astleys left Versailles with something even more valuable – a royal patent for exclusive performances in Paris for eight years. The Astleys took the two-hour coach trip back to Paris where they performed several times in the Faubourg du Temple, meanwhile looking around for a suitable site for a permanent base. In September, Astley notified the London public that he was closing his Westminster venue for the summer. He thanked them for their support, adding that he would be very happy to welcome his customers at his new Amphitheatre Anglais in Paris. On 16 October he finally achieved his long-cherished ambition of opening the first permanent circus in Paris in the Faubourg du Temple, just a short walk from the French capital's theatreland, the Boulevard du Temple.

Astley was at the heart of a city discovering how to have fun again. In Paris, as in London, theatre had been in the stranglehold of censors and magistrates, but now the shackles were loosened. The Boulevard du Temple was the new home of mass popular entertainment, a maze of dimly-lit medieval streets with every inch of space occupied with the business of pleasure. A travelling Englishman, Arthur Young, described the shows in this neighbourhood as 'music, noise and *filles* without end'. There were hundreds of street performers with roadside trestles supporting performing animals, including Munito the fortune-telling dog and a white rabbit with a talent for algebra. Among the stars of these miniature variety shows were duelling fleas, somersaulting birds and tightrope-walking rats. Human celebrity performers of the Temple show-business fraternity included a girl who danced with eggs tied to her feet and La Petite Tourneuse, 'the human spinning top.' There was a flameproof Spaniard who drank boiling oil and walked barefoot on red-hot iron and

Jacques de Falaise, a consumer of live frogs. The ironically named Beauvisage made a living by gurning, while jugglers and high-wire artists tested their skills to the limit dressed in heavy wild animal costumes. The 'pissing puppet', a marionette of a boy urinating, and 'the Virile Boy', a precocious four-year-old with 'beyond the finest proportions in the virile organ', took their places alongside 'the boy who could see underground' – his talent was accredited by several learned journals – and a man who could walk on water: 'St Peter himself could not have done better, perhaps with no more grace, nor with more assurance.'

Among the throng of peddlers, ticket touts, conjurers, pickpockets, prostitutes and conmen there were diversions for all tastes and interests, including live animal fights where bulls with their horns removed were set upon by dogs and wolves. Human life in Paris was cheap, too. One of the more grotesque privileges of the aristocracy was their licence to hit and run. The carriages of the wealthy mowed down pedestrians without stopping, even if they had caused serious injury or instant death. Visitors to Paris were appalled by this daily hazard; even more shockingly, the privileged passengers only asked their coachmen to stop if they thought the horses had been injured. The Temple also stank of animal and human ordure, hence the emerging consumer market for scent, the *parfum* for which Paris became famous. Brothels all around the district did brisk business, as did the quacks with cures for venereal disease, sweetening the sting by lacing their mercury with chocolate syrup.

There was a seemingly inexhaustible supply of new things to see in Paris and the public couldn't get enough of them, irrespective of rank or station. The Russian traveller Karamzin noted: 'Not only the rich people who live only for pleasure and amusement, but even the poorest artisans, Savoyards and peddlers consider it a necessity to go to the theatre two or three times a week.' The French royal family was as much in thrall to these exciting new entertainments as anyone else. The King forbade his wife's frequent trips to the Paris theatre as a breach of decorum, but she continued to do so, or at least until the audience reaction to her presence was so unfriendly that she no longer dared show her face.

Like Astley, the Paris theatre managers had a nose for profit and they knew how to please. Here, too, was the Caverne des Grands Voleurs – literally the Cave of the Great Thieves – the forerunner of Madame Tussaud's waxwork Chamber of Horrors, exploiting the public fascination for a juicy murder and a dramatic execution. One of Astley's most successful neighbours, and unarguably his toughest competitor, was the legendary theatrical impresario Jean-Baptiste Nicolet, owner of the *Théâtre des Grandes Danseurs du Roi*.[55] Nicolet was a tyrant, managing his troupe with an iron hand and firing performers on a whim. Like Astley, Nicolet was said to have had little education and knew nothing of music or playwriting, but he was a shrewd businessman with a theatrical instinct. He had also learned to survive fierce struggles against the competition at a time when rival Paris company managers wouldn't hesitate to resort to blows, or even to arms. Just as in London, the commercial theatre in Paris was subject restrictions on form and content. Nicolet was banned from performing any play in five acts – the classical form that was the prerogative of the Comédie-Française and the Opéra. The entertainments he staged had to be in three acts and the players were banned from speaking in verse. Nicolet also mixed acrobats and rope-dancers with ballet and music, night after night playing to packed houses. Among his troupe was Turcot the tightrope-walking monkey, who apparently trumped Astley's original acrobatic monkey General Jackoo by displaying not only

---

55 Coincidentally in 1772 Nicolet was also summoned to play before King Louis XV, who allowed him to call his theatre the *Spectacle des Grands Danseurs du Roi*, a title it retained until Nicolet retired in 1795.

his balancing skills, but also an imitation of the leading classical French actor of the day, Monsieur Molé.

Astley's new Amphitheatre Anglais was a round, roofed, wooden structure with a ground plan laid out in the shape of a horseshoe. As usual the ring was set at forty-two feet in diameter and was surrounded by two tiers of boxes and a musicians' gallery, the whole illuminated by three hundred candelabra lit by twelve hundred flames. It was generously equipped to handle extravaganzas featuring his usual mixture of clowns, tumblers, dancing dogs, fireworks and, the star attraction as always, horsemanship.

Astley's circus had been to Paris to perform many times before, but then it was the riding of Astley senior that astonished one and all. With Philip now assuming the full-time role of ringmaster, Astley junior again took the starring role. While Philip made announcements in his very best French, John charmed the ladies with his graceful, athletic horsemanship and his striking good looks. The impact of Marie Antoinette's patronage was immense, too. Even members of the aristocracy abandoned the Opéra and sneaked off to Astley's to see the entertainments that, as one sage observed, 'everyone claims to despise, and which everyone frequents.'

There was soon a new member of Astley's company in Paris, one whose contribution to the development of the circus in France would become almost as great as Philip's. Antonio Franconi was an expatriate Italian from a noble Venetian family. Like Astley, he was a striking physical presence with a broad chest and a booming voice. Accounts of how he came to be in France vary. According to one version, when Franconi was a teenager his father killed a senator and was condemned to death, his possessions forfeited to the state. His own life threatened by the prospect of a family vendetta, Antonio fled abroad. Another report has it that Franconi left Venice to avoid the legal consequences of a duel in which he himself had killed a young opponent. He certainly had a violent temper and a talent for making enemies. Franconi earned a living for several years as an itinerant juggler and a wandering physician. In 1758 he arrived in Lyons, footsore and starving, and offered his services at a menagerie as a lion tamer. This novelty proved very successful until a lion bit a chunk out of his arm. Figuring that canaries were a safer bet, he hit the road again with a travelling bird act. In Spain, the Duke of Duras introduced him to bullfighting, an Arab sport newly popular among the Spanish aristocracy. For a while Franconi organised bullfights in the south of France. One day in Toulouse his toreadors, protesting the low wages he was paying, walked out and threatened to set up on their own. Franconi stepped in and tamed the bulls himself. In 1783 and in his forties, he found himself in Paris. Eager to be part of the burgeoning theatre scene in the Boulevard du Temple, the mercurial Italian made his way to Astley's where he was hired on the spot. He spent the next three years there, demonstrating his acclaimed canary act and studying circus craft, before galloping off to Lyon to try to set up his own.

Every Autumn, as soon as his London amphitheatre closed in accordance with the law protecting winter theatres, the Astleys left Lambeth and took themselves off to Paris in the Amphitheatre Anglais for two or three months. To begin with this annual pilgrimage didn't give their Paris rivals any cause for alarm – there were more than enough customers to go round – but the presence of an Englishman with royal patronage became a growing source of resentment. Every time his troupe returned to the French capital the surrounding theatres were emptied of their patrons as they defected *en masse* to see horses dancing minuets at the Amphithéâtre Anglais. English circus was all the rage and the Parisian theatrical establishment didn't like it one bit.

In 1786 Philip Astley found that royal patronage was a double-edged sword. Europe was suddenly gripped by a scandal unfurling at the French court. A diamond necklace of immense value, containing over six hundred precious stones and weighing two thousand eight hundred carats, had gone missing. It was the most expensive piece of jewellery in France; conservative estimates valued it at 1.5 million livres. It was commissioned by Louis XV for his mistress, Madame du Barry, but the king died before the necklace was completed. Naturally its creators, the crown jewellers Boehmer and Bassenge, were eager to offload the finished article but its extraordinary cost meant the French royal family was the only potential buyer. The jewellers made an official approach to Louis XVI, offering him the necklace as a gift for Marie Antoinette but she declined to acquire it: she tried it on, but that is as far as it went. Nevertheless, the finger of suspicion was pointed at the unpopular, spendthrift Queen. By the time truth about the 'theft' of the necklace finally emerged – that it was all a hoax and the Queen herself was entirely guiltless – she was already irreparably damaged.

With the *ancien* régime lurching from one public relations disaster to another and respect for the royal family unravelling by the minute, Astley was vulnerable and his enemies in the Paris theatrical world emboldened. Nicolet figured out that, although the English circus owner had been granted a monopoly on presenting equestrian displays, he had no licence for presenting acrobats, clowns or rope-dancers. In 1786 he made an official compliant to the Paris Lieutenant-General of police against Astley for trespassing on his entertainment rights: the Englishman was operating outside French law. The *Garde* called on Astley to remind him that his licence limited him to displays of horsemanship: all performances not on horseback were henceforth forbidden. Denied the use of his clowns, his tumblers and of John Astley, who had been laid low with a knee injury, audience numbers at the Amphitheatre Anglais fell away dramatically. On some evenings, takings were as low as sixteen pounds and it seemed that closure of the Paris venue was inevitable, to the great satisfaction of his competitors.

They had, of course, underestimated Astley's resourcefulness. Presently, Philip and John summoned their carpenters and showed them a sketch they had made with instructions for the assembly of a new piece of apparatus unlike anything they had seen before. After a couple of weeks of feverish activity behind closed doors the project was complete. Astley's had a new playbill printed. From 27 December his tumblers, acrobats and rope-walkers would be performing as usual 'by permission of the KING and the Lieutenant-General of the Police.' There would also be a mysterious new feature, a '*pont* équestre'. The Parisienne theatrical world held its breath to see what would happen next. Would the maverick *pére Astley* defy the police order? When the day arrived half of Paris was eager to know the answer. After the regular equestrian entertainments, a gasp of astonishment echoed around the amphitheatre when into the ring marched eight horses, bearing a huge wooden platform on struts fastened to their saddles. On top of this platform, acrobats tumbled, rope-dancers danced and clowns clowned as ever before – all on horseback. Astley had brilliantly and cynically outwitted the authorities.

Having circumvented the law, Astley's '*pont* équestre' served him well for the next three years and he was able to present his full circus programme without further interference from the French authorities. His reign in Paris, however, was soon to be cut short, abruptly and permanently, by events beyond even his control.

9

MONSTROUS CRAWS AND CLEVER PIGS

The Monstrous Craws played a few nights at Astey's while touring London with their 'unnatural' physical deformities. Courtesy of the Wellcome Collection.

Back in Lambeth, Philip Astley was ready for his next big challenge. He was determined to do whatever it took, at any cost, to trounce his troublesome rivals down the road, even if that meant stealing all of their best ideas.

First, he needed the materials to rebuild. Timber was expensive, but then another bargain came his way. It was a General Election year. Most people did not have the right to vote but it didn't stop them getting involved and expressing their grievances. Elections were extremely rowdy and boisterous events as partisan crowds, inflamed with alcohol, threatened the peace of the district. For as long as anyone could remember, as soon as polls were closed, the mob would demolish the speaking platforms, steal the wood and celebrate with a bonfire. Guards were often paid to protect the timber and fearful brawls ensued. In Covent Garden, Astley promised free beer to anyone who would help him carry the timber from the hustings across the river to his venue in Lambeth. The thirsty mob took up his generous offer: now he had enough wood at a fraction of cost price, to completely remodel his amphitheatre. Astley was inordinately pleased with himself and still chuckling about it thirty years later.

A press preview for the upcoming season of 1784 noted that Mr Astley had built a large extension to his amphitheatre. There was a new dome-shaped roof, two tiers of boxes, a pit and a gallery. There was also now a stage – in direct competition with the Royal Circus. Thanks to the installation of new lighting, performances could continue beyond midnight. The interior was also completely redecorated. The celebrated scene painter John Henderson Grieve was poached from Covent Garden, to repaint the walls and ceiling with images of tree branches and leaves – giving the building yet another new name, The Royal Grove.

Having appropriated Dibdin's innovation of a combined ring and stage and a regular orchestra to replace the basic fifes and drums that usually accompanied his acts, Astley could now also copy the Royal Circus's ambitious mixed programme of burlettas and pantomimes. He was also developing his own version of a peculiar form of entertainment, also pioneered by Hughes and Dibdin, called hippodrama. These were equestrian melodramas in which the horses were the stars; they rescued damsels in distress, apprehended villains, playing dead and so on. Critics often took delight in pointing out that the horses frequently outshone their two-legged co-actors in their acting abilities. These hippodramas, with a cast of hundreds of actors and horses and a full orchestra, provided a great deal of noise and spectacle, even if they didn't make a great deal of sense. Astley was always keen to emphasise the authenticity of the events he recreated – the battle of Emsdorf, for example – and was at pains to explain that he had travelled far and wide 'for the accurate information of the public'. But authenticity wasn't allowed to get in the way of a good show. Every opportunity was taken to insert horses into the action whether it was appropriate or not. One of his most bizarre efforts was his epic Grand Equestrian Dramatic Spectacle depicting the tragic death of Captain James Cook, whose three voyages of discovery to the Pacific were cut short in Hawaii (Astley spelled it 'O-why-ee') when he became the main course of a native buffet. There were no horses in the North Pacific when Cook died.

Hughes and Dibdin had had good reason to feel pleased with their first full season at the Royal Circus. They wound up in late September for a break, but opened again for the Christmas holidays – in open defiance of the law – offering 'The Fairy World, splendid Equestrian Exercises and entirely new music, composed and conducted by Mr Dibdin.' Newly licensed, they were looking forward to the Easter season with great optimism. Their reaction is easy to imagine when Astley opened on Easter Monday with a venue and a format almost entirely based on their own.

Astley's makeover received mostly glowing reviews in the newspapers but some of his audience were puzzled to find themselves faced with a largely unfamiliar programme. He began with a dance called 'The Distressed Milkmaid', followed by a play, 'The Dressing Room'. It also featured a hippodrama 'Jupiter in Disguise, or the Rape of Europa'. This was indeed a strange choice of popular circus entertainment. Perhaps Astley was hoping to impress the 'nobility and gentry' who might be completely familiar with classical Greek mythology but it went completely over the heads of most of his audience. After that they were back on safer ground. There were dancing dogs from France and Italy and a 'Gigantic Spanish Pig' ridden by the now-famous monkey General Jackoo. They were followed by tumblers leaping over mounted horsemen and ranks of soldiers with fixed bayonets, 'the best mandolin player in the world' and 'nine strong men performing real Venetian exercises'. There was a near tragedy on the opening night when a performer on the slack rope, while adjusting himself to swing by one leg, lost his grip and was catapulted over the orchestra pit. He lay unconscious for some time but was carried away and revived, returning to finish his act to great applause.[56]

With Hughes and Dibdin stealing from Astley and *vice versa*, there wasn't a great deal to choose from. The performances given in both establishments were a mixture of equestrian and physical feats, music, song and dance, usually followed by some form of hippodrama to complete the evening's entertainment. In their desperation to find something that would set them apart, Hughes and Dibdin took to staging actual fox and stag hunts in the circus ring, with packs of hounds and huntsman chasing animals through woodland scenery. And so it went on, an ever-escalating conflict as the two venues battled over advertisement boasts and competing attractions. Astley was prepared to try anything that might create attention or make money. This is his advertisement for a demonstration of a rudimentary telegraph in 1794:

Explanation of the TELEGRAPHE (sic), to be exhibited every Evening...the TELEGRAPHE is an instrument at present used in France, for the conveyance of certain intelligence, at the rate of

---

56 Although there were many reports of serious injuries at Astley's there were only two fatalities and neither occurred in Philip or John's reign. By the mid-1800's lion tamers were a regular fixture at the venue. The only human death was caused by a lion owned by Mr Crockett 'The Lion Conqueror' in 1861. The victim was a groom called Jarvey, who was caught unawares by one of Crockett's three lions when they escaped from their cage. Jarvey's dismembered corpse was retrieved and that evening the performance went ahead as normal. In 1888 eight wild Siberian wolves were caged in one of the stables behind the amphitheatre in the vicinity of several horses. One night all of the wolves escaped and attacked one of the performing mares, called Shrewsbury. It was a publicity stunt, set up by the proprietor.

200 miles an hour, and which is effected without the knowledge of any persons, except those at two extreme distances. The Scene is supposed to represent the country between Lille and Paris: and to try the effects of the Machine, four distances are appointed, as sufficient to convey a true idea of the ingenuity and utility of the Telegraphe.

How successful this demonstration was is hard to know: the first working telegraph wouldn't be invented for another twenty-two years. Not all of his money-making ventures came off. For instance, in 1784 he opened a 'Floating Bath for the reception of Bathers' – basically a very large public bathing-machine, which he stationed on the Surrey side of Westminster Bridge. Despite being enormously fat, Astley was still an expert swimmer and he promoted his new enterprise by floating down the Thames on his back from Westminster to Blackfriars, while waving a Union Jack held in each hand. It didn't go swimmingly. Although no-one ever forgot his publicity stunt, the enterprise it promoted sank.[57]

With Philip incapacitated by his war injury and restricted to small equestrian roles, his teenage son John emerged from under his father's wings as a truly star performer. In the 25 October 1785 edition of *The Morning Chronicle*, Astley's ran an advertisement promising;

For the first time, and never performed in England, an exercise called still vaulting, invented by young Astley (John) and performed by himself, demonstrating what ought to be practised by every

---

57 Plans are occasionally floated for a new swimming baths on the Thames so it is interesting to find that such things actually existed a couple of hundred years ago. They were basically swimming pools moored on the Thames containing thousand gallons of filtered water, drawn from the river. Astley's floating bath was still operational in 1804 as listed in John Feltham's guide *The Picture of London*, but he had fierce competition. There were two more floating baths on the Thames between Westminster and Blackfriars bridges.

horseman in order to familiarise more effectively the body to the various actions of the horse.[58]

Astley's next big innovation was training horses to dance in time to music, an idea he developed from studying London's cart and wagon drivers. He had taught John to perform minuets on horseback, the horse moving 'with surprising grace' with 'each keeping time to the music, in a manner truly extraordinary'. These graceful routines resulted in 'full houses and unbounded applause'. It was joked in one newspaper that Astley was 'engaged for the next season as Ballet-master to the Opera-house.' Hughes went to great pains to ridicule horse-dancing in the press, implying that John Astley was effeminate. Georgian audiences were a remarkably intolerant bunch and if his innuendo had taken root there was a good chance he would be booed out of the ring.[59] Hughes was barking up the wrong tree: as anyone who read the papers knew, the young rider was burnishing his reputation as a great womaniser.

In 1784, Philip Astley's head was full of balloons. In September of the previous year he was in France when the Montgolfier brothers Joseph and Etienne oversaw one of the first ever public exhibitions of a hot air balloon from the courtyard of Versailles. The brothers had found that heated air trapped in lightweight material caused it to rise. They really had no idea why: at this point they thought the process was caused by black smoke, which they gave off by burning a mixture of straw and wool, creating such a terrible stench that many of the spectators, including

---

58 Still-vaulting' involved putting your foot in the stirrup using the leverage to vault but over the years the term took on a different meaning and came to refer to the gymnastic act of launching from a springboard. Bill Smith of Astley's was still still-vaulting in 1825, when he landed badly and broke his neck.

59 Thomas Dibdin's old writing partner Isaac Bickerstaffe had feared for his life after he was outed as gay.

the French royal family, retreated from the scene in horror. At precisely 1pm a sheep, a duck and a cockerel were loaded into a round wicker basket tied to the balloon by a rope. Eleven minutes later at the blast of a cannon they were sent skyward. To wild applause and general disbelief, the vessel soared 600 metres in the air and remained aloft for just under ten minutes before descending in a forest a couple of miles away. The surprised livestock, evidently none the worse for their journey, were hailed as 'heroes of the air' and rewarded with a place in the Royal Menagerie in Versailles. The Montgolfier brothers became instant celebrities and news of their astonishing achievement travelled quickly around the world.

Astley may have been one of those who witnessed this eighteenth-century miracle of flight. He was quick to spot a trend and exploit it and it wasn't long before he was organising his own hot air balloon flights. After buying at great expense three small balloons and the apparatus to fill them, he began advertising his New Curious Aerostatic Experiments, admittance 2s 6d. Amid huge excitement, on Friday 12 March 1784, at around half past one in the afternoon, under the very noses of his competitors at the Royal Circus, Astley launched three unmanned balloons from St. George's Fields. *The Morning Post* speculated that the turnout might be 'the biggest crowd that had ever been assembled on any other occasion' with 'spectators of all descriptions, from the Peer to the pickpocket'. They were among the first ever balloon flights staged for public spectacle in Britain.[60]

The first balloon snagged in some nearby trees and burst: the second shot off towards Essex. The third, much larger balloon,

---

60   To the great disappointment of Mr Scott, a chemist from Edinburgh, who by a curious coincidence set off by his own hot air balloon from Herriot's Gardens about an hour and a half after Astley's. According to *Gentleman's Magazine* a Mr Blaggini also launched a balloon from Finsbury on 16 November 1783; the journal added 'but what practical use may result of it cannot yet be foreseen'.

a maroon-and-white striped silk affair about twenty-five feet in circumference, was supposed to set off a series of small explosions via a slow fuse to indicate its location when out of sight. Although no explosions were heard, the balloon sailed skyward and soon vanished. Witnesses speculated that it would remain aloft for several days. Astley offered a silver tankard to anyone who found the large globe and returned it. The big balloon eventually came down in Faversham but the prize went unclaimed. *Gentleman's Magazine* pointed out that Astley's launch would live in the memories of all the spectators since 'a more ample harvest for the pickpockets never was presented', adding that 'some noblemen and gentlemen lost their watches and many their purses'.

In July 1784 Astley's was promoting a new display titled 'The Air-Balloon, or All the World in the Clouds, in the second Scene will be presented the Manner of travelling through the Air in the Triumphal Car, and a most beautiful Firework, in which will be introduced a Salamander'. England was in the grip of balloon mania. Six months later the Italian aviator Vincenzo Lunardi flew a balloon from north London, the first manned flight in England. On 4 January 1875, a Mr Harper set off in a balloon from Birmingham and travelled 50 miles, the longest manned flight at that time. He got completely lost and landed near Newcastle in Staffordshire, coincidentally only a mile or so from Astley's birthplace. On 29 June that year the actress Laetitia Sage became the first English female aeronaut when she ascended in a balloon from St. George's Fields. She was a very large lady and had to overcome the embarrassment of a public weigh-in before she was allowed to get into the balloon car. She wore a very low-cut silk dress, apparently to 'aid wind resistance'. The balloon rose to a height of about 50 feet from the ground and made straight for Astley's Amphitheatre, into which it would have undoubtedly crashed had her co-pilot Mr Biggin not thrown out a large quantity of ballast.

On 31 August 1785, an aeronaut called Stuart Amos Arnold, a former seaman who had given a limb in the service of his country, attempted to take off in a hot air balloon from St. George's Fields and cross the Channel to France. Balloon mania had probably peaked by this time but the novelty of seeing a one-legged sailor go up in a huge balloon, ten times bigger than anything previously seen, was enough to draw a big crowd. Charles Hughes, jealous of the attention his rival was getting from his balloon experiments, got in on the act, offering to tickets to watch the event from the nearby Royal Circus coffee house.

With Arnold were his son and an associate, George Appleby, who was to descend from the balloon in a parachute. It all went horribly wrong. An assistant, who climbed a pole to release the ropes at the apex of the balloon, was blown over by a gust of wind and left floundering on top of it. It took half an hour to get him down. Disaster struck on launch when the balloon caught on some railings, causing Appleby to plummet to the ground shortly before Arnold himself was ejected along with the ballast. The out-of-control balloon ascended rapidly before bursting, flinging Arnold's son into the River Thames somewhere near Blackwell. The roads surrounding St. George's Fields were so congested with carriages that very few of the paying public were able to get near and only thirty-seven pounds was taken on the gate. On the bright side, the misadventure almost certainly saved the life of George Appleby. His parachute, which was basically a very large umbrella, would have failed and sent him to his death. Although Hughes failed to cover his expenses he offered a benefit on the next two Saturdays 'as a small assistance toward enabling him [Mr Arnold] to repair the damages he sustained in his Balloon.'[61]

---

61 Benefit performances gave performers an opportunity to supplement their income. They were allowed to keep full value of any tickets they sold to the benefit. Notices of benefit were displayed at the top of handbills and advertisements, alerting fans to buy tickets directly from the beneficiaries.

At least Astley made money on his balloon experiment and he repeated the entertainment several times elsewhere, but with manned balloon flights now crossing the Channel to England the novelty of his simple unmanned flights soon faded. He wasn't entirely finished with ballooning, however, and he incorporated Vincenzo Lunardi, whose appearance over the rooftops of London had caused an outright sensation, into the bill at Astley's. Having been the first to present ballooning for public entertainment, several years later Astley became the first to present parachute jumps. In 1802 his son John presented:

> Mons, Garnerin and Capt. Soden's Aerial Voyage in a BALLOON, with an exact Representation of its Appearance OVER LONDON, and its Descent near Colchester, in the REAL CAR, as presented by Mons. Garnerin to Mr Astley.[62]

Astley always had another card up his sleeve. By 1785 he was confident enough in his abilities as a conjuror to publish a magician's manual entitled *Natural Magic: or Physical Amusements Revealed*. Critics point out that it bears an uncanny resemblance to *The Conjuror Unmasked*, a translation of a book by the French illusionist Henri Decremps, including a very similar cover illustration. The frontispiece depicts 'the card nailed to the wall with a pistol shot', which involves the conjuror firing a nail at a pack of cards that have been thrown into the air and skewering the card selected by the audience. He made use of the latest science to assist his sleight of hand. One of his tricks, the Magic Nosegay, involved artificial flowers made from animal

---

62 Decades later, balloons would become a regular feature of the circus but their pilots were under pressure to perform in ever more difficult conditions. In 1840 an aeronaut at Astley's shared his basket with a leopard. In 1871 an acrobat named Professor Torres was performing tricks on a trapeze hanging from a balloon when it exploded. Torres survived the crash, only to drown in another balloon accident later that year.

intestine dilated at will by pumping air through the hollow stems. The blossoms would then swell 'like little aerostatical Balloons'. In his book Astley also claims he invented one of the most dangerous and dramatic tricks in the repertoire of any magician, the bullet-catch.[63] This is still debated by historians of the sleight-of-art, but his colourful account is worth retelling. According to Astley, while he was serving in the army in Germany, a couple of his colleagues got into an argument which they elected to settle with a pistol duel. Astley, acting as a second, colluded with his opposite number to avoid bloodshed. He removed the live bullets via a method still regularly used by magicians to this day.

There is another rather odd anecdote in Astley's magic book that should also be taken with a pinch of salt. He claims his first major scrape with the authorities occurred in 1765 when a warrant was issued summoning him to Kingston for trial on a charge of 'dealing with the Devil'. The trigger for this rather bizarre episode was supposedly an investment he had made in 'a most elegant Piece of Machinery with four Fronts, made by the ingenious Artists Mr Martinet, of Clerkenwell.' Mechanical automata were all the rage in Europe and it was only natural that someone with Astley's keen sense of showmanship should want to own one for display in his amphitheatre. His automaton, according to local informers, played a German flute and a harpsichord suspiciously 'in a manner beyond conception'. The authorities smelled brimstone: Astley set off for Kingston Assizes in procession with his entire troupe, Little Billy and all. When the truth emerged that Astley had stolen the idea from some figures he had seen on the clock at St. Dunstan's in Fleet Street, the court collapsed in laughter and the charge was thrown out. Or so he claims in his book but, like many Astley

---

63   The effect known as the bullet catch is officially the world's most dangerous magic trick having allegedly claimed the lives of fifteen people, including the most famous bullet-catching death, that of William Robinson aka Chung Ling Soo, shot on stage in 1918. So shocking was the death of Robinson that even Harry Houdini never attempted to perform the trick.

anecdotes, the story doesn't stand up. In 1765 he was still a sergeant-major in the army. Besides, the laws against demonology were repealed in 1736.[64] Perhaps it was own heavily embellished version of his appearance at Kingston assizes in 1777 and he (or his proof-reader) got the dates wrong.

Astley did face accusations of demonic involvement, figuratively speaking. His spectacular trick-riding was often described as 'devilish' in the press. One journalist complained, 'What a wicked age this is, and likely to continue so! For no less than two thousand persons nightly walk and ride to the Devil at Astley's.' Another noted that the audience's 'delighted astonishment' was 'tainted by the suspicion that spectacularly visible accomplishment could readily be associated with devilry in disguise'. This was very effective advertising but Astley was uncharacteristically keen to play it down. He went to great pains to point out that his apparently supernatural power over horses was the simply the result of a lifetime of very hard work and training.

In the spring of 1887 he went on an extended tour of Europe, finishing in Belgium, where he caused quite stir, as a letter from the *Brussels Gazette* on 6 March related:

> Astley and his troop are the general topic of conversation here in all the polite circles and assemblies; and true it is, there never was his equal seen in Brussels; all those who have been here before him in his line, are in comparison to him, what a puppet shew (sic) is to a good play. The surprising feats performed by his troop, and especially by his inimitable son, appear to some, to be the ne plus ultra of the art of horsemanship and equestrian exercises, while other people, of weaker minds, imagine them to be supernatural, and that they are really assisted by a little magic.

---

64   In the reign of Elizabeth I lived the famous Banks, whose miraculous tricks featuring his famous horse Morocco led to accusations that he was a sorcerer and he narrowly escaped being burned at the stake in France.

Wild animals and human oddities – 'wonders of Nature' –
were not prominent features at Astley's during his lifetime, but
as a theatre manager with profits to consider he was pragmatic.
In August 1787 his handbills introduced the 'Three Monstrous
Craws... wild born human beings'. The three Craws were
described in the London newspapers as:

> Two Females and a Male, of a very small stature, and most
> extraordinary shape and form, with large Craws under their throat,
> full of moving balls, or glands, which play all ways as directed,
> and stimulated by either their eating, speaking, or laughing. Their
> speech, country, and language are unknown to all.

The Craws caused quite a stir. They were said to have been blown
out to sea in a violent storm, then picked up by a Spanish ship
and carried to Italy, and from there to Holland and then London.
In actuality, the 'most extraordinary bipeds that perhaps ever
visited this country' came from a town in the Italian Alps known
for a local iodine deficiency. All three had large goitres – swollen
thyroid glands. For several nights, the Craws were led around the
ring on horseback by Philip Astley while carrying illuminating
candles so the audience could get a good look at their undoubtedly
distressing disfigurements. *The Morning Herald* reported that the
Craws were 'extraordinary and curious savage beings' while the
Morning Post considered them 'the most astonishing prodigies
of our nature ever beheld by all the known world', likening one
female Craw to an 'ourang outang'. Astley employed the Craws
through October. The lady billed as the 'Wild Born Female
Monster' become so 'tame' that she rode two horses at a full
gallop while standing upright. The Duke of York came to see
them incognito, accompanied by General Grenville and Colonel
Lake. After being subjected to the inconvenience of a crowded
house, their presence was made known to Astley, who ordered the
performances repeated in private for his distinguished guests.

In the mid-1780s, London was hit by a wave of performing pigs. Astley showed his first porker on 23 May 1784. This was probably Mr Nicholson's original Toby the Learned Pig, 'who has been the admiration of the nobility and gentry of this kingdom all the winter'. It did all the things crowds expect from a clever swine: it could spell, calculate, do card tricks, tell the time and read minds, although one suspects that from a distance the card tricks were unimpressive. The show was a great success and the pig went on to tour the provincial towns, returning to London later in the year and then moving on to Europe. The following year this porcine prophet appeared at Sadler's Wells as the headline act on a mixed bill of entertainment featuring accomplished tightrope dancers and acrobats Signor Placide, Mr Redigé 'The Little Devil'[65], Mr Dupois, Mr Meunier and la Belle Espanola. The human performers, outraged at finding themselves second billing to the pork pretender, told the theatre manager Richard Wroughton, 'either the pig goes or we do'. They found themselves looking for new jobs. Happily, the disgruntled troupe quickly found new employment at Astley's. This was followed by a heated newspaper campaign from both theatres over the legality of their new employment at the Royal Grove.

In April 1785, the Royal Circus responded with their own automaton 'pig of knowledge', along with a mechanical monkey which did revolutions on the tightrope. In 1787 another real pig appeared at Astley's, this time under the stewardship of Sieur Garman. According to the newspapers, this pig could speak French. Or at least he 'articulated *oui, oui,* with an uncommon fine accent, proof of his having an early polite education'. Astley took his pig on tour and in December that year they appeared in Manchester as part of a show, 'By his majesty's royal letters patent... at the riding house in Tib-street... a grand display of

---

65 Not to be confused with a performer called Nevit, who also appeared at Astley's as The Great Devil.

various exercises, by Astley's company of dancers, tumblers, vaulters, and musical performers, on several horses.' Also featured on the bill were 'a minuet by two horses', the 'Metamorphose of the Sack by Mr Lansdale' and 'several feats on horseback by a young lady, Miss Vangibles. Performances are peculiar to herself – first appearance in Manchester.'

According to one report, Astley's 'Toby the learned pig' grunted its last in 1788. By the following year, however, it had risen from the dead and was 'just returned from France' following the revolution and was ready to 'discourse on the Feudal System, the Rights of Kings and the Destruction of the Bastille'. By this time there was a drove of performing pigs and Toby was the generic name for any porcine prophet worth his salt.[66]

Astley's celebrated performing monkey, General Jackoo, a staple act as early as 1768, was still going strong in the mid-1780s. In 1785 Jackoo was a simian sensation in Paris and across the Continent, amazing audiences by standing unassisted on horseback, carrying a candelabra balanced on a stick held between his teeth, or dressed as a Prussian Hussar and brandishing a sword. In 1788 he had a dance named after him, *The General Jackoo*, written in D Major and performed in 2/4 time. In Paris, in a rarefied precedent to the chimp's tea party,

---

66 In 1784 Samuel Johnson, as quoted by James Boswell, noted that education, however painful, has at least prolonged the learned pig's life. In 1817 another learned swine, Toby the Sapient Pig, appeared at Astley's, saving the bacon of his canny handler, Nicholas Hoare, a failed magician who had turned to training novel animal acts: he would later appear in company with a Learned Goose. Toby captivated audiences with his ability to 'spell and read, cast accounts, play at cards; tell any person what o'clock it is to a minute by their own watch... tell the age of any one in company', and most remarkably, 'discover a person's thoughts', a trick 'never heard of before to be exhibited by an animal of the swine race'. Hoare probably showed his first black pig in 1785, reinventing the act when the need arose. One black pig looked pretty much like another, so it is likely that the demanding programme of 'four performances a day' – was fulfilled by two or three Tobys taking turns.

Jackoo enjoyed an elaborate public breakfast with 'a canine Mme de Pompadour' while waited on by humans. The General also attracted groupies. Horace Walpole reported that Madame de Choiseul ('lover of Monsieur de Coligny and Prince Joseph of Monaco') was so in thrall of the rope-dancing, cross-dressing anthropoid that she offered to buy it. Of course, there was never any question of Astley giving up his show-stealing monkey and he politely declined her offer, so poor Madame de Choiseul had to settle for second best. She bought another trick monkey who had been brought up in a kitchen and 'learned to pluck fowls with inimitable dexterity'. Madame de Choiseul never forgot her first love and named her new pet General Jackoo II.

The 1780s were General Jackoo's heyday and from then on he was eased into obscurity. By 1824 he was washed-up as a headliner and receiving third billing as 'the Clown' in a pantomime, but by that time he was at least fifty-six years old and too arthritic to perform acrobatics. That's show business.[67]

In the early summer of 1788, Astley acquired another show horse, a magnificent Andalusian grey, a present from his old commanding officer General George Augustus Elliot, now ennobled as first Baron Heathfield.[68] This wasn't just any old horse, this was the mount that carried Elliot through his epic defence of Gibraltar during the Great Siege of 1779-83, when combined French and Spanish forces failed to starve out the desperately poorly supplied British garrison. Lasting three years

---

67 If indeed it was the same monkey. In 4 April 1785 the *Gazetteer* announced Jacko's (Jackoo's) show in unmistakably identifying the monkey as a new arrival on the London scene: 'The Second Week's Exhibition will Continue until Saturday, the 9th of April [*and will include*] General Jacko, (never exhibited in *England*) from the Fair of St. Germain's, Paris, who has been celebrated for his astonishing Performances on the TIGHTROPE, and other Exercises, which are beyond Conception.' My Googling skills reveal that the oldest monkey on record was a black spider monkey named Buenos, who died of heart failure in 2005. She was 52.

68 *Morning Post and Daily Advertiser* 4 June 1788.

and seven months, it was the longest siege in British history and it made the battle-honour 'Gibraltar' one of the army's most-prized. Astley's 'Gibraltar Charger' enjoyed instant celebrity status when it was first displayed in June and it was the headlining act for the entire 1788 season. The horse was such a huge draw that one commentator speculated that it would net around £1,000[69] profit in the first year alone.

Every 4 June from 1783, at his own expense, Astley held an annual outdoor firework display to honour King George III's birthday. These events, skilfully combining the latest pyrotechnics with the usual patriotic equestrianism, were considered hugely successful, despite the odd fatality. In 1792, three days before the king's birthday display, Astley's head carpenter John Horner was killed by an explosion of gunpowder while preparing some fireworks and was buried in the ruins of his laboratory.

Gibraltar's debut was timed to coincide with Astley's most ambitious fireworks display to date, held to celebrate the King's fiftieth. The fireworks were set off from a series of barges anchored in the Thames directly in front of Westminster Bridge, Astley directing the event from another barge stationed just in front of them. What made this unusual is that he did it while mounted on Gibraltar. This was surprising enough; what made the performance more astonishing is that when the fireworks were lit, horse and rider were repeatedly and randomly 'entirely covered with fire'. Whether accidental or otherwise this sight was very well received by the watching crowd and was immediately adopted into Astley's regular amphitheatre programme. Throughout the season Astley and Gibraltar performed a similar, albeit smaller indoor version designed by his pyrotechnics expert Johannes Hengler. The unflappable Gibraltar, who by this time must have seen it all and was surprised at nothing, appeared in the ring surrounded by a circle of fire, with Astley mounted on his

---

69   About £150,000 in today's values.

back, energetically letting off a cascade of 'golden rain, crackling stars and Roman candles'.

Throughout the 1780s, competition was emerging from other directions. Of all the city's minor entertainment venues, Sadler's Wells in Clerkenwell was one of the most successful by adapting to the changing tastes of Londoners. It began with the chance discovery of a well in the garden of one Richard Sadler in 1685. As Clerkenwell was known for its supposedly health-giving spa waters, Sadler claimed his well was effective against 'dropsy, jaundice, scurvy, green sickness and other distempers to which females are liable – ulcers, fits of the mother, virgin's fever and hypochondriacal distemper'. By the end of the summer London's most fashionable were flocking to Mr Sadler's garden to sample his waters. He built a wooden Music House where visitors could listen to performers, 'filling the air with... pipe, tabor and dulcimer.' He soon found himself facing stiff competition from rival wells, at which point artistic sensibility went out of the window. Before long he was showing prize fights and anything else he thought might drum up a crowd, including the Hibernian Cannibal who could devour a large, live cockerels – feathers, feet and all – with a side order of oats, all washed down with a pint of brandy. In 1740 the venue was offering rope-dancing, tumbling, singing and pantomimes with elaborate stage sets and machinery. By this time the Sadler's Wells audience was different, too. One visitor described the regular crowd as 'vermin trained up to the gallows'.

The Wells' traditional dependence on liquid refreshment as a means of drawing an audience also changed. The waters once touted as promoting health were now being used in the brewing of beer. Public drunkenness at Sadler's Wells was so rife that it was now operating more as a drinking establishment with entertainments on the side. By the 1780s Sadler's Wells was a serious rival to Astley's with a very mixed bag of entertainments including Scaglioni's troupe of performing dogs led by Moustache, the canine matinee idol of his day, two horses dancing a minuet, a singing duck and the ubiquitous learned pig. Competition between Astley's, the Royal Circus and Sadler's Wells was sharp, each attempting to gain the upper hand with original and ever more daring acts.

One of the most thrilling aspects of these early circus performances was that the players routinely put their lives on the line for the sake of entertainment. Near-death experiences, broken cheekbones and cracked skulls were commonplace.[70] Few in the profession forgot the fate of a popular tight-rope dancer at Astley's and Sadler's Wells in the 1780s, Paulo Redigé a.k.a. The Little Devil. According to the show bills, the Little Devil could 'dance with wooden shoes; then, without the pole, will kick a half-crown piece into a drinking glass upon his head; after which he will exhibit the tricks of the hat, stick and hoop; and other capital manoeuvres.' He was married to another Astley's performer, a busty Spanish lady called La Belle Espagnole who could dance a Fandango on the rope while playing castanets. They had a son, Paulo junior, described as 'clown to the rope'. His father died tragically while performing as the character Harlequin: he jumped through a window and the top of his skull collided with a protruding screw when stage-hands failed to catch him. Paulo senior was forty-two years old.

At the Royal Circus, cracks were beginning to show. It had been riven with internal disputes almost from the beginning. Each of the backers had brought to the gathering a measure of self-interest. The sporting investors were simply expecting to make a profit. Sir John Lade was hoping to pay off some of the debts he had accrued through his wild and unconventional

---

70 An Astley's performer of the day was 'St. Clare the celebrated foreigner', who took London by storm with an optical illusion called Phantasmagoria. John Astley offered him to a theatre manager in Liverpool but then had to cancel, explaining that 'St. Clare has fallen through a trap and dislocated his collar bone'.

lifestyle. In Colonel West's case, he rather fancied himself as a playwright and had penned a couple of plays himself. Suffice to say they weren't very good, which introduced a certain amount of awkwardness to the relationship. More corrosively, the two managers Hughes and Dibdin didn't get on at all. Hughes for his part made no attempt to ingratiate himself with Dibdin. Hughes didn't leave any memoirs, but Dibdin doesn't mince words in his: he described his business partner as 'a weak, unstable absurd creature' and 'a leech'. The two were constantly fighting over their share of the profits and methods of operation. Dibdin was a talented manager of the stage department but had poor people skills and worse judgment in financial matters. Their backers were mostly businessmen and lawyers with no experience of any theatrical enterprise and were overwhelmed by the cost of operations at the Royal Circus. Hughes, Dibdin and the proprietors were constantly in court suing one another over badly worded contracts. Hughes, meanwhile, was craftily pitting the proprietors and actors against Dibdin. After three years of frustrating conflict, in 1785 Dibdin decided he had had enough and walked away from the circus business, never to return. His departure should have been a source of immediate worry for his financial backers because, although Hughes was a great showman, he didn't have much of a business brain.

The Royal Circus was now completely under Hughes' control, but he still didn't own the site and he was engaged in a state of perpetual conflict with Lady Jane West, the site's new proprietor. Her husband had died after being thrown by his horse. This mount had been selected for him by Hughes, who had reassured the Colonel that it was a safe, docile ride. The grieving widow accused Hughes of causing his death by deliberately giving him a dangerous horse. She tried to turn him out of the Royal Circus but her co-investors rallied to defend him, concerned that the business would fail without its horse trainer and star rider. By the end of the 1780s the power of the Royal Circus as a rival to

Astley's was diminishing almost daily. In his desperation to find a local audience, Hughes acquired a liquor licence and his circus became what his stage manager Thomas Read described as 'a bear house... a scene of nocturnal orgies, riot, dissipation (sic) and confusion'.

Astley, meanwhile, was still struggling to stay one step ahead of the law. He and Hughes enjoyed a sort of quasi-legal status inasmuch as they were licensed by Surrey magistrates to perform equestrian displays but could do little else. Local magistrates had the power to grant annual licences to non-patent theatres for singing, dancing and the performance of burlettas. A burletta was defined as a drama with music: so long as the actors didn't speak dramatic dialogue but sang or delivered their words in rhyme, they were within the letter of the law. At Astley's and the Royal Circus, whenever a line of dialogue was considered absolutely necessary, someone would walk on stage holding up a banner with the spoken line printed on it. Or at least that was the theory. For the most part, they got away with doing pretty much whatever they liked because entertainments on the South Bank were still nowhere near as rigorously policed as they were in Westminster and the City.

In July 1787 the absurdities of the arcane licensing laws were revealed in all their glory when an Italian clown called Carlo Delpini strayed from a sentimental ditty penned by Henry Fielding about a cut of meat and spoke the words 'roast beef' on a non-patent stage. Writers have a well-known dislike for actors who mess with their words but this time the wrath wasn't Fielding's. Delpini was arrested and jailed, along with his theatre owner. This strange dispute had an unexpected silver lining. The owners of Sadler's Wells, realising that they too were technically in breach of the law and could also find themselves in prison at any time, petitioned Parliament for the right to present pantomimes and burlettas with dialogue. Astley's and the Royal Circus quickly followed suit. Their argument was simple: if

Sadler's Wells was allowed to have a licence then they should have one too. Old hostilities were temporarily put aside as the Royal Grove and the Royal Circus joined forces to petition parliament for the right of their businesses to exist.

In setting out his own case, Astley relied heavily on his honourable military record, backed up with a character reference from the late Colonel Nangle with whom he had served in the 15th Light Dragoons in Germany, attesting to Astley's valour at Emsdorf and Friedberg. Decisively, it was Lord Thurlow, defender of Astley and the slave trade, who came to the rescue again. The management of Sadler's Wells argued that, as their establishment was the oldest, they should be treated preferentially. Thurlow disagreed: all the minor theatres should be given legal status or none at all. On payment of double the usual sums and sureties, Astley and Hughes were each granted a special licence to exhibit 'performances of singing, dancing, pantomime and music' and 'other public entertainments of the like kind' – broadly interpreted to include displays of equestrianism – to run from Easter Monday to the 15 September. For the first time the two rival circuses could operate legally. For the best part of twenty years Astley had been regarded as little more than a showman, an outlaw barely tolerated by the authorities, scorned by the Westminster theatrical establishment. He was now a legitimate theatre manager and show business impresario.

In 1788 Philip Astley decided to build himself a mansion fit for a theatrical potentate. He leased a triangle of land just a stone's throw from his home in Bridge Row, next to his amphitheatre[71] and in the centre erected a gated mansion surrounded by a shoulder-high black iron fence with spokes on top. He called it Hercules Hall, a fond tribute to one of his earliest and most successful acts, a human pyramid trick called the La Force d' Hercule. The architecture of Hercules Hall reflected the owner's

---

71   Now bounded by Hercules Road, Kennington Road and Cosser Street.

considerable wealth and his eccentricity: the building was topped by three conical, flat-topped turrets like giant upturned plant pots with bulls-eye windows. It was a noisy, vibrant household and visitors ringing the doorbell were greeted with a chorus of horses and snarling dogs. Soon afterwards, he extended his property portfolio by building the Hercules Buildings, a row of comfortable three-storey terraced houses with private gardens front and back. On two of the corners he built inns, the Hercules Tavern and The Pineapple.[72]

By now a network of houses and public buildings covered the old Lambeth marshland and, with two circuses within a few hundred yards of each other, the area was so thickly populated with performers that it became something of a thespian ghetto known locally as the Theatrical Barracks. Stangate, at the back of Astley's, was a favourite meeting place for the sons and daughters of actors and as a residence for the pantomime and equestrian fraternity. The Hercules Buildings were said to house a theatrical family in almost every room. One of the best-known tenants was Astleys' famous clown, the Liverpudlian Dicky Usher. Usher was the first ever carpet clown – that is, he was in the ring from the beginning to the end of the performance and it was his job to interplay with the audience and keep everyone laughing when nothing much else is happening. Usher trained a team of cats to pull him in a cart around the ring. He once caused a stir by sailing up the Thames from Westminster to Waterloo Bridge in a bathtub drawn by four geese. It wasn't discovered until many years later that the tub had actually been towed by a boat, sailing unnoticed a few dozen yards ahead.

From the summer of 1791 Astley was a near-neighbour and landlord of William Blake, who lived happily with his wife Catherine at Number 13 Hercules Buildings, just a few minutes'

---

72 Hercules Hall was demolished in 1841 but at the time of writing The Pineapple was still a thriving pub.

walk from the riverside wharves 'near where the chartered Thames doth flow'. The house was one of the largest in a row of twenty-four, with eight or ten rooms. Blake worked in the front and back rooms on the first floor. Blake's 'dark Satanic Mills' described the once-famous Albion Mills in nearby Blackfriars Road. When Blake moved to Hercules Road the mill had just been burned down, supposedly by arsonists, and was a blackened shell, but the Blakes generally enjoyed the pastoral surroundings of Lambeth. At the end of Blake's private back garden was a small summer house. Calling on his friend one day, Thomas Butts was surprised to find Blake and his wife stark naked. They were reciting passages from *Paradise Lost*, apparently 'in character.'

One day, Blake looked out of his window and was shocked to see a boy in Astley's garden with a log tied to his foot. It was the type of device commonly used to shackle a horse. Even in an age that believed strongly in the improving qualities of corporal punishment, Blake thought that this was a bit extreme and he went round to Hercules Hall and hammered on the door to remonstrate with its owner. Patty Astley answered and, when Blake told her what he'd seen, she explained that the boy was doing some work for her husband – she assumed the log was a punishment of some sort. The boy was released and Blake went home. When Astley heard about his neighbour's interference, his blood was up. He charged round to the poet's house and the two men had a heated exchange which almost came to blows. In the end, Astley admitted that the punishment was too harsh and the two men departed as friends. The treatment of the boy was upsetting to Blake but, in an age when boys were routinely whipped, it was hardly surprising. The Georgians loved their children and they took care of them but they also expected their obedience and if they didn't give it, they expected to be punished.

William Blake was Astley's tenant for ten years and during that time produced some of his greatest work; *Songs of Experience, The Marriage of Heaven and Hell, Visions of the Daughters of*

Albion, America a Prophecy, The First Book of Urizen and much more. He must have visited Astley's Amphitheatre during those years, too. Blake wrote a satire called *An Island in the Moon* in which one of the characters was called General Jackoo, a tribute to his landlord's famous performing monkey. No trace remains of Hercules Buildings or Blake's studio where he made his extraordinary works during 1790s. In 1918, No.13 Hercules Buildings was razed, along with the rest of the terraced row in which Blake lived.

10

IF THEY DON'T KNOW MANNERS,
WE CAN'T TEACH 'EM

Philip Astley in middle age. Father and son were once said to be 'remarkably handsome, the father being a veritable giant but of perfect symmetry'. Reproduced with permission of the National Portrait Gallery.

The best contemporary likeness of Philip Astley is an anonymously produced etching in the archives of the National Portrait Gallery in London (see previous page). According to the records it was made in the early 1800s but it is more likely that it shows him as he was around the early 1780s. From this portrait it is hard to imagine him as the broad-shouldered, athletic, handsome performer who once dazzled with his eye-popping horsemanship. We see someone in early middle age who has grown in reputation and girth. He has long since given up trick-riding because of his injured leg and has put on weight, the buttons on his waistcoat straining to contain his huge stomach. Astley's corpulence was often remarked on but gluttony was the hallmark of a Georgian gentleman. He would have been pleased to be fat and resigned to gout. In later years, when he became even more plump and prosperous, his cheeks were puce and he looked uncomfortably likely to explode, which perhaps was not far from actuality.

He has discarded his trademark regimentals and his three-cornered hat and is wearing the uniform of an eighteenth-century riding instructor, a coat with gold buttons and trim, a white waistcoat and breeches with black riding boots that came up to the knee. On his head is a black top hat and he is holding some reins and carrying a whip. This outfit, instantly recognisable to any modern circus-goer, was probably worn by him in his new permanent role as equestrian director – ringmaster, as it became known – introducing his acts and keeping his horses on track around the ring. Later, he occasionally displayed the arms of the French monarchy on his tunic, a right he claimed was given to him by royal ordinance.

He was in every sense a huge man – 'Philip the Big' was one of the many nicknames attached to him. Contemporaries would probably have heard him long before they saw him: think Brian Blessed on steroids. His booming voice was unmistakeably that of a powerfully built man with a commanding demeanour and it made the timid shrink. He was often mocked for his accent and his manners. The proper way to speak in Georgian London was English as spoken 'among the better sort', according to Dr Samuel Johnson, as long as it avoided the worst of Cockney. It certainly wouldn't have included the broad North Staffordshire dialect of Astley's youth – if indeed he retained any of it – which was actually a relic of Anglo-Saxon Old English and much closer to that spoken by Geoffrey Chaucer.

He peppered his conversation with salty oaths and imprecations, mangled his grammar and misplaced his 'h's'.[73] Apparently he once noted that 'these ere orses heat most vociferously.'[74] It was said that if he came across a new word or phrase he liked the sound of he used it liberally. The story goes that, having got hold of the word 'cadence', he dropped it everywhere. 'You don't act in cadence, Sir' he once lectured a pantomime performer. 'Cadence, Sir, everything should be done in cadence. My horses perform in cadence, as well as singers sing, Cadence is the staminer (sic) of everything, Sir.' To underline the point, he took a piece of chalk and wrote on the wall, C.A.D.U.N.C.E. – 'Cadence, Sir, remember that another time.' So throughout his career and for a long time afterwards he was the butt of amusing jibes about the way he spoke, his legendary malapropisms, his lack of education and his boorishness, which all helped add up to create a cruel and undeserved caricature of an ignorant buffoon.

The likes of the satirist Henry William Bunbury and Charles Dibdin the Younger, among others, made a great deal of Astley's supposed lack of schooling and his generally uncouth behaviour.

---

73 *Annals of the Liverpool Stage* by R. J. Broadbent. H-dropping (and h-adding) was a trope in comic literature from Victorian times to the early 20th century and was always used to portray common, uneducated types, e.g. in the musical *My Fair Lady*, 'In 'Artford, 'Ereford and 'Ampshire, 'urricanes 'ardly hever 'appen'.

74 The same source has him talking about 'a crocodile what stopped Halexander's harmy and when cut hopen had a man in harmour in its intellects'.

Dibdin described Astley as 'a humane hog'. Long after his death accounts of his career written during the Victorian era describe him as 'uneducated' or even 'illiterate'. The circus historian Maurice Willson Disher, writing in the 1930s, described him as 'extremely ignorant'.

These characterisations are at best ill-informed and at worst pure snobbery. Astley was plain-spoken and lacked refinement but somewhere along the line he had an education. According to the military historian Richard Holmes, in the 1760s Astley's rank as sergeant-major would have been given to him as much for his literacy and numeracy as for his bearing or skill at drill because the post involved a lot of administrative work and clerical skills. Astley also wrote seven books – not bad for an illiterate – and most of his early show scripts (although a cynic might say that some of what has survived is doggerel). He also had at least conversational French, which is more than can be said of most Britons today.

Astley wasn't without a sense of humour. He was well aware of his reputation for gaffs and perhaps invented a few for comic effect, but he didn't like it when people took liberties. Sadler's Wells overstepped the mark when they hired a comedian called Rees to do a stage impression of 'Old Astley'. John Astley, like his father, not the sort of man to mess with, went round to sort them out. He waited in the audience until the impressionist had taken the stage, then stood up and brandished his horsewhip, promising to thrash Rees in full view of the public if the act went ahead. The management dropped the curtain, disappointing many who had hoped to see a good fight. The ensuing riot took a full thirty minutes to quell. Astley senior thanked his son for defending the family honour in an open letter to *The Times*. The terrified Rees lodged an official complaint and John Astley was fined five pounds and bound over to keep the peace.

Samuel Johnson, who came to London from Staffordshire with David Garrick, was described by James Boswell as 'much of a

John Bull, a blunt true-born Englishman', and the same could be said of Astley. He was a huge, outrageous, booming, opinionated man and it is reasonable to assume that he wasn't always a paragon of affability and amiability. He inherited his father's hot temper and could switch from charming to threatening in an instant. The very first edition of the *Dictionary of National Biography*, published in 1885 just over sixty years after Astley died, described him as a man 'of violent temper, peremptory of speech and rude of manner'.[75] At times he was difficult company and an overbearing conversationalist. Charles Dibdin junior once regretted sharing a coach with Astley for four hours. During the whole length of the journey Dibdin sat mute as his boss bawled out a 'curious rant' with his opinions on everything from music, writing, theatres, the courts, parliament and the nation.

His politics, especially his deep and fierce loyalty to king and country, attracted a great deal of mockery too. He was very proud of his credentials as a war hero and wasn't shy about playing the part. He told his paying customers, 'I have bled for my country many times, and I will gladly bleed for it again'.

His contemporaries laughed at his pretentions. Patronage was essential, as every stage manager knew well, but Astley loved to embellish his own royal connections, often incorporating impressive lists of noble patrons in all his publicity materials. As he grew older and richer the name-dropping and displays of loyalty to king and country, and his frequent obsequious entreaties to 'persons of quality', became ever more ostentatious.

He was a patriot but never a xenophobe. He worked all over Europe and made Paris his second home. As early as 1771 he was bringing French, German, Italian, Spanish performers to his amphitheatre and during his lifetime would provide work for people from all over the world. The early circus had so many performers from overseas that British artistes often took on

---

75   But also adds, 'of great energy and notable integrity.'

foreign-sounding names to add to their mystique in the ring. Generally, there are very few prejudicial references to black and ethnic performers in British newspapers from the time. Thomas Horne, the Chaplain of the Showman's Guild, recalling the black circus showman Pablo Fanque, noted, 'In the great brotherhood of the equestrian world there is no colour-line... the camaraderie of the Ring has but one test, ability.'[76] It wasn't only ethnic performers who enjoyed an unusual degree of independence and professional success in the early circus. Women also enjoyed freedoms in Astley's circus that would have been unthinkable in broader Georgian and Victorian society.

Astley was quick to bawl out slackers or anyone else that didn't meet his high expectations. He demanded the best from the dozens of performers and musicians, writers, scenic artists, carpenters and stable hands who worked for him and those who under-performed could expect the worst. If his human performers quit in protest he could replace them quickly and easily. He found horses a lot easier to manage. As one circus historian pointed out, 'Given a comfortable stall, a few bucketfuls of oats, and an occasional pat on the nose, they were the most uncomplaining employees imaginable.'[77]

He loved a fine Bordeaux claret, in moderation, but was especially intolerant of drunks. For a while he employed an inebriated hack called Oakman who supplied original dramas for a guinea each. Astley withheld his pay and doctored his manuscripts as he saw fit. Oakman walked out in disgust and, as he left, wrote in chalk over Astley's office door, 'Mangling done here'.

---

76 This was true in the UK, but sadly not in the 19th-century American circus, where even those black people serving as P. T. Barnum's attractions who had been technically freed were kept in *de facto* servitude, thanks to slave-nappers and the legal hostility toward claims of vagrant freedman. In Barnum's shows, blackness was an integral part of the show, such as deliberately unkempt enslaved people who posed as 'wild men of Borneo'.

77 A. H. Saxon, *Enter Foot and Horse.*

Astley reveled in his reputation as a despot and enjoyed a joke at his own expense. One day a theatre manager called Harris complained to him that one of his actors wasn't was pulling his weight. The ringmaster replied: 'Why don't you do with your performers as I do with mine? Never let them have anything to eat 'till they've done acting.' This story first appeared in a collection of stage anecdotes published long after Astley's death and was repeated in the memoirs of Charles Dibdin junior, the son of his old Royal Circus rival and certainly not a fan of Astley, a quarter of a century later. It is the origin of the legend, now more or less hardwired into circus folklore, that he literally starved his performers.

Like all stage managers he was very careful to keep his costs down, but he looked after his stars. The comic actor and singer of popular bawdy songs Richard Johannot was a great Astley favourite. He had worked for Charles Hughes at the Royal Circus in 1783 but jumped ship a couple of years later. According to Dibdin junior, Astley was paying Johannot seven guineas a week all year round, which would have netted him around £600 a year – £86,000 in today's values. Astley also gave him benefits in London, Dublin and Liverpool, paid all of Johannot's travelling expenses and provided him with 'a pleasure horse for his recreation'. It is also worth noting that while under contract to Astley, Johannot was still allowed to perform freely elsewhere, including the Haymarket Theatre in London and Crow Street in Dublin. According to Jacob DeCastro, thanks to his income from Astley's, Johannot 'rolled in the lap of inconsiderate luxury'. Despite these favourable terms the singer was an ungrateful and disloyal employee. In 1798 he quit Astley's to try his luck as a solo performer. He failed but was allowed to return to Astley's, albeit at a reduced salary.

One of Astley's most popular clowns was the Frenchman Jean-Baptiste Laurent. Laurent wasn't just any old clown because he was responsible for bringing to the clown's sartorial repertoire huge floppy clown shoes. He was held in such high regard by Astley that when young Laurent became homesick and absconded to Paris it was the manager himself who hunted him down among the show booths of Boulevard du Temple and brought him back to London. Astley took him under his wing and helped to make him very wealthy.

It is fair to say that this generosity didn't extend to everyone. Another thing that Astley shared with his Staffordshire kinsman, the potter Josiah Wedgwood, was a faith in good copywriting.[78] He was the first theatre manager to employ a full-time 'stock author' to write new stage pieces as well as to devise and deliver 'puffs' and advertisements to the newspapers – an innovation that was quickly copied by all the minor theatres in London.[79] Charles Dibdin junior was one of Astley's main writers in the 1790s. He was one of many illegitimate children fathered by Dibdin senior and the eldest of two born to the actress Harriett Pitt, just one of several women he treated badly, then abandoned: she died in Clerkenwell Poorhouse. Dibdin junior was a cheerful, industrious young man with literary ambitions. He put himself forward for his first writing job at Astley's because he had been told that the fat old circus owner would 'buy anything'. Dibdin offered him a pantomime based on *Don Quixote*. Hoping to increase his chances of a sale, he built a mock-up of every one of the show's twenty-four scenes then lugged them all the way to Hercules Hall in Lambeth. His preparation work paid off; the pantomime was purchased and Dibdin was offered a three-year contract.

---

78 Wedgwood has been called 'the man who invented marketing'. He was the first to find that celebrity endorsements and influencer marketing engage prospects and was the first to use customer testimonials. Most importantly he also introduced the brand – literally stamping his name on the bottom of each piece of ceramic.

79 He also performed his own newspaper-clippings service, which can be viewed today in the British Library.

When he got around to reading the fine print, however, he was shocked to discover that working for Astley, to paraphrase Dibdin, was going to be more like slavery than employment. The young writer was expected to write twelve burlettas, twelve 'serious pantomimes' and twelve harlequinades a year, as well as composing eight or nine daily newspaper 'puffs'. He also had to supply Astley's resident clown with a constant stream of amusing songs. His reward for this enormous output was a weekly salary of a guinea and a half – and only for the weeks when the circus was open. When Dibdin tried to negotiate a better deal, Astley was unyielding, although he did add a clause in the contract agreeing that Dibdin's wife Mary, whom Astley also took on as a dancer, would never have to appear on stage wearing breeches. Fortunately, young Dibdin was a prodigiously fast worker.

Astley as proprietor, critic and censor had the final word on every piece of stage dialogue written for him. Whenever he came across a passage he didn't approve of he would put the author in his place with a blunt: 'You must cut that out by God, Sir,' then dictate something to substitute the offending passage. Dibdin conceded, however, that he was occasionally prepared to listen to reason. When the author stood his ground and refused to publish anything that wasn't entirely his own, Astley relented and never again asked to see a line of any piece Dibdin wrote for him.

From the earliest days of his enterprise Astley always understood the value of publicity and the mechanisms of marketing. His eyes and ears were permanently attuned to commercial opportunities. A hundred years before P.T. Barnum did it, he was shouting his wares on the street and courting controversy in the press. In the early days he relied heavily on handbills, usually handed out by Astley himself, often to the consternation of the more genteel passers-by. As well as promoting the evening's performances, handbills doubled as programme, preview and, occasionally, a forum for a war between himself and anyone else who had rubbed him up the wrong way.

He instructed his handbill writers to keep it simple: 'John Bull, Sir, won't understand that. John Bull never thinks for himself, therefore if we want to catch him, we must think for him. He won't know what five successive evenings means, whether next week of the week after, or the year after: nor will he trouble his head about it. No Sir, if you want John Bull to understand you, you must say Monday next, with the day of the Month, the next day, Tuesday, and the day after, Wednesday, and so on, or you won't catch John Bull, Sir.'

He reserved his greatest scorn for musicians, whom he regarded as a necessary but irritating expense. He complained, 'Any fool can handle a fiddle but it takes a man to manage a horse. Yet I have to pay a fellow who plays upon one fiddle as much salary as a man that rides upon three horses.' Many of the anecdotes regularly told about the showman concerned his supposed ignorance of music. His favourite, and often only, musical instruction was 'play it loud'.[80] Famously, he once berated a musician for not playing in the middle of an orchestra piece. When the man explained that was a rest in his part, Astley exploded: 'I don't pay you to rest, I pay you to play!' According to A. H. Saxon, a very similar anecdote was told of the nineteenth-century circus manager Andrew Ducrow. In 1794 Astley was proposed for honorary membership of the Royal Society of Musicians, so make of that what you will.

In his own lifetime Astley was a national legend partly thanks to his own relentless self-promotion. He always gave good copy to journalists and we was the inspiration for countless stories in the press. Not all of the publicity was positive. It was widely reported that some performing dogs at Astley's were starved and trained to

---

80 Although some of his musical directions were more detailed. He once requested his bandleader to arrange a few bars of music for a broad-sword combat: ' a rang, tang, bang; one, two, three; and a cut sort of thing, you know!'

Likeness of Philip Astley wearing the Sergeant Major's uniform of the 15th Light Dragoons, by Andrew Edwards. The artist used forensic methods to recreate the portrait from existing images of Philip and his son John. Courtesy of the Van Buren Family (Org) Collection, with thanks to Andrew van Buren.

Above: *General George Augustus Elliot, Lord Heathfield, shown here in the thick of the battle astride his famous white charger Gibraltar; after Lord Granby and the Duke of Wellington, judging from his occurrence on public house signboards, he was 18th-century England's most popular war hero. Public domain.*

Left: *Map of Lambeth in 1807. Astley's amphitheatre, shaded yellow, is at the foot of Westminster Bridge at the junction of Westminster Bridge Road and Stangate Street. Reproduced with permission London Borough of Lambeth, Archives Department.*

Jacob Bates, one of the original English trick-riding superstars, performed as far afield as Russia (1764–65) and America (1772-73). New York Public Library Digital Collections.

Domenico Angelo Tremamondo, expert swordsman and Philip Astley's army riding instructor. Illustration from L'Ecole des Armes *published 1787.*

Fig. 275. — Le capitaine Lunardi.

Above left: *Print showing a view of the Royal Circus, on the right, from St. George's Fields at the time of the ascension of Arnold's balloon on 31 August 1785. Public domain.*

Above right: *The Italian aviator Vincenzo Lunardi was a sensation at Astley's in the 1880s. Public domain.*

Below: *The first female aeronaut Mrs Sage and her ascent in 1785. To the right is the obelisk in St George's Fields. Public domain.*

Above: *Interior view of Astley's Westminster Amphitheatre in 1777. Courtesy of British Museum.*

Below: *The young John Astley performing acrobatics on horseback, from an engraving by William Hincks. Reproduced by permission of the London Borough of Lambeth, Archives Department.*

Above: *The Palace of Versailles in the 18th century. Astley's performed there for the Queen of France in 1782. Public domain.*

MYNHEER WYBRAND LOLKES, *the celebrated Man in Miniature, from West Friesland, & Madame Lolkes, his Wife, by whom he had Three Children, all live born and christened.*

Left: *Mynheer Wybrand Lolkes, the dwarf watchmaker from Holland, and his wife, who was three times his height. They performed at Astley's on Easter Monday 1790 and then every evening for the rest of the season. Although very small Mr Lolkes was remarkably agile 'and possessed uncommon strength, and could with the greatest ease spring from the ground into a chair of ordinary height'. Courtesy of the Wellcome Collection.*

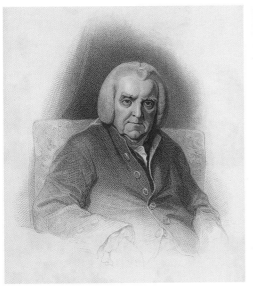

Above left: *Astley's saviour Baron Thurlow, Lord High Chancellor. Luckily, Philip had taught his daughters how to ride. Public domain.*

Above right: *Charles Dibdin the elder, who first used the word 'circus' in its modern sense. He made a fortune from writing popular sea shanties although he'd only ever been to sea once, very briefly. Public domain.*

Below: *A show at Astley's in 1808. Houghton Library, Harvard University.*

ASTLEY'S AMPHITHEATRE.

ROYAL CIRCUS.

Above: *A Rowlandson print showing the interior view of Astley's rival, The Royal Circus. Public domain.*

Left: *The entrance to Astley's amphitheatre in Westminster Bridge Road, 1819. Courtesy of British Museum.*

Right: *Hercules Buildings, Lambeth, home of English painter and poet William Blake. From 1793 until 1800 Philip Astley was his landlord. Public domain.*

Below left: *Jacob DeCastro, actor and memoirist, shown here with a small portrait of his former employer Philip Astley. Public domain.*

Below right. *William Blake (1757–1827). Public domain.*

Portrait of John Conway Philip Astley, painted by James Saxon in approximately 1810 when John was about 43 years old. Courtesy of the Garrick Club, London.

FATIGUES OF THE CAMPAIGN IN FLANDERS.

Above: *This satirical print by James Gillray shows Astley's patron and commander-in-chief, the 29-year-old Duke of York, head of the British forces in Flanders, celebrating a rare victory – too soon and too vigorously. Public domain.*

Right: *This poster shows John Bill Rickets and his famous horse Cornplanter, which was acquired from George Washington. Houghton Library, Harvard University.*

Whoever shall look upon has like again

The celebrated Cornplanter *taking a flying leap over Silva a Horse of his own height*

BY

Mr. RICKETTS

The images on this page are details from a poster for American circus trick-riding, early 1900s. US Library of Congress.

Right: *The greatest clown Joseph 'Joey' Grimaldi. Print by George Cruikchank, public domain.*

Below left: *The formidable 'Betsy' Billington went head-to-head with Astley's sparring contests in Dublin. James Gillray print, public domain.*

Below right: *Madame Teresa, The Corsican Fairy, billed as 'one of the most perfect and admirable productions of human nature in miniature'. She spoke French and Italian with the 'greatest vivacity'. Courtesy of the Wellcome Collection.*

Mr GRIMALDI, as Clown.

A Bravura Air

MANDANE.

Engraved by R.Cooper.

MADAME TERESIA.

The Corsican Fairy

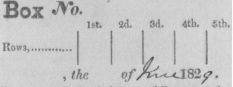

Above: *Theatre riots in London and Dublin happened regularly in the Georgian era. This print shows a disturbance at the King's Theatre, Haymarket, provoked by the non-appearance of the singer Catalani. Courtesy of the Wellcome Collection.*

Left: *1820s box seat ticket for Astley's Royal Amphitheatre. Unlike the pit and galleries, a seat in one of the boxes could be reserved for a fraction of the cost, but if the theatre goers arrived late, they might lose their claim to it. Houghton Library, Harvard University.*

Above left: *A rare and previously unpublished photograph of Astley's Amphitheatre a few days before it closed for the last time in 1893. Standing on the balcony is the owner of the famous old building, 'Lord' George Sanger. Van Buren Family (Org) Collection, courtesy of Andrew van Buren.*

Above right: *Pablo Fanque and the playbill that inspired John Lennon to write The Beatles'* Being For the Benefit of Mr. Kite! *Fanque's real name was William Darby and he made his professional London debut at Astley's in 1847. These benefit performances were usually for circus workers down on their luck or struck down by injury. Fanque became Britain's first black circus owner but died destitute. Public domain.*

A rare copy of Philip Astley's book Natural Magic. *Author's own edition.*

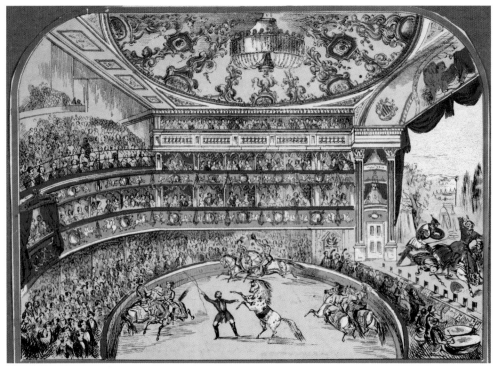

Shakespeare's Richard III on horseback performed at Astley's around 1856. Public domain.

Above: *Tokens for Astley's Amphitheatre. They were usually purchased on the door then handed over on entering the relevant part of the auditorium. Ivory season tickets were also issued to box subscribers with their names inscribed on the reverse. Courtesy of the Wellcome Collection.*

Left: *Paving stone in the gardens of St. Thomas's Hospital, Lambeth marking the exact location of the entrance to Astley's at the southern end of Westminster Bridge. Author's photograph.*

storm a miniature castle on stage with such eagerness because they knew that there was some food on the other side. In another act regularly performed at Astley's, a bulldog learned to clamp its jaws on a rope attached to a pulley, then the dog was hoisted thirty feet into the air while fireworks were set off around it, 'representing a heavy discharge of small arms and artillery'. Human sensitivity to animal suffering, it has to be said, was not widely shared in Georgian England. The extremely cruel treatment of animals was everywhere on the streets of London, from 'throwing at cocks' to bear and badger baiting: it can be seen in the first of Hogarth's series of prints, *The Four Stages of Cruelty*.

As a trainer of horses Astley was without equal and his treatise on schooling them still stands today. It begs the question, was there cruelty involved in making his mounts perform tricks? This was the advice he gave in his book on breaking horses:

> A little obedience from a horse is very great, therefore if somewhat tractable the first morning, take him into the stable and caress him; for observe this as a golden rule, mad men and mad horses never will agree together.[81]

If some of the stories told about him are to believed, he was a great deal kinder to his animals than he was to his human performers. Astley got things done by a mixture of bullying and goodwill – a sort of benign dictatorship. To some he was an overbearing, ignorant thug, but he was generous and genial to others. It was said that he had few friends, but others found that he could be a kind host and great company. The fact that these two conflicting versions of him exist isn't surprising. A great

---

81 Writing a hundred and seventy years later, the legendary circus mogul Bertram Mills concurred: 'Training secrets? There are none. Patience, understanding, and carrots are the eternal triumvirate. There is no other way with a horse, and never was.'

deal of what we presume to know about the man comes from just two memoirs written by former employees, the first by the comic actor Jacob DeCastro and the second by the younger Dibdin, published eight years and sixteen years respectively after Astley's death.

Let us consider Dibdin first. He clearly loathed Astley and perhaps with good reason. Dibdin's father was Astley's bitter business rival for many years. Putting family enmities aside, Astley gave the younger Dibdin a job, but Dibdin still felt much put upon, as young men do, and thought he deserved much more. Astley also fired Dibdin's wife – apparently when she failed to put away her sewing when commanded to do so during rehearsals. This, as Dibdin's memoirs make clear, was understandably the source of great and lasting resentment.

Then there is Jacob DeCastro. He was one of a large contingent of performers at the amphitheatre at that time known colloquially as 'Astley's Jews'. He worked for Philip on and off for many years and was with his company right up to his old employer's death. DeCastro's memoirs, it is only fair to point out, are riddled with inaccuracies. He gets dates wrong and conflates stories about Astley's famous performing horses – and so on. But DeCastro's judgment of Astley's character was authentic. When the actor first informed his friends that he was engaged to work at Astley's, they told him that he must be mad: the circus proprietor, they warned him, was by reputation the sort of man who would give you a horsewhipping if you so much as looked sideways at him. But DeCastro, who got to know Astley as well as anyone, found otherwise. This is what he wrote in his *Memoirs*:

Our Adventurer (DeCastro) was led to believe that Mr Astley, senior, was a very quarrelsome, arbitrary man, and coercive in his measures; however, he experienced to the contrary, for to him he was a very facetious, liberal person; for, in thirty-eight years that he was with him, he had never any difference, upon any account whatever, either pro or con. He was obstinate at times, to be sure, and would not give up his opinion to anyone, but very forgiving the moment after.

Astley's occasional rudeness, DeCastro suggested, perhaps with tongue firmly in cheek, was because 'he was inclined to be a little deaf now and then.'

On the whole, Astley's employees and associates seem to have regarded their employer with a mixture of amusement and respect. Even Dibdin junior never questioned Astley's courage, couldn't help but admire his energy and conceded that he was occasionally capable of great generosity. There was no sugar-coating the fact that Astley was a ruthless competitor, but he needed to be tough to survive in the cut-throat world of Georgian showmen. His experience at home and in the army had exposed him from an early age to the harsh realities of life, so building up a family business on the tough and edgy south bank of the Thames was just another challenge to overcome. His precarious childhood gave him a fierce determination never to be poor. He was as frugal as he was industrious, ploughing his profits back into continual reinvestment of his multiplying empire. He retired to bed early and rose at five in all seasons. Every evening he took his customary seat under the portico as soon as the doors were opened to keep an eye on his evening's takings. In financial matters he was inscrutable. One creditor who came to him requesting overdue payment of a large bill was astonished to see the showman produce the cash from a secret stash of guineas – 'rainy day' money that that no-one knew about and presumably had been hoarded for years.

He guarded his interests suspiciously. When Hughes trespassed on his territory he was ferocious in defending what he regarded as his 'birth right'. He kept every entrance of his venue locked during rehearsals to in case his enemies crept in and stole his ideas, meanwhile maintaining his own team of spies to keep an eye on theirs. He was ever-vigilant around his own ever-growing cast of performers in case they, too, harboured informers. One day during rehearsals he caught sight of a stranger dressed in a riding habit. Astley called the man out and was on the verge of booting him out of the door when his son pointed out that that stranger was the Duke of Gordon delivering a couple of horses that Astley was breaking in for him.

It was essential to be thick-skinned to survive the bear-pit cruelties of the Georgian stage. A modern visitor to an eighteenth-century theatre would find it a chaotic, intimidating experience. Today, the height of rudeness is a failure to switch off a mobile phone, but in Astley's day they had rather more startling ways of ruining your evening's entertainment. The Georgian theatre-goer asserted control over how the house should entertain them. They booed if a favourite act didn't appear or called on players to 'speak up!' If a particular tune went down well they would demand it was played over and over again. In most theatres could even pay a bit extra to sit on the actual stage. Performers were pelted with orange peel, or worse. The actor Thomas Hollingsworth was almost killed when he was hit in the eye by an apple skewered on a knife. The action in the pit was very often more memorable than anything taking place on stage. A 'terrible alarm' of fire at Drury Lane that caused a near-fatal panic began with an argument when two gentlemen drew swords. Horace Walpole once witnessed a boxing match between two ladies in the boxes; the pit 'hinted to the combatants to retire, which they did into the lobby, where a circle was made, and there the champions pulled one another's hair, and a great deluge of powder ensued; but being well greased like Grecian pugilists, not many curls were shed'.

The mood of the audience could move swiftly from lively to riotously violent. The patent theatres in Drury Lane and Covent Garden had rows of iron spikes across the stage front to guard the actors against personal attack. At the Haymarket Theatre, seats were ripped up, scenery destroyed and the wreckage carried into the street and made into a bonfire. Some theatres hired grenadiers to take up position on either side of the stage at the start of a performance to act as a deterrent and to step in if behaviour got completely out of hand.

In this febrile atmosphere, it was Astley's job as ringmaster to pacify a potentially riotous audience, but he was fearless, weathering storms of disapproval with disdain. If the crowd hissed and hooted at anything, he would stand at the side of the stage at the prompters' entrance with a large quarterstaff and thump the stage floor with it: the more they booed, the louder he would thump. If there was a particular passage where he thought the audience should have applauded, he would hammer at the floor with his staff until the audience took the hint and began clapping. Generally, as long as the people were still coming, he didn't really mind what they thought. 'Ladies and Gentlemen pay their money, and they have a right to hiss if they like it,' he would say. 'If they don't know manners, we can't teach 'em'.

His life experiences gave Astley the grit to overcome adversities that would have defeated most people, so dealing with recalcitrant punters was all just grist to his mill. And he would be severely tested again in ways that he had never expected.

11

REVOLUTION

King George III and John Follett, one of the most popular clowns of the day with his carrot-eating routine, a huge royal favourite. Wikimedia Commons.

1789 would be a tumultuous year for the Astleys, the first inkling of which was a famous fireworks fiasco in Dublin.

King George III was a big fan of the London theatre all of his sane life. He was especially fond of a bit of slapstick. The clown John Follet once made the king laugh 'almost to suffocation' by swallowing whole carrots. George was slightly less inclined to visit the theatre after one of Astley's regiment tried to kill him. On the evening of 15 May 1800, as the king was taking his seat in his royal box at Drury Lane, he was shot at from the stalls below. The bullet struck a wooden pillar fourteen inches above his head. It was the second bullet to have narrowly missed him that day. The first whizzed by just after breakfast as he reviewed the 1st Foot Guards in Hyde Park, passing straight through the thigh of a clerk of the Allotment Department of the Royal Navy Office, who screamed and bled profusely. After his second scrape with death, George calmly stood up and stepped forward so that everyone in the Drury Lane stalls below could see he was unharmed. A musician who saw the gunman fire then drop his pistol, pulled him over the rails into the orchestra pit, then he and several others dragged him backstage and dealt him a good hiding. The king was apparently so unfazed by events that he followed his usual practice of having a short doze at the end of the play. His would-be regicide, James Hadfield, was brought to trial for high treason five weeks later. Hadfield served under the Duke of York in the 15th Light Dragoons at Flanders and was left for dead on the battlefield after sustaining a deep sabre wound to his skull. The injury had left him severely brain damaged. When asked why he had tried to kill his monarch, he replied that he had no beef with the king, he was just tired of living. When the Duke of York was called to give evidence, the pitiful Hadfield cried out; 'God bless the Duke, I love him!'[82] Astley's former army colleague would spend the rest of his life in Bedlam.

---

82 The jury found James Hadfield not guilty by reason of insanity. It was a landmark case in trials where a plea of insanity had been entered and led to a change in the law.

It was 1789 when the King, after his own long period of mental derangement, suddenly returned to sanity. The previous October he had suffered a violent bilious attack. His condition alarmed everyone who saw him. The veins in his face stood out; he chattered feverishly and continuously and he foamed at the mouth. In an astonishing display of loyalty, old friends rallied around by pretending to be mad themselves. The regular court physician, Dr Baker, reported that the King's condition was deteriorating rapidly; he was violent and abusive toward his family and his courtiers and generally 'quite unlike his normal self.' At first it was thought that the King was suffering from 'flying gout' – the Georgian medical profession's stock-in-trade diagnosis for anything they didn't understand, which covered pretty much everything. This mysterious affliction was thought to be relatively harmless unless you were unfortunate enough to get it in your head. The King's flying gout, it was asserted, had somehow travelled to his brain and got stuck there. The answer was to apply blisters to the royal head to drive the gout back down again. When it became all too obvious that this was a painful waste of time, six more doctors were called in to the King, none of them any wiser than the last. They bickered, they placed leeches on his forehead, gave him large doses of James's Powder to make him sweat and stuck his feet in hot water. The only thing that everyone could agree on was that the King was suffering from temporary insanity. Finally, and very reluctantly, they agreed to stand aside and let a so-called expert on the treatment of the mentally ill have a go.

Enter the Rev. Fr. Francis Willis, former rector of St John's Wapping. His thinking on mental derangement was that it could be cured by restraint and punishment. At his private lunatic asylum in Gretford, the insane were broken with considerably less compassion than Astley's horses. Willis's state-of-the-art equipment for the treatment of mental illness comprised a straitjacket, iron clamps, a chair and a length of rope. Additional treatment was in accordance with conventional guidelines: frequent bleedings, forced vomiting, a starvation diet, salivations and afterward a cold bath.

Remarkably, in February 1789, the King's condition improved and he was well enough to walk arm in arm in Richmond Gardens with his wife, Queen Charlotte. The Lord Chancellor visited him and reported back to his Prime Minister that the King was completely recovered. Parliament struck an official medal to celebrate this joyous event.

In March, Philip Astley was just about to wrap up his season in Dublin when he was offered two hundred pounds to supervise a display of fireworks to celebrate the King's recovery. Astley, now universally acknowledged as the go-to for this type of event, was only too happy to accept. The celebration was to take place on St. Stephen's Green, a popular Dublin venue for all kinds of public events. There had been a fireworks display there for the King's coronation in 1761. You could go to St. Stephen's Green to listen to a military band playing on Wednesday afternoons or watch a hurling match on Sundays. On Saturdays, until recently, you could have attended a public hanging at the top of nearby Baggot Street, although your enjoyment might have been interrupted by crowds of vagrants, basket-boys and servants shouting obscenities. There were also beadles about to keep beggars like Billy the Bowl from bothering you. You might chance upon Billy propelling himself across the Green; born without legs, he had devised a method of propulsion in a wooden, iron-clad bowl. Despite his deformity he was a fine-looking fellow with 'dark eyes, aquiline nose, a well-formed mouth, dark curling locks, and a body and arms of Herculean power.' Given the opportunity he would rob with violence; it was for such an assault that he was sentenced to hard labour for life in Green Street Gaol. The Green itself was also a valuable perk for the lord mayor who personally held the grazing rights. Protestant and Catholic alike took their Sunday walks there, but each kept to their own path. The ladies you found strolling might have been a respectable woman taking the air or a prostitute out looking for business. The London Coffee House in St Stephen's Green combined caffeine and sex in a notorious brothel.

Astley's fireworks display didn't go at all well. As the *Dublin Evening Post* reported later, 'Never was disappointment more universal, never was disgust more general'. To begin with there was a great deal of dissent because the event had been commissioned by the corrupt and deeply unpopular Lord Lieutenant of Ireland, the Marquis of Buckinghamshire. Astley had just overseen the set-up, assisted by his German pyrotechnical expert, the former artilleryman Johannes Hengler, and was on his way to nearby Dublin Castle to inform a group of waiting civic dignitaries, including the Marquis himself, that the fireworks were ready for their arrival. A bystander overheard the showman instructing Hengler to be ready to set off a rocket at his command. As soon as Astley was safely out of earshot, the bystander gave the awaited command himself, mimicking Astley's dialect, 'Halloo you 'tilleryman, let auf that there rocket'. The whole display went off prematurely. By the time the dignitaries arrived from the Castle there wasn't a single firework remaining, to the great amusement of the Dublin crowd and Astley's mortification. The showman swore a great deal and offered twenty guineas for the hoaxer's name, but none was forthcoming. For the next eight years, every time Astley showed his face to the Dublin public he was guaranteed to hear someone shout, 'Halloo you 'tilleryman, let auf that there rocket!'

One of the fireworks from the display hit Astley on the leg, leaving him badly burned. He neglected to treat the wound properly and it festered, leaving him lame and unwell for several months. Compounding his misery, an exceptionally severe winter had hit his profits that year in Dublin and in Paris. The temperature sank so low that the Thames froze. A ship, anchored to a riverside pub in Rotherhithe, was dragged away from its mooring by melting ice and then capsized on a nearby building, killing five people who were fast asleep in bed.

Across the Channel, the health of the monarchy itself was in jeopardy. In 1789 hunger was the common enemy of the French people. A long, hot summer the previous year had caused drought and severe crop failure. It was followed by an uncommonly brutal winter. As living costs soared, in Paris, famished peasants turned to protest and violence. The Bastille was a fourteenth-century fortress which had been converted into a state prison, a place to which people who had offended the government or broke the law were spirited away, often never to reappear. In more recent times the prison had become more a symbol of royal repression than a place of correction. The Marquis de Sade, an inmate of the Bastille until a fortnight before it fell, was allowed to hang his family portraits on his cell walls and kept a wardrobe of fashionable clothing and a library of books. Rather than being held in chains, like the 'man in the iron mask', prisoners were even encouraged to make use of the exercise area on the roof with its lovely views of the city. On the day of the attack, the fortress contained just seven prisoners; four forgers, the incestuous Comte de Solages, whose own family insisted on having him locked up to protect them from him, a mad Englishman and an even crazier Irish aristocrat by the name of Clotworthy Skeffington, who had his own suite on the first floor. On 14 July, their leisurely stay was rudely interrupted by twenty thousand Parisians who stormed the so-called fortress, then stabbed the governor to death, hacked off his head with a pocket knife and mounted it on a pike.

John Astley, who was in Paris at the time of the fall of the Bastille, sent his account of the dramatic events in Paris back to London. Within days, his father was putting the finishing touches to a new show:

An entire new and splendid spectacle ... 'Paris in an Uproar; or the Destruction of the Bastille. One of the grandest and most extraordinary Entertainments that ever appeared, grounded on authentic facts.'

This extravagantly produced pantomime featured a model of central Paris based on drawings sent by John Astley, filling the floor of The Royal Grove. Philip took a starring role, wearing an actual National Guard uniform, also sent from Paris by his son, as he and his troops re-enacted the attack on the Bastille. Despite its revolutionary subject matter, the play was as loyalist as all other Astley productions, ending, improbably, with the Paris mob singing 'Hail Britannia, tis to thee / We owe our Liberty.' Astley had somehow turned a story about a violent and out-of-control mob into an equestrian musical about the virtues of English liberty.

The show was a huge success but within weeks it provoked rival, even more lavish productions at the Royal Circus and Sadler's Wells. A 'Bastille war' erupted all over London as theatre managers pitched in with their own versions. Astley as ever was ready to do whatever it took to upstage them. As a near-neighbour of Madame Tussaud he was handily placed to take advantage of the lurid souvenir industry that was emerging in Paris.[83] In September Astley's had a new star attraction:

Finely executed in wax by a celebrated artist in Paris, the heads of Monsieur de Launay, late Governor of the Bastille, and M. de Flesselles, prevôt de marchands (sic) of Paris with incontestable proofs of their being striking likenesses.

In the interest of authenticity these heads were to be exhibited 'in the same manner as they were by the Bourgoisie [sic] and French guards' – stuck on the end of pikes, presumably.[84] The wax heads,

---

83   There was a vast range of commemorative merchandise, from Bastille bonnets trimmed with fabric towers to Bastille shoe buckles - even Bastille bed linen, possibly not the ideal gift for an aristocrat seeking a decent night's sleep.

84   According to Madame Tussaud, as soon the Governor's head was pulled from the pike, it was rushed to her at her salon for modelling. In her memoirs, she claimed that she sat with the bloody head on her knee taking the impressions of de Launey's features. Several days later, Astley ordered waxed copies of the men's heads and smuggled them across the border.

displayed along with an actual uniform worn by the late Bastille governor, were a horrifying hit with his Lambeth clientele, so much so that his later advertisements boasted:

> The head of the Governor which Astley has brought from Paris is so finely modelled that almost every artist in London is anxious to take a drawing, for which purpose several of them have been attempting to take sketches as we suppose for magazines, print shops etc.

Astley's Bastille show was a great success. On 31 August 1789 *The Times* commented on the huge popularity of his stage presentations, as well as the stupidity of the licensing laws:

> By all accounts [Astley] has netted more money this season than in any preceding one, and to say the truth of him, his industry has been great, and his assiduity unparalleled and as all entertainments improve by time, so we find that the horsemanship which was the first is now but a second consideration, and the interludes and scenery, much more attended to than riding and vaulting: and were the law to be so generous as to permit the actors on those stages to use their mother tongue as nature and literature direct, the *petit pieces* of those stages, would tend to the refinement of the public, and serve the purposes of morality as well as the great pieces on the Winter Theatres, but whilst they are clogged with recitative, and sense so basely mangled by order of Law, we laugh at the absurdity of such legislative trammels, and make every excuse for merit working under such great disadvantages. And yet even hampered with this recitative we find genius breaking out, and the public endeavouring by the patronage to give it all the encouragement in their power. What the Squeeze for St. Paul's has done for Wroughton at Sadler's Wells, the Bastille is likely to do both for Astley and Hughes. We must not close the account of this place without mentioning what almost everybody will join in affirming that young Astley is, without exception, the most graceful rider in the universe.

This was extraordinarily strong language for a paper such as *The Times* and it makes clear that Astley was more than holding his own against the bigger, licensed patent theatres.

All the same, events in France had hit Astley's profits hard, forcing him to abandon his beloved Paris circus, but like most people in Britain he was broadly supportive of the revolution. The fall of the Bastille was seen as a symbol of the overthrow of absolutism, pushing England's traditional enemy towards a more British model of constitutional rule. The Whig leader Charles James Fox spoke for the national mood, describing it as 'the greatest event it is that ever happened in the world!' The Prime Minister William Pitt was sure that revolution would make France a much better neighbour.

Within a year doubts set in. This revolutionary spirit might be infectious; it could spread across the Channel if left unchecked. Alarm increased as the British heard of more riots in France and the appalling behaviour of the *sans culottes*. Every month the press reported new horrors of crowds jeering and spitting at aristocrats as they were wheeled to the guillotine. A rumour reached the Home Office that French Jacobins disguised as waiters were plotting to storm the Tower of London and the Bank of England. Meanwhile French refugees poured across the Channel, each bringing fresh tales of bloodshed.

In 1792 Astley's amphitheatre was refurbished and renamed the Royal Saloon. Philip, fifty years old and in ill-health, also handed over permanent management to his son John, while keeping half the profits for himself.

Meanwhile events abroad were escalating. On 21 January 1793 King Louis was executed in Paris. Within days, on the streets of London handbills were distributed with details of his gory demise. His decapitation was seen as a threat to every crowned head in Europe, including Britain's own much-loved King George. By 12 February, the country was once again at war with France. In the preceding century Britain had fought France many times;

in the War of the Spanish Succession from 1702-13; the wars of Jenkin's Ear and the Austrian Succession from 1739–1748; the Seven Years War from 1756 – 1763; the American War of Independence from 1775–1783. This war was rather different. The National Convention in France had announced a *levée en masse* and all able-bodied Frenchmen were obliged to defend the state. As Frenchmen outnumbered Englishmen by almost three to one this was a seriously troubling development. At a stroke, Britain's enemy had an army of 800,000 men who could be trained within a year. The idea that a whole nation could go to war, rather than professional soldiers fighting on their country's behalf, was very frightening. The British army was desperate for volunteers – so desperate that when Philip Astley volunteered his services to king and country he was allowed to re-enlist in his old regiment at the grand old age of fifty-one.[85]

Staging patriotic pantomimes to raise public morale was one thing; putting your life on the line by signing up was quite another, but for an old war horse like Astley the opportunity to wear the regimentals of his beloved 15th Light Dragoons in anger once again was impossible to refuse. Shrugging off illness, his advancing years, lame leg and the protests of a wife and son who must have assuredly thought him insane, the now internationally famous theatrical manager was shipped off to the continent as the company's resident Horse-master.

Another who felt the tug of glory was a debt-ridden student called Samuel Taylor Coleridge, who signed up as a private alongside Astley in the 15th as Silas Tomkyn Comberbache. He was a terrible soldier and didn't know one end of a horse from the other. He also suffered terribly from an eruption of boils on his

---

85   To put that in some context, although the British army was famously full of very elderly officers, the average age of recruits fighting on the front line was twenty-one years old, with over a quarter of the men aged fifteen to nineteen.

backside and so was declared unfit to ride, and put in charge of nursing a man with smallpox, meanwhile making himself useful to his fellow troops by using his literary skills to ghost-write love letters to their girls back home. After three months of misery he was rescued by his brothers and discharged as 'insane'.[86]

The urgent need was to stop the French marching into Britain's ally the Netherlands, threatening North Sea trade and the Dutch-held Cape of Good Hope, a vital staging-post on the British route to India. The British army set sail for Flanders to aid the Netherlands and William V of Orange under the command of the King's second son, twenty-nine-year-old Frederick, Duke of York. This was the royal duke immortalised in 'The Grand Old Duke of York,' doggerel that just about summed up his contemporaries' faith in his competence as Commander-in-Chief of the British army.[87]

The Duke's continental foray was successful at first. They drove south, besieging the border fortress of Valenciennes, vital for its position on the Scheldt flowing north to Antwerp. Astley rejoined his regiment in time for the charge at Ribecourt on 7 August 1793. Typically, he was soon in the thick of it once again, single-handedly recapturing a gun carriage that had been taken by the French. As a reward for his gallantry, the Duke of York gave him the four horses drawing the piece of retrieved ordnance. Astley auctioned the horses off and donated the proceeds to buy wine for his comrades in arms. There were more acts of kindness for his fellow soldiers. Although they fought through the summer in a sweltering heatwave, the following winter was one of the worst anyone had ever experienced. Rivers froze, men were killed

---

86 Four years later, Coleridge's famous poem, *The Rime of the Ancient Mariner*, was published as part of the Lyrical Ballads with Wordsworth and so the Romantic movement was born.

87 The nursery rhyme commemorates an ignominious defeat that he suffered at Tourcoing in Flanders, in May 1794: his loss to an outnumbered revolutionary rabble who had had the effrontery to guillotine their King was considered shocking.

by the cold in their sleep, disease was rampant and the soldiers' uniforms fell apart. The colonel of each regiment was responsible for clothing but many had scrimped on the money allocated to them in order to make a profit. Some soldiers marched without coats, wearing only linen shirts. The army was also starving due to collapsed supply lines. Astley spent a considerable sum of his own money to provide his regiment with better clothing. He bought a large quantity of flannel and set all the women at his amphitheatre to work making a waistcoat for every man in his regiment. Sewn into each garment was 'a friend in need' – a new shilling. He also gave each man a large supply of needles, thread, buttons, twine, leather – everything required for mending clothing and shoes. His generosity was widely reported in the British press, doing no harm at all to ticket sales at the Royal Saloon.

Meanwhile, from the battlefields of Flanders, Astley was also sending back descriptions and sketches of actual military engagements so his son John could dramatise them in quick order for presentation on stage in Lambeth. He was the nearest thing Georgian England had to a contemporary war correspondent, giving Londoners a chance to experience recreations of battles fought by British troops abroad. In September 1793, the audience at the newly-renamed Royal Saloon could watch a dramatised version of the siege of Valenciennes, just over a month after the town fell. In the play, John Astley exploited his father's first-hand knowledge of the actual battlefield site including 'on the spot' drawings, meanwhile burnishing dad's reputation as a war hero. To give some idea of the tone and content, in this song, to the tune of 'Oh dear, what can the matter be!' a cowardly soldier – the Fop – duets with the 'Serjeant' – presumably the brave, stoic Philip Astley himself.

Fop – Oh, dear! what will become of us!'
Serjeant – Damn me, how the Frenchmen will run from us!
Fop – Dear! dear! they'll kill ev'ry one of us!

Serj – Let them come on if they dare.

Fop – They'll take us for certain, and kill us and eat us Instead of soup-meagre;

Serj – But first they must beat us.

Fop – Dear, dear, where are we straying, Sir?

Serj – To the siege without murmur repair.

Fop – To the siege I dare never repair; I wish I was home, and in Tavistock-street again.

Serj – By my soul it is a pity you ever should meet again.

Fop – I fear the Monsieurs, sir, will never retreat again.

Serj – We'll make them, my dear, in a panic retreat again.

Fop – O that I had something, dear sir, but to eat again.

Serj – By the Lord, how we'll lather away.

Fop – O Lord, let us both run away.

The show was a smash hit and ran until the end of the season, hastily reconfigured with the tragic news that Colonel James Moncrieff, a distinguished hero at Valenciennes, had been mortally wounded by a shot through the head just a couple of weeks after the siege.

As it turned out, Valenciennes was the high point of the Flanders campaign. The French Republican armies regrouped and drove the allied forces back to the coast. Astley fought in Europe for just over a year, dealing with the inevitable hardships of army life, poor food, sleeping on hard ground and freezing cold nights. His continental adventure, however, was cut short when he heard that his business had fallen to the scourge of all London theatres.

12

ASHES TO ASHES

Exterior view of Astley's Westminster Amphitheatre in 1777.
Public domain.

Fire struck cruelly and haphazardly in Georgian Britain. It was one of the great anxieties of the age. London theatres tended to combust and kill their patrons with depressing regularity, going up like tinder and taking their neighbours with them. People were corralled in their thousands into wooden buildings with only one or two exits and no evacuation procedures to stem the inevitable panic should the worst occur. Even if the buildings were made of stone or brick, everything inside was wood and fabric and lit by naked flames from candles or oil lamps. Special stage effects were achieved with the help of volatile lightning machines, trays full of burning spirits, not to mention large amounts of indoor fireworks.[88] The few, privately funded fire-engines that did exist were pitifully ineffective against a large blaze, so once a fire had gained a hold there was little chance of saving the building. The London theatre, a contemporary noted, had assumed a role previously taken on by bakers.[89] Even the threat of fire was lethal. At Sadler's Wells theatre, hearing shouts from the pit of 'Fire! Fire!' the audience of two thousand panicked and stampeded; many in the gallery hurled themselves into the pit below. Eighteen people lost their lives and many more were badly injured.

In the early hours of Sunday 17, August 1794, a fire broke out on the Surrey side of Westminster Bridge, lighting up the south bank and St. George's Fields beyond. Astley's amphitheatre and nineteen adjoining houses including a public house were destroyed in the blaze. The cause was not known and no lives were lost. The horses were saved thanks to the efforts of Mr Searle, the boat-builder from nearby Stangate Street. Astley's burned along with all the contents including scenery and props and 'three excellent wigs' once the property of David Garrick.

Philip Astley was still serving in Flanders when his commanding officer, the Duke of York, read about the fire in a British newspaper. The Duke granted him leave of absence and

---

88 One of the most famous theatrical fires was at Shakespeare's Globe in Southwark in 1613 when a real cannon, loaded with gunpowder and wadding, was fired during a performance of *Henry VIII*. Sparks set fire to the thatched roof, which collapsed causing the wooden stands to burn. Remarkably, nobody was badly hurt; a man's trousers caught fire but he was saved by a friend who threw beer over him.

89 In 1792 The Pantheon in Oxford Street burned down and was reopened by Astley's neighbour, a gentleman who rejoiced in the name of Crispus Claggett, proprietor of the Apollo Gardens in Westminster Bridge Road, Lambeth. Claggett disappeared owing a year's rent and was not heard of again. The theatre's shareholders complained to the Bow Street justices that Claggett had done a runner, but their suspicions were unproven. His skeleton turned up forty years later under the Pantheon stage, nailed down presumably by someone also long dead.

an immediate return to London. Astley hurried to Westminster Bridge where only a charred desolation remained. While he was away, the running of the business was in the hands of his son John, whose oversight had left the building barely insured, if at all. It was a devastating loss, bringing the Astleys to the brink of ruin, but Philip was not the sort to dwell on misfortune and he bore the blow with typical stoicism.

The following day he called the company together. Standing amid the wreckage of his life's work, everyone was struck by his composure as he addressed them.

> Now, girls and boys we must begin again. No deserters among you, I hope. Stick by me, I'll give you all half salaries till we commence once more; and if any of you wish to take benefits, I'll do what I can for you.[90]

The rebuilding work began immediately, with Astley performing the duties of architect and foreman. As usual he set about his task with military orderliness, drilling his workmen as though they were raw recruits. The rebuilding project was expensive and no-one, possibly not even his wife, was quite sure where the money came from or how he acquired the credit to accomplish such a vast undertaking. To keep at least some of his company and stud employed, John Astley rented the Lyceum Theatre in the Strand for a couple of months in partnership with the showman Benjamin Handy to stage equestrian performances.

The great topic of Easter 1795, pushing the war out of the headlines, was a royal wedding like no other. The marriage of the Prince of Wales to Princess Caroline of Brunswick-Wolfenbuttel was an unmitigated disaster. Prinny's sole motivation for getting married was to pay off his enormous debts of at least £630,000, enough to fund an army. Parliament was reluctant to bail him

---

90 *Memoirs of Jacob Decastro.*

out again, having already shelled out a fortune on princely fripperies, but agreed to do so if he promised to get off his very ample backside and find himself a wife. The bride chosen for him was a squat, rather slovenly German princess with a personal hygiene problem. After embracing her for the first time, Prinny quickly retreated to the furthest corner of the room, instructing the Earl of Malmesbury: 'Harris, I am not very well, pray get me a glass of brandy.' His intended was similarly unimpressed. 'By God, is he always so fat? He looks nothing like his portrait.' The groom arrived for the wedding dead drunk and at one point looked likely to make a run for it. They tolerated each company's company just long enough to produce a child born nine months later, then went their separate ways.

Just two days before the royal wedding on Easter Monday 1795, Astley's new Amphitheatre of the Arts opened its doors to the public for the first time. Few people who knew the showman well ever doubted that he would have his London venue ready in time for the new season. All the same, a building on that scale should have taken at least a year to build: it had taken him just six months. When he put his mind to something he made it happen, even it meant taking a few risks with the construction work.

The new venue was much bigger than before, with the ring and stage almost surrounded by pit benches and three massive tiers of boxes or galleries. He celebrated the opening with another staged representation of the Siege of Valenciennes, featuring actors rigged out in the uniform of Astley's regiment and the actual recaptured cannon from Ribecourt. The production was the talk of the metropolis, acclaimed in the London press for its astonishing authenticity, the director having fought in the actual battle only a year or so earlier. It was great publicity for Astley's but it also went down extremely well with the British government, still troubled by the threat of imported republicanism from France and relieved to see someone flying the flag for Britain against the evil of the *Assemblée Nationale* in Paris. Another regular show in Astley's repertoire was a musical pantomime called 'English Bravery: Or, the Victorious Tars' in which English sailors triumphed over some 'savages' through a 'manly display of the broad sword'.

To be fair, Astley was far from the only theatrical manager presenting this sort of xenophobic light entertainment. The Georgian public was mad for a bit of no-holds-barred patriotism and the Lord Chamberlain's censors were more than happy to let them get on with it. The robustly loyal Jack Tars, heroes of so many Astley entertainments, served as recruiting propaganda for the British army and navy, badly in need of additional manpower and muscle. London's best artists moonlighted as scene painters, transforming stages into heroic depictions of victorious battles in faraway lands. Competition for scene-painting work at Astley's was fierce and the amphitheatre employed some of the biggest names of the era, including the great marine artist Clarkson Stanfield. Astley was also a safer bet than their usual regular customers, the Georgian nobility, who were notoriously bad at settling debts.

Meanwhile, Astley's Amphitheatre and the Royal Circus stepped up their rivalry to source the best performers and the biggest audience. The following season, Astley's promised 'thirty-five new acts' including 'two surprising females,' in addition to pony races and a novel act by a performer named Carr, a former Royal Circus employee who could stand on his head in the centre of a globe and ascend thirty feet 'turning around in a most surprising manner, like a boy's top.' The plundering of talent ran both ways. One of Astley's star equestrian performers at this time was a lad called Young Crossman, who could 'leap from a single Horse over Two Garters, twelve feet high, and alight again on the Saddle, and Play the Violin in various Attitudes'. Crossman defected to the Royal Circus, an acquisition of some importance for Hughes and a bitter blow for Astley.

On 23 August 1796, the twenty-one-year-old Jane Austen wrote to her sister Cassandra to let her know that she had safely arrived in London, adding; 'We are at Astley's tonight, which I am glad of.'[91] Jane was in time to see Astley's latest coup, the first ever native Americans to appear in an English circus; two Indian Chiefs from the Catawba nation. Described as 'copper-coloured gentlemen', they performed a war dance and a variety of martial exercises with tomahawks and bow and arrow. By the end of the 1790s ethnic 'exotics', copper-coloured or otherwise, were scant diversions from what was for most Londoners an increasingly miserable existence. In January 1799, as food shortages threatened again, householders were shocked to learn that Prime Minister William Pitt had introduced an entirely new tax, not on wigs or other property, but on income. It was a general, temporary tax at ten per cent – two shillings in the pound – on all annual incomes over two hundred pounds.

At the end of October 1799 there was distressing news for Patty Astley. Her fifty-nine-year-old brother Thomas, a Captain in the Merionethshire militia, had been shot dead in a duel at Whitchurch by a local apothecary, twenty-eight-year-old Richard Pate Manning. Duels occupied a strange position in law. They were illegal but the judiciary was broadly tolerant of them. If you killed someone in a duel, at worst you faced a manslaughter charge and often you would be acquitted outright. Thomas Jones's killer was fined 6 shillings and eight pence and sentenced to six months' imprisonment. Later, Manning was declared insane and was removed in 1812 to an asylum where died at the advanced age of seventy-eight.

A tax on the rich meant very little to people who were going hungry. As the new century dawned, Britain was still at war and Napoleon seemed indestructible. With the falling cost of

---

91 Jane Austen in her 1815 novel *Emma* credits a visit to Astley's for bringing about the reconciliation and engagement of Robert Martin and Harriet Smith.

wages and the price of bread rising, for most people they were the worst times in living memory. The summer of 1801 saw the sixth bad harvest in a row. Throughout the summer, French and English envoys had been in secret negotiations. Then suddenly, to everyone's surprise, on 2 October the government announced a peace deal with France. Mail coaches spread the good news with the legend 'Peace with France' chalked on their doors and coach drivers wore celebration ribbons tied to their clothing. When details of the terms were released there was general dismay among old troopers like Astley at how badly Britain had done out of it. She had to give up most of what she had won but France was allowed to keep Holland, the graveyard of so many men in his own regiment, leaving Britain once again vulnerable to invasion. Despite these reservations, Britain was war weary and the national mood was immediately lifted. Towns, villages and cities were once again full of returning soldiers.

With the coming of peace after so many years at war, the delights of foreign travel and the commercial opportunities it presented once again seized the nation. Everyone, it seemed, was off to Paris to see how it had changed in the past ten years. Businessmen rushed to renew old contacts and the British aristocracy flocked *en masse* to rekindle their love for all things French. They had never given up their smuggled wine and brandy but now the latest French fashions were available to them once again. The French capital was full of British celebrities; James Watt, who went to inspect the Marly aqueduct, William Herschel went to be elected as an associate of the French Institute, Turner, filling his notebooks with sketches, William Wordsworth, back to see his daughter, now nine years old, for the first time. In September there were reckoned to be 12,000 British visitors in Paris. Napoleon held an audience for the most eminent among them. Many found the First Consul disappointing: instead of the mighty warrior they had heard about they encountered a small, careworn man with a pale face.

In 1802 Astley's old regiment returned home. He set aside a number of free seats every evening so that men who had taken part in the actual Siege of Valenciennes could see his spectacular stage representation of the campaign. A couple of months later he brought over a company of ballet performers from Paris. For many Londoners this was a step too far and the presence of 'Frenchies' aroused such hostility that they were only allowed to perform after Astley reassured his public that their engagement was only for four weeks.

Philip was off to France, too, but not to gawp at Paris and its pleasures. When he was forced to abandon Paris at the start of the Revolutionary Wars there was no-one left to represent his interests. He turned for help to his former employee, the popular French clown and acrobat Jean-Baptiste Laurent. A message was smuggled to Laurent's mother in Paris asking her to keep an eye on the Amphitheatre Anglais and the house attached to it. The building, however, had already been commandeered by the new revolutionary government as an army barracks.

In May 1803 Astley returned to Paris accompanied by his two eldest nieces to demand from Napoleon the return of his amphitheatre and ten thousand pounds compensation for lost and damaged property and fourteen years of back rent lost during the French Revolution. To everyone's amazement, and probably Astley's as well, remuneration was granted. Perhaps it was because the First Consul was a fan of the circus[92] or maybe he was amused by the Englishman's breathtaking audacity. Either way, it didn't do Philip much good. Almost as soon as the

---

92 Napoleon's favourite performer was a rope dancer called Madame Saqui, who is referenced in William Makepeace Thackeray's *Vanity Fair*. She walked a wire as fireworks exploded around her, depicting battles won by her benefactor. During a performance to celebrate the birth of his heir, she wire-walked between Notre-Dame cathedral's towers. In 1816 she was hired to perform at Astley's Westminster amphitheatre, according to John Astley's advertisement 'at a considerable sum'.

reparations were agreed upon he learned that hostilities between England and France had resumed.

The peace, fragile from the start, was like the eye of a hurricane, a temporary respite before the winds of war renewed with a ferocity even greater than before. On 18 May 1803, Britain confirmed that the short-lived treaty of Amiens had failed by declaring war on France, sending the population into a frenzy of fearful speculation about imminent invasion. There was talk that Napoleon was digging tunnels under the Channel; there were supposed to be fleets of giant balloons that could carry three hundred French soldiers apiece, and giant rafts a thousand feet long that could carry sixty thousand soldiers.

The British navy captured two French frigates off Brittany and seized French ships in British ports. The move caught Napoleon on the hop but he was swift to retaliate. In Paris, panicked British visitors packed their bags and the road to Calais was jammed with carriages taking them to safety. In the early hours of 22 May, Napoleon issued an order that all Englishmen still in France between the ages of eighteen and sixty were to be regarded as prisoners of war and interned. Philip Astley was among just a few hundred British subjects caught in the scoop, including an entire delegation of tradesmen at an industrial exhibition in Paris.

While under house arrest, Astley bribed a doctor to certify that he was ill and needed to take the spa waters at Piedmont. Once safely outside Paris, he drew a pair of pistols on the driver of his postilion and told him to head for the German border. From there he took a boat down the Main river, then descended the Rhine to Holland. Shocking news awaited him. His new circus had once again been destroyed by fire. He raced back to London, only to receive another revelation that he could barely take in. His wife Patty had died the week before.

Astley had an almost childlike fascination for fireworks. He and his son used them regularly in their shows, especially in the 'blow-up' endings that were much in vogue in his military equestrian spectacles, despite surrounding themselves and their audience with auditoriums entirely constructed from wood. The cause of the fire this time was a spent firework from the previous evening's performance. Sparks had fallen on some tow stored in the lamp room. In the early hours of Friday 2 September, at around half past two, neighbours saw flames burst from the roof of the building like a volcano, illuminating the whole London horizon. The flames could be seen shooting from the amphitheatre roof twenty miles away. By dawn the whole building was engulfed, by noon it was a heap of charred ashes. There was barely time to save the horses. It was reported that one of the mounts, having survived the fire of 1793, remembering his former peril, had allowed himself to be led away and the others followed. Little else was saved aside from a few props stored in an out-house. The music room was entirely destroyed along with the entire catalogue of original scores and all the company's musical instruments, mostly the valuable property of band members who could ill afford to lose their livelihoods. Forty neighbouring houses were also destroyed, their inhabitants left shivering in the street, but glad to escape with their lives. One of the displaced was Chevalier D'Eon, French spy and transvestite, who was living at 33 Westminster Bridge Road, just a few doors from Astley's.[93]

John Astley, asleep with his wife at their country house in Surrey ten miles away, was woken with news of the fire and he raced to the scene, arriving at around 5am, just in time to see the roof collapse. Having lost his mother a week earlier, he was told that his sixty-year-old mother-in-law had burned to death. Old Mrs

---

93 D'Eon was the subject of great speculation. One version has it that this man of noble birth and distinguished military career was sent on a delicate diplomatic mission to England, which went badly wrong. In order to extricate himself and to escape from his enemies without leaving a trail, he adopted the brilliant ruse of pretending to be a woman. On the other hand he might have just have enjoyed wearing women's clothes.

Woodman, as Hannah Astley's mother was generally known, had performed at Drury Lane, Covent Garden and the Haymarket as an actress and a singer. Retired from the stage, after her daughter's marriage in 1800 she lived above the shop at Astley's Amphitheatre. She was last seen inside the burning building, running from window to window, frantically gesticulating that she needed help. A couple of neighbours placed a ladder against an upper floor windowsill to rescue her. She appeared to indicate she had forgot something. She went back inside the building, it was speculated, to retrieve the previous two nights' takings hidden under her bed. She returned to the window just as the floor fell in. Her headless torso was dug out of the ruins later that day.

Almost overshadowed by the drama of the theatre fire was the Astley family's loss of a wife and mother. Patty and Philip were married for more than thirty-seven years but Mrs Astley left only a faint footprint, just a couple of passing mentions in the reminiscences of old circus hands such as Jacob DeCastro and a few dozen references in handbills and in the early press. Charles Dibdin junior recalled her in his memoirs as a ladylike, good-natured woman but she had steel, too. The Georgian circus was one of the very few arenas in which a woman could achieve near-equality with men. For at least eight years she performed alongside her husband and her son John on an equal footing, competing with them in feats of 'manly horsemanship' and had become a much-admired staple of Astley's repertoire of the strange and wondrous. Moreover, this remarkable lady had to do everything they did wearing full skirts – not the ideal costume for trick-riding. She was also, of course, the first woman ever to appear in the ring and a very important figure in the early circus. Philip was immensely proud to boast in his advertisements that his wife had performed for royalty in England and France, 'being the only one of her sex that ever had that honour'.

The First Lady of the circus was in her sixty-second year when she died, the cause of her death unknown. It wasn't entirely a shock to her family. *The London Gazette,* on the announcement of her death, mentions that she endured 'a long and severe illness'. A few years earlier, in a letter preserved in a scrapbook in the British Museum, she wrote to a friend hinting at a long-term debilitating malaise, specifically:

> A violent pain in my heart shot throw to my shoulder could not turn in my beed, scears breath without screaming continued so 2 or 3 days.

The press lamented the fact that 'Old Astley' wasn't even able to see his wife buried because he was detained by 'the Corsican monster'. Philip's sudden reappearance in London came as a huge surprise to everyone. It was widely assumed he was still Napoleon's captive, or dead. The Astleys' appalling personal loss was once again compounded by chronic under-insurance. John Astley had provided for a building worth £30,000 with cover for just one-sixth of its value. Two fires and the complete destruction of his business twice over in ten years and the doubly cruel loss of his wife would have crushed a lesser man, but 'father Philip' was indomitable. He immediately began the process of rebuilding all over again.[94]

Once again Astley was his own project team; architect, building engineer and foreman. Through the winter he drilled his labourers in the rain, snow and freezing cold. Londoners came just to watch and applaud the heroic efforts of his workforce. Old animosities were set aside and Charles Dibdin junior's Sadler's Wells theatre

---

94 In 2018 the bottom half of a letter written by John Astley went for auction, in which he writes, presumably to their patron the Duke of York, pleading for financial help to rebuild the amphitheatre. It transcribes, '(we) are reduced from this melancholy catastrophe to this mode of application and that by your Royal Highness' humane interference we may be once enabled to rebuild the amphitheatre for our future support. Trusting on your Royal Highnesses goodness and greatness of heart I beg leave most respectfully to subscribe myself Your Royal Highness Most Humble and dutiful Servant John Astley, 6 September 1803 Westminster Bridge.'

gave a benefit for Astley's performers laid off by the theatre fire, raising seventy pounds to be shared between them. Meanwhile, John Astley helped keep some money coming in with a series of shows in temporary accommodation in the East End of London.

Everyone knew about Philip Astley's prodigious work ethic but there was still widespread astonishment when his new Royal Amphitheatre of the Arts rose Phoenix-like in just a couple of months, in time for the traditional start of the new season, Easter Monday 1804. Although not especially impressive from the outside, with a simple wooden portico for an entrance, inside it was palatial, hailed by the press as 'the handsomest pleasure haunt in London'. At the top of the stairs there was a sixty-foot wide lobby with a large stove in the centre and seating around the walls. All around were stacked crates of oranges for refreshment. The auditorium was a 2,500-seater, lavishly painted in crimson and gold and fully lit by a great chandelier ablaze with hundreds of candles – a present from the Duke of York. Below was a ring of sawdust, separated by the orchestra from a stage 130 feet wide. It was reputedly the biggest yet built in the whole of England, strong enough to take the weight and stress of dozens of galloping horsemen and flying carriages.

The grandeur of the new Astley's was largely illusory. Despite the reassuring appearance of some brickwork and lots of flashy interior embellishments, the whole edifice was held up by recycled ship's masts and spars. The fine ceiling, although it looked like solid stone and plaster, was made of canvas-draped scaffolding covered with pitch and tar and framed on fir poles, lashed together with ropes and nails. It was remarkable, Astley no doubt chuckled to himself, what Mr Grieve could achieve with painted wood and canvas.[95] The safety of his amphitheatres in general left

---

95   Astley also offered work to a new scene-painter, twenty-one-year-old David Cox from Birmingham. For some reason the job fell through but Cox went on to become one of England's greatest landscape painters.

a lot to be desired, but this new venue left every visiting architect and builder in London scratching their heads: how on earth did the building stay up? And he was still building firetraps. Although not in Philip's lifetime, in 1841 this huge structure, too, like its two predecessors, would catch ablaze and was entirely consumed within three-quarters of an hour.

On Boxing Day 1804, Astley's opened with a special holiday bill that included the six-feet seven-inch Giovanni Belzoni, 'the Patagonian Samson', with his 'surprising Feats of Strength, accompanied by a 'Groupe of Savages.' One evening Belzoni crashed right through the stage, having attached an iron girdle to his body and invited eleven men to climb on board. The show proved very popular and its run was extended for another week. The following summer, the strongman Belzoni was back for three weeks and once again he was a smash hit. At the end of his first week a Sunday newspaper reported:

> What with the attractions of the grand Spectacle of the Castle of Otranto, the surprising Horsemanship of the Equestrian Roscius, the almost more than human feats of Strength of the astonishing Troop of Indians, led on by the Giant Belzoni... the Royal Amphitheatre, Westminster Bridge, has nightly overflowed with company during the whole of the last week; and we may venture to say, that, as the whole of these performances are to be repeated to-morrow evening, the house will be found to exhibit a crowded audience in every part of it.

This was Belzoni's final appearance at Astley's. The great Venetian strongman gave up the circus and became an explorer. He was among the first to have a go at finding the source of the Nile, setting off for the African interior in 1823 in typically flamboyant fashion; 'God bless you, my fine fellows and send you a happy sight of your country and friends!' Having covered only ten miles, Belzoni died of dysentery.

The new Astley's was nicknamed the 'ample-theatre' because it gave customers more than their money's worth. The setup was much the same most evenings. At 6.30pm the curtain rose on a featured piece, usually a hippodrama with some eye-catching title such as The Brave Cossack or The Blood Red Knight. At 8.30pm spectators paying half price were admitted. If there was already a full house they were allowed to watch the final scenes of the spectacle from the empty ring. Next came a forty-five-minute session featuring gymnasts, contortionists, clowns and strongmen, followed by the ever-popular trick-riding displays. The action then reverted to the stage where a burletta or pantomime of equestrian drama finished off the evening's bill. Throughout, a musical accompaniment was provided by an orchestra. These entertainments often ran on until midnight or even after 1pm.

With this tried and trusted schedule, Astley's third and last Lambeth amphitheatre began its long and distinguished career as the venue admired and cherished by Charles Dickens, William Thackeray and a host of Victorian writers.

13

ST. PETERSBURG TO PHILADELPHIA

One of the earliest American circus playbills, an advertisement for Ricketts Circus in 1797. The Taylor's Ride to Brentford has been plagiarised as The Taylor's Disaster; Or, Johnny Gilpin's Journey to Brentford. Public domain.

By 1790, Charles Hughes, exasperated by endless run-ins with his business partners, was rapidly losing interest in the Royal Circus. He was almost ready to throw in the towel when he had a chance meeting at the Newmarket races with Sir John Dick, ambassador, horse-lover and adventurer.

The life of the much-travelled Sir John was more colourful than that of your average British diplomat. He made his fortune as a merchant in Rotterdam before taking up appointments as British Consul at Livorno in Italy and St. Petersburg. He had important connections all over Europe, not least of which was the Russian Empress Catherine II. She rewarded him for services rendered by making him a Knight of the order of St Anne of Russia. It was rumoured that Dick had made himself useful to the Empress by organising the abduction of her rival to the Russian throne, Princess Tarakanova.[96] This adventure was allegedly accomplished by Dick with the help of Catherine's confidant, the Russian nobleman Count Alexei Orlov, a giant of a man, six feet six inches tall, a celebrated duellist – as befitting his nickname 'scarface' – and one of the most influential men in Russia.

Horse racing brought together all ranks of Londoners and Dick was one of many aristocratic gamblers seeking a substitute for the gaming tables of Mayfair by trying his luck at the annual festival at Newmarket. He informed Hughes that his friend Count Orlov was in England on business for the Empress Catherine, buying bloodstock for the imperial stables. Someone with Hughes' knowledge of horseflesh, Dick suggested, could make himself very useful. The diplomat arranged for Orlov and Hughes to meet. A deal was struck at the first interview. Hughes would buy the horses and take care of them until they were safely lodged in

---

96 The mysterious Princess Tarakanova was an impostor claiming to be Empress Elizabeth's love child with her favourite, Prince Razumovsky. In 1775 she was imprisoned in the Peter and Paul Fortress in St. Petersburg and died there the same year of tuberculosis. Dick was implicated in an evil plot to kidnap her.

the Imperial palace at St. Petersburg. Within a matter of weeks Charles Hughes was on a boat bound for St. Petersburg and an unlikely appointment with the most notorious woman of the age.

The reign of Catherine 'the Great' began with an assassination carried out, or at least facilitated by, Hughes' new friend Alexei Orlov. The Empress was German by birth and at the age of fourteen was betrothed to the heir to the Russian throne, Grand Duke Peter, nephew of the Empress Elizabeth. Her intended was an unappealing, smallpox-scarred youth said to resemble a monkey. Peter succeeded the Russian Imperial throne as Czar Peter III on the death of his elderly aunt on Christmas Day 1761. Catherine by this time had long since abandoned any pretence of marital fidelity and was consoling herself with a series of lovers, mostly officers from the Palace Guard. The new Czar really wasn't equipped to deal with the nuances of Russian court intrigue, unlike his very resourceful young wife who was already plotting to get rid of him. Even as the old Empress Elizabeth was hovering at death's door, the Palace Guard was quietly plotting to replace Peter with his much more popular spouse. In June 1762, just six months into his reign, Peter was disposed of in the time-honoured Russian manner – a palace revolution.

The conspiracy was organised by Alexei Orlov and his brother Grigory who was at the time Catherine's regular lover. The Orlovs were born into distinguished Russian nobility and were serving officers in the Imperial Guard. By Romanov standards it was a rather tame coup. Czar Peter was away with his mistress at his summer home at Ropsha when the Orlovs had Catherine proclaimed Empress in St. Petersburg. When Catherine's supporters eventually tracked him down they found him dead drunk. He meekly gave way, requesting only that he be allowed to take his mistress, his dog, his black servant, his pipes and his fiddle to prison with him. Frederick the Great noted that Peter III had 'allowed himself to be overthrown like a child being sent off to bed'. Nine days after the abdication, Alexei Orlov went to Peter's room and together they had a drinking session well into the night. According to legend, Orlov waited until Peter was too drunk to defend himself, then throttled him with a pyjama cord. The official announcement was made, in the inimitable fashion, that the ex-Czar had died of an acute attack of colic during one of his frequent bouts of hemorrhoids. Orlov was rewarded handsomely for his part in the coup. Catherine elevated him to Count and gave him an estate with several hundred serfs and a lump sum of two hundred thousand roubles. He went on to become a war hero and statesman before retiring to devote his time and his considerable wealth to the breeding of horses.

Charles Hughes arrived in Russia with the Empress's livestock, along with his own trained horses, accompanied by several apprentice equestrians. In the party, too, was Philip Astley's father Edward, employed as ostler to take care of the horses. In St. Petersburg they found a home from home. A small but thriving ex-pat English community drank English ale with oysters in one of three English pubs located in the city, or visited one of many English barbers that used the famous Sheffield razors. Many of them rented houses on 'the English Embankment', making few concessions to their surroundings: 'Furniture, meals, establishments,' wrote a chaplain, 'everything is English – even to the chimney fire. Here where wood is in such plenty, the Englishman fetches his coal from home.' Very few of them bothered to learn Russian. Even ex-pats who had left England to escape scandals or criminal charges looked down on their Russian hosts whose manners were, in the opinion of one visitor, 'far inferior to that of a well-taught bear'.

Hughes found an enthusiastic audience for his horsemanship. He was introduced to the Empress and, ever the showman, was able to convince her that he had brought over his horses at great expense so that he might perform equestrian exhibitions never before been seen in Russia. This was disinguous. He would have known that there had already been a steady stream of English equestrian performers arriving in Russia through the mid-1700s. Jacob Bates introduced trick-riding to Russia as early is 1764 and, since then, the Russian public had seen similar performances by James Price and Old Sampson and his wife. All the same, Hughes charmed Catherine into inviting him to entertain at the Winter Palace before a grand assemblage of Russian nobility.

The Russian court Hughes encountered was a mixture of fantastic extravagance and medieval squalor. The Winter Palace was one of the biggest and most opulent royal residences in the world with sixteen hundred rooms, housing four thousand staff. It was also perpetually alive with vermin and so was occupied by a large army of feral cats employed to keep in check the rats chewing on Catherine's expensively imported furniture.

The Empress was particularly interested in exchanges with Britain, with whom she was an ally against the French. Early in her reign she dispatched some of her architects and designers to England with instructions to observe, learn and copy. There was lots of goodwill towards her personally in the British press and a great deal of interest in Russia generally. Josiah Wedgwood was one of many who had reason to be grateful for Catherine's Anglophilia. She placed an order at his Staffordshire factory for plates and tureens for a palace she hadn't yet built, after some unsubtle lobbying by the British ambassador and his wife, who spent years doing the rounds in Moscow wearing Wedgwood cameo brooches. Josiah was delighted but it was a risky commission. The terms were not generous and he was justifiably worried that another Russian coup might prevent his patron from living long enough to pay her £2,700 bill, but he took a gamble and mobilised an army of painters to decorate a huge service of plain creamware views of the British Isles. Fortunately, the Imperial patronage paid off and his tableware became hugely fashionable among the Russian gentry.

The biggest thing for a Russian gentleman was to own an English horse. During the time Hughes was in Russia around three hundred horses a year were imported from England. Alexei Orlov did more than anyone to make English thoroughbreds popular in his homeland by buying up former winners of the Derby and St. Leger, while English grooms, ostlers, blacksmiths and dealers were also in great demand. Everyone in the Russian court wanted Hughes to teach them the English style of riding. In his memoirs, Jacob DeCastro hints that the Empress enjoyed more than just riding lessons from her English guest. By this time she was in her sixties and most her teeth were missing but her appetite for tall, handsome young men was notoriously intact, so it is entirely possible that they had an intimate relationship. She was certainly unstinting with her favours to Hughes. Catherine ordered a permanent residence built for him and his company in her palace at St. Petersburg, with plans for a second in Moscow. Hughes also drew a huge sum from Catherine's treasury for the upkeep of his troop and his own living expenses. He lived in the lap of luxury for almost a year, occasionally performing at the Empress's command, meanwhile breaking horses and giving riding lessons to the Russian aristocracy. He also played a big part in promoting horse-racing in Russia. In July 1792 he organised a race on Vasili Island for a silver cup worth one hundred and fifty roubles – the first ever recorded in Russia.

There was plenty of incentive for Hughes to stay in Russia permanently, but trouble was brewing back in London. While he was away he had let his circus out to a number of independent equestrian troupes, but Lady Jane West was suing him for ground rent. Hughes begged Catherine for permission to return home to attend to his business. The Empress gave him temporary leave of absence on condition that he left his horses and stable hands, including his ostler, Edward Astley, behind in Russia. Hughes sensed that this might be a good time to cash in his chips. There were some signs that the novelty of trick-riding was beginning to wear thin. During his time in St. Petersburg he supplemented his income by putting on some *ad hoc* performances in a theatre in Old Isaac Street. According to the local newspapers he relied greatly on the skills of his young boy riders who performed numerous, but by that time very repetitive, tricks. Hughes hinted to Catherine that his horses and stable-hands might be for sale. He struck a favourable deal and they became Russian crown property.

Charles Hughes is often given the credit for introducing the circus to Russia but that would be overstating his influence because his shows only consisted of trick-riding and there were no acrobats, clowns, jugglers or any other side shows that we associate with it. But he does deserve credit for bringing the main attraction of the circus, which was always the riding act in the ring, to the attention of the Imperial court. Without the Empress's patronage the Russian circus would never have taken off so quickly or become so all-conquering. So it is fair to say that Charles Hughes was a very important mainspring of an institution that would one day become one of Russia's greatest cultural exports.

While Hughes was at least forging the beginnings of the circus as a popular art form in Russia, at precisely the same time, one of his former apprentices was trying his luck at the other end of the world. John Bill Ricketts was born in Bilston in Staffordshire in 1769.[97] His unfinished portrait by the American artist Gilbert Stuart shows a strikingly handsome, dark-eyed young man gazing steadily from the canvas from under his powdered wig. He served at least some of his education as an equestrian apprentice under Hughes at his original Riding School near Blackfriars Bridge. Jacob Decastro saw Ricketts perform and remembered him as 'the first rider of real eminence that had then appeared.' He was about twenty-three years old when he went to the newly formed United States of America in 1792.

---

97 He has often been described as a Scotsman, a mistaken assumption arising from the early years he spent performing in Edinburgh.

As in Europe, individual circus performance arts existed in America long before anyone tried to present them in one format for a single entrance fee. There are records of rope-dancers and stilt-walkers in the colonies as early as 1724. England's Jacob Bates was an equestrian star in the US in the 1760s, as was America's own Thomas Poole twenty years later.

Ricketts opened America's first ever circus on 3 April 1793 in Philadelphia. It was the capital of the US and hungry for entertainment. On the corner of Twelfth and Market Streets he built a roofless wooden arena based on Astley's principles, a ring surrounded by box seats with standing room behind. His company comprised himself, his younger brother Francis and a couple of horses, but within a couple of months he was taking on new acts including Mr Franklin, another British defector from Hughes' Royal Circus in London, Signor Spinacuta, a famous rope dancer and animal trainer in Paris and London, and a clown called Mr McDonald.[98]

The performances Ricketts presented owed more or less everything what he had learned from Hughes and Astley, a mixture of equestrianism, acrobatics, rope-dancing and clowning. The star attraction of the show was Ricketts' brilliant trick-riding. He was renowned for his astonishing speed and athleticism and was performing stunts on horseback with a degree of acrobatic skill never before attempted by any of his fellow equestrians, not even the Astleys, father or son, in their pomp. He stood erect on two horses without breaking 'two eggs fastened to the bottom of his feet', leaped from a kneeling position on horseback over a ribbon suspended high above the ground, stood on his head and performed somersaults while mounting and dismounting, and somersaulted from a springboard over the heads of a row of thirty men and six horses. His most eye-popping feat was his

---

98 Disappointingly, not the inspiration for 'Ronald McDonald, the Hamburger-Happy Clown', invented by a marketing department in 1963.

ability to juggle four oranges while standing on the back of a galloping horse. There were direct steals from Astley's repertoire, too. Ricketts' version of the 'flying Mercury' routine featured an apprentice, Master Hutchins, who stood on Ricketts' shoulders as the horse galloped around the ring, with both balancing on one foot for the finale.

Ricketts' circus had its own version of Little Billy, a trick horse named Cornplanter, who could 'at the word of command, ungirth his saddle, and take it off his back. He will also pick up a handkerchief, gloves, etc.' Ricketts also performed the classic Taylor's Ride to Brentford and a variation, The Drunken Sailor. Both of these skits would endure as popular staples in American circus for generations. One of the few aspects of his performances that Ricketts could completely call his own at this point in his circus career was his choice of costume. He was much admired for his smartness when he was riding, dressed in a mode generally assumed to be that of a typical 'English gentleman'. An early chronicler of the American circus recorded his 'pantalets, trunks full disposed, and neat cut jacket which were sufficient to make ample display of his figure for all purposes of agility and grace.'

Ricketts' Philadelphia circus received some very important patronage. America's first President, George Washington, visited it with his wife Martha at least twice. Washington's famous white horse, Jack, which he rode during the years of the Revolution, became the very first sideshow attraction of the American circus when Ricketts bought it for $150 a couple of days after Washington's second visit in 1797. The president probably thought he was a pretty good horse-trader because Jack was now in his twenty-eighth year, but the showman had seen the publicity value of Astley's 'gift horse' Gibraltar and was more than happy with his deal.

In 1796 Ricketts hired a tight-rope and slack-wire artist called Jack Durang on a salary of twenty-five dollars a week. Durang wrote a fascinating account of his experiences as Ricketts' right-hand man, multi-tasking as performer, painter, set designer, music writer, handbill maker and treasurer. Unlike his feuding fellow British circus compatriots back in London, Ricketts seems to have been well liked by everyone. Durang's memoirs describe him as socially skilled enough to become the President's riding companion but someone who was also prepared to get his hands dirty on an equal basis with his employees.

After a couple of years Ricketts' original building in Philadelphia was replaced by a huge new venue in Chestnut Street, a circular tent of wood, ninety-seven feet in diameter, with white walls and a conical roof with a stage and a seven-hundred-seater auditorium. In New York, Ricketts built another amphitheatre on Broadway. His shows were now so popular that some theatres postponed to avoid going head-to-head with him. A local dramatic author complained that 'Sheridan and *The School for Scandal* had been forced to give way to Ricketts and the Clown!' In March 1795 Ricketts added to its attractions: 'The Indian Chiefs, lately arrived, [who] will with Mr Ricketts, perform on horseback, drest (sic) in the character of warriors,' thereby anticipating the much later successes of Buffalo Bill's Wild West Show.

Ricketts brought to the circus a couple of really important innovations. Firstly, his advertisements encouraged parents to bring their children. It may seem strange now, but this was considered highly unusual for eighteenth-century circus performances. Secondly, he got back to the basics. As in England, elaborate, large-scale stage spectaculars came to play an increasing part in his programmes. By 1796 Ricketts' small ensemble of four or five performers had grown to seventeen, plus a crew of painters, carpenters and a thirteen-piece orchestra. The operation had become too bloated for him to make a profit, so he decided to ditch the equestrian dramas and pare his staff down to a much smaller, more economic outfit and concentrate on the physical skills: trick-riding, clowns, acrobats and jugglers.

This was the template on which all subsequent American circuses – and eventually those all over the world – were built.

Ricketts spent the rest of the decade touring up and down the Eastern seaboard blazing the trail for the travelling American circus show, but he was following Astley's tour model. Wherever he went he erected speedily built, semi-permanent wooden buildings, selling them off at half price when he left. North American circus audiences were just as rowdy and demanding as their London cousins. One night in Montreal, one of Ricketts' crew fired a pistol loaded with dried peas at a group of punters who had clambered on the roof to watch without paying. He put out the eye of a young man who subsequently sued Ricketts for $800. The shooter had to flee for his life and rejoin the troupe across the US border.

It seemed that Ricketts was set fair for a great career as a circus impresario, but he soon experienced first-hand just how fickle the business could be. In 1798 the roof of his Philadelphia circus collapsed. The following year his circus burned down when a drunken carpenter left a lighted candle in a scenery room. The horses were saved but little else. The fire with losses estimated at $20,000 effectively ended Ricketts career in the United States.

Ricketts' run of bad luck continued. Dejected by his losses he took a break and withdrew from his company, but after a more than a year of inaction he decided to give it another go and perhaps lift his spirits by taking his show to the West Indies. In May 1801 he departed on the schooner *Sally* bound for Jamaica with ten horses and a small company of performers. His ship was captured by French pirates and taken to Guadeloupe in the Leeward Isles where their possessions were sold as prize money. Intervention by a sympathetic merchant allowed the troupe to recover some of its property and to begin performing, but disaster struck again. Two of the company, including a ten-year-old boy, died of yellow fever. Ricketts' brother Francis was jailed after allegedly marrying then rapidly deserting a West Indian girl – the circumstances surrounding these events are murky. In 1803, the star-crossed Ricketts decided he had had enough. He sold his horses and chartered an old vessel to take him back to England. On the way home, his ship was hit by a storm mid-Atlantic and he and everyone else on board was lost at sea.

So ends the story of America's first circus proprietor. An appetite for the circus, however, had been whetted and large numbers of European performers, mainly French and English, flocked to the States to continue where Ricketts had left off and exploit the dearth of competition. By the end of the nineteenth century, the US circus had grown to become a vast business empire, supported by great names such as Ringling, and Barnum and Bailey. Its lineage, though, was traceable directly back to Lambeth: John Bill Ricketts, the man employed by the man employed by the man, became 'the father of the American circus'.

Charles Hughes' Russian adventure proved to be his swansong. While he was away in St. Petersburg, his audience in London began to drift away. When he returned he found the Royal Circus in a dilapidated state. For a while he tried to make a living by turning his arena into a menagerie, exhibiting various animals brought back from Algiers by his friend Sir John Dick – mules, asses, sheep and silver-haired goats – hardly the sort of spectacle that would draw a crowd. In 1794 Lady West had her revenge for her husband's death, repossessing her property and leasing it to James and George Jones.[99] That same year, Philip Astley's father, Edward, recently returned from Russia in the service of Empress Catherine, died and was buried in the churchyard of St. George's in Southwark. In October 1796 Hughes lost his licence to the new owners, effectively terminating his role is a circus proprietor and so ending the most acrimonious rivalry in Georgian show business. He died just over a year later, a prematurely aged fifty,

---

99   The Royal Circus remained in their hands until it was destroyed by fire in 1805.

of a heart attack, which many thought had been brought on by the loss of his licence. He was buried in the same churchyard as Edward Astley in Southwark. Little is known about Hughes' surviving family except that he had one daughter, Wilhelmina, who was about seventeen years old at the time of his death.

It may have been Astley who gave birth to the modern circus but Charles Hughes, as his deadliest rival, at least deserves credit, too, for motivating Astley to ever-improve his performances to surpass him. If Philip was 'the father of the circus', Hughes was its dark, complicated uncle.

Hughes' former business partner, Charles Dibdin, was going through a period of financial turbulence, too. Having walked away from the Royal Circus in 1785, Dibdin put all his money into the building of a new theatre that was destroyed by a gale. He turned his hand to journalism and began a weekly periodical, which also failed. He went on a tour of England giving performances of his music but the public didn't believe the famous Mr Dibdin would play the provinces and he was denounced as an imposter; the tour was an embarrassing financial failure. In 1788 he decided to try his luck in India[100] but only got as far as Torbay. The vessel he was sailing in was forced to put in because of bad weather, so the world's most famous writer of sea shanties gave up and went home. He opened a music shop in the Strand but that venture failed too. In 1808 the public took pity and a dinner was held to raise money for the elderly and destitute composer. With the proceeds he retired, but five years later he was paralyzed by a stroke. The man who gave the modern circus its name died on 25 July 1814.

---

100 Dibdin's best known song Tom Bowling was written in honour of his brother, Tom, who had drowned in the India trade.

14

CROPPIES LIE DOWN

James Gillray's print of Daniel Mendoza. 'The Fighting Jew' dared knock Philip Astley on his backside. Public domain.

Like all good military men Philip Astley was thrilled by the prospect of invading enemy territory. By the late 1780s he had toured most of continental Europe and had permanent amphitheatres in two capital cities, London and Paris. He was soon to add a third.

Dublin and London were the twin capitals of Georgian theatre. The former was the junior partner in terms of size but it was still a very important part of the economy of the English-speaking entertainment world. Their performing communities were intrinsically linked; most of London's best-known performers played Dublin at some point in their careers and *vice versa*. Astley took his circus to Dublin for the first time in December 1772 and was a sensation when he appeared at the Inn's Quay, charging an admittance of two shillings.[101] He stayed in Dublin until June the following year, performing and attracting more pupils to his riding lessons than he could possibly handle. From then on Astley's troupe performed in Dublin regularly for a couple of months at least every winter in various temporary venues. In 1789, he acquired a permanent home when he bought Molyneux House on the corner of Peter Street and Bride Street.

Astley's new Dublin Amphitheatre, as it became known, was one of his craziest structures. Molyneux House was in the fashionable part of the city, just a stone's throw from the archbishop's cathedral. It was once one of the most imposing buildings in Dublin but it had seen better days. The main part of the new amphitheatre was an enormous lean-to built against

---

101 As well as his regular circus performances there were other *ad hoc* money-making opportunities. Astley and his horse Little Billy were engaged to appear at Capel Street Theatre and Little Billy was hired to appear in a brief double act with a female dwarf billed as the Corsican Fairy. At thirty-four inches tall, a newspaper describing her as 'a beauty, her exact proportion and symmetry, may without the least falsehood, allow her to be called one of the most perfect and admirable productions of human nature in miniature.' It was also noted that she spoke French and Italian with the 'greatest vivacity'.

the back of the crumbling old mansion. Instead of slate or tiling, the roof was covered with large plates of old sheet iron. A commentator noted that the roof was 'a curious one indeed, (it) already exhibits a stupendous figure, forming an uncommon and lofty segment of a prodigious circle; in short, nothing that ingenuity can devise, or money execute, is wanting to accomplish the work'. In fact the project cost Astley £10,000 but it was a gamble he was happy to take. He had successfully lobbied some of his influential friends, including the Irish politican Sir Capel Molyneux from whom he bought the Peter Street site, for a Dublin performing licence. In April 1788, his hard work paid off when he was granted a Royal Letter Patent – only the second awarded in Dublin. It gave him permission to stage theatrical entertainments through the winter season from the end of October to the end of January for fourteen years. It drew Astley into another increasingly acrimonious feud with a rival theatre manager.

The only other venue with a patent in Dublin was owned by the infamous Richard Daly.[102] There were surely few more sinister figures in theatre history than 'Dick the Dasher'. He was an Irish buck: tall, dandified and considered strikingly handsome despite being alarmingly cross-eyed. Daly's pronounced squint came in useful during his frequent duels with sword or pistol (as many as sixteen years in two years according to one source) because his opponents found it impossible to read where he intended to strike. Daly was born in Galway, the son of a prosperous farmer and had studied at Trinity College, Dublin. After squandering his inheritance, he turned to the stage. He failed in England as an actor and returned to Ireland, joined a company in Cork and

---

102 There's an apocryphal story that Daly invented the word 'quiz'. He allegedly bet that he could invent a new word which would be used by everyone in the city within forty-eight hours. He wrote 'quiz' on a card and asked his staff to write it on walls all over town.
Quiz most likely derives from the Latin: 'Qui es?' or, 'Who are you?'

then moved to Dublin. Daly was ruthless and brutal in pursuit of women. His seduction technique was to advance money to young actresses then, when they were unable to repay the loan on time, demand they make good on the debt with sexual favours. If they refused to acquiesce he would threaten to have them arrested or offer them violence.

In 1780, Daly bought at a knock-down price the abandoned, dilapidated Theatre Royal, known locally as Smock Alley. It was one of the most dangerous buildings in Dublin. Built on reclaimed ground from the River Liffey, it was prone to collapse – and had done so several times, killing and injuring many people in the process – and was also the site of some of Dublin's worst riots. However, it also gave Daly an exclusive fourteen-year royal patent to perform drama in Dublin, at a stroke removing all competition from rival theatres. In the feudal world of Georgian theatre, managers ran their businesses like personal fiefdoms and sleeping with the cast was their *droit du seigneur*, but Daly relished the power his new position gave him with unparalleled enthusiasm. The author and actress Elizabeth Inchbald was among his prey; when she refused to sleep with him, Daly sacked her on the spot. His most infamous conquest, Dorothy Jordan, joined his company in 1781. His own wife was heavily pregnant when Daly seduced – or more likely raped – the seventeen-year-old actress. Dorothy fled to England to escape the abusive theatre manager while pregnant with his child (though Daly may have accompanied her at first).[103]

In 1788 her seducer transferred his exclusive patent to the refurbished theatre in Crow Street, but the new Theatre Royal had a profitable but short career – its receipts were soon diminished by the arrival of Astley's Amphitheatre. Daly

---

103 Dorothy or Dorothea Jordan was famed for her high-spirited comedy and tomboy roles. She performed in Dublin and London, and retired to France. She had a daughter by Daly, three children by Richard Ford, and ten children by the Duke of Clarence (later William IV). The children by the duke were ennobled under the name of FitzClarence.

vehemently opposed his rival's application for a patent, arguing that Astley's musical acts were an encroachment on his own patent. At the hearing, Daly tried to work out some kind of deal but the Englishman was in no mood for compromise. Astley roared, 'I am no man of straw, Sir! I have fought and bled for my country and my King has rewarded me for it!'[104]

Astley knew that he held all the cards. Dublin theatregoers were even more rebellious than their London cousins. Daly's establishment was a down-at-heel, unruly place with poorly paid actors and shoddy scenery. His customers showed their displeasure by pelting his performers with missiles from the upper galleries. They did this at their peril because Daly was a violent thug. In November 1789, when a couple hissed and booed him while he was on stage, he and a huge actor called Kennedy dragged them out of the stalls and took them off for a hiding. A press correspondent warned the Dublin public they had 'better not presume to hiss or even squint or sneeze at those gentleman, unless they have a fancy for being cudgelled in to civility by... The Theatrical Bludgeoners, so active on the business last season.'

Astley's extremely well-run circus was thought to be a welcome addition to Dublin's culture, promising to provide a more respectable alternative to Daly's disorderly venue. And should things did get out of hand, if anyone could quell a potentially riotous Dublin crowd, Astley could. There was also another motive behind legal recognition for his circus. It was thought that his ultra-loyalist entertainments would mobilise local support in the interest of the Crown and the Empire. The British government attached so much importance to the Dublin Amphitheatre that it was even rumoured that it was secretly helping Astley secure the services of top entertainers from London to advance the Crown's agenda in Ireland.

---

104 Jacob DeCastro *Memoirs.*

Astley's new venue in Peter Street caused a great deal of excitement and speculation in the local press, who anticipated a showdown with Dick the Dasher. A commentator noted:

> Mr Astley's Circus is not yet nearly finished … what the event of the contest between the Theatre and him will be, it might be hazardous to predict, but the opposition hereto has certainly been of use, causing a degree of exertion that without it probably would not have existed.

Astley's first season in his new Dublin amphitheatre was delayed by a terrible winter storm, resulting in the late arrival of scenery and other props imported from his venue in Lambeth. He opened two months late, on 12 January 1789, promising a host of startling innovations such as 'scenes and machinery… such as has never been known in this country' and a Dublin stage debut for Monsieur Henry, 'that learned professor of Natural History Philosophy, whose abilities and knowledge of an extensive diversity of variegated inflammable air, stands unrivalled'.[105] Despite the bitterly cold weather, on the day before the grand opening, Astley sent out small troupes of artists to put on short, impromptu street shows in the surrounding area to draw in the crowds. Acrobats braved the frost to perform daring stunts on the railings of Molyneux House while dogs danced below and trick-riders roamed the plazas at Christ Church and College Green, weaving through the crowds while standing on horseback. All of this, of course, was literally jaw-dropping to anyone who had never before seen a circus, and the feeling of excitement and anticipation it generated on the streets of Dublin was intense. A review of the opening performance noted: 'The amphitheatre was completely filled before the curtain drew up and the audience

---

105 The puff goes on to describe M. Henry as 'the original inventor of fireworks produced from air, without smell, smoke etc.'

were kept in a continual roar of laughter during the whole of the performance.'

As in London, Astley's Dublin company might be more correctly called a troupe, because its members almost always performed multiple functions as actors, riders, dancers and singers. One of most versatile performers in Dublin, and one who would go on to become Britain's second most pre-eminent clown after Joseph 'Joey' Grimaldi, was a six-foot Frenchman named Jean-Baptiste Dubois. He was one of the most athletic and courageous performers of the age. He first arrived in Britain in the 1770s as a trick-riding clown at Astley's London amphitheatre. In these early performances he demonstrated the skills that would make him a circus star, vaulting over seven horses and their riders ('one more than any person ever vaulted over in England'). He could also tumble, act, mime, sing, dance a hornpipe and even 'imitate birdsong in a manner far superior to anything of the kind ever performed in this kingdom'. He danced on the rope with two boys tied to his feet, performed clown routines on a donkey and introduced a comic gender-swapping riding act called the French Post Boy's Journey from Paris to London (yet another variant of the Taylor's Ride) in which he changed his clothing from male to female (or possibly the other way around) while inside a mailbag. As 'Gobble the Eating Clown', Dubois guzzled vast amounts of food for comedic effect. He and his great rival Joey Grimaldi were often locked in a stage duel to see who could eat the most: Dubois packed away pies and sausages while Grimaldi downed quarts of beer, competing for laughs.

Dubois once saved Astley's entire company from drowning. The Dublin season was often delayed by bad weather, which made crossing the treacherous Irish Sea even more hazardous than usual. On one trip back from Dublin, a ferocious winter storm blew up. On this occasion Astley had hired the cheapest transport he could find, a packet called *Venus*, but didn't have the time to check it out beforehand. There were holes in the sails, it had compasses that didn't work and just two broken life boats, one bottomless, the other with a side caved in. The seven-hour trip to Holyhead turned into a forty-eight-hour nightmare when the weather turned nasty and the ship began to flounder. The terrified captain was forced to admit that he had never navigated the Irish Sea before and was quite out of his depth. Fortunately, a former naval officer called Fitzgerald, ably assisted by Dubois, took command and steered the *Venus* safely into Holyhead.

The outcome for some who attempted the crossing to and from Dublin was less propitious. One of Astley's regular equestrian performers through the 1790s was the Irishman Benjamin Handy, praised for his 'unparalleled vaulting horsemanship'. Handy started out as an ostler working for Charles Hughes but established his own company starring his wife, Signor Riccardini – whose *tour de force* was standing on her head on top of a spear while surrounded by fireworks – and their thirteen-year-old daughter Mary Ann, an equestrian billed as The Child of Promise. In December 1797, Handy's company of twenty-five men, women and children and twenty show horses embarked to join him at Astley's Dublin amphitheatre on *The Viceroy*, a sailing packet used on the Liverpool to Dublin run. The vessel was loaded nearly to gunwhale height when it left Liverpool, sailing directly into a gale. *The Viceroy* was not heard from again. Handy's wife and daughter were among the drowned, along with John Astley's brother-in-law and sister-in-law.

Astley's Dublin patent didn't permit him to stage performances after 31 January each year, although he occasionally overstayed his welcome by the odd day or two. He was back in November 1789 with a new extravaganza called 'The Royal Naval Review at Plymouth', during which a squadron of ships passed in review and fired their broadside, producing 'an effect charming beyond description'. The Dublin press marveled at the army of carpenters, blacksmiths, tailors, glaziers, painters and upholsterers required to pull this off, all directed under Astley's iron hand. 'There is nothing like generalship in a Theatre, it commands subordination, and we know no man more indefatigable and obliging than Mr Astley.' In December 1789 we find Astley's faithful memoirist Jacob DeCastro at the Dublin Amphitheatre starring in a musical titled, alarmingly, 'The Jew In The Dumps'.

1790 was a very busy year for John Astley. In his second season at Peter Street he made his acting and directorial debuts in Dublin as the character in the old favourite 'The Death of Captain Cook'. It was reviewed favourably as 'one of the most charming, comic, heroic and tragic pantomimes ever presented on the Irish stage'. The younger Astley continued to pack them in as the hero of 'The Convention: or Free Trade', a topical new pantomime apparently based on the British government's new trade deal with Spain in the South Seas. A Dublin critic enthused:

> The last scene is the most beautiful and enchanting picture ever seen on any Theatre. Young Astley's super-excellence throughout the whole Pantomime, gives it a high colouring. His combats with the Savages are such as we never witnessed before; in short, this week's entertainment seems to attract all ranks, for last night at an early hour not a place was to be got.

In addition to his acting and directorial duties, John was also still performing on horseback. A programme from February that year promised: 'Young Astley's hunter will leap thro' a hogshead covered with paper: after which he will in a most surprising manner take a flying leap over another horse's back.'

Astley's regular practice was to present the same programme for a week from Monday through Saturday, then change it the following Monday. During the early years of the Astley's Dublin venture most of the acts presented were tried and proven successes from his London amphitheatre, but in 1792 Philip made an exciting addition to his show.

Prize-fighting emerged as a spectator sport in England in the early 1700s along with cudgel fights and wrestling at fairs and wakes. The English loved a good scrap. 'Anything that looks like a fight' observed the Frenchman, Henri Missan, 'is delicious to the Englishman'. There were bare-knuckle fist-fights between men, or between women in petticoats. Surgeons were often called upon to attend serious injuries, justifying the combatants' colourful nicknames such as 'Jawbreaker' and 'Gravedigger'. When 'Bruising Peg' took to the ring she 'beat up her antagonists on a terrible manner.' In London, pugilism increasingly rivalled trick-riding as a crowd-puller. In 1772 prize-fighters took over Old Sampson's trick-riding ground in Southwark charging *6d* each for admittance, from which they earned 'a good sum'.

Another south London venue, Hockley in the Hole, doubled as a famous bear-baiting and bare-knuckle boxing venue until Christopher Preston, the proprietor of the ring, fell in and was mauled to death by his bears. In 1738 a wig-maker was trampled to death while trying to get into the Great Booth at Tottenham Court Road to see a boxing match between Jack Broughton and his challenger George Stephenson.

The first major contributor to the growth of boxing as something more like a respectable sporting contest was the setting down of Broughton's Rules in 1743. These 'rules' still allowed an alarming degree of brutality but they were an improvement on the previous free-for-alls and represented some degree of restraint, making it a sport on which a gentleman might wager. Jack Broughton insisted on chalk lines to separate the protagonists before the start of each round, umpires picked from 'among the gentlemen present' and proposed that 'no person is to hit his adversary when he is down, or seize him by the ham, the breeches or any part below the waist'. From now on 'heroes of the fist', as the pugilists became known, were courted and feted by the upper classes, a dangerous world collectively known as 'The Fancy'.

The boxing superstar of the late 1700s was the Londoner, Daniel Mendoza, billed as 'The Fighting Jew'. Before Mendoza, boxing was artless. In essence, two combatants stood toe-to-toe, trading heavy blows until one went down and stayed there. Mendoza was not your usual lumbering heavyweight. At five-feet seven-inches tall and weighing one hundred and sixty pounds he was at a massive disadvantage to his opponents in height, reach and weight, but unlike his flat-footed adversaries, Mendoza relied on speed and footwork, feinting, ducking and weaving between punches. There was still nothing in the rules, however, to forbid hair-pulling. Unlike most fighters, who wore their hair close-cropped, the vain Mendoza let his dark curly hair grow long. He came to regret this during one particularly brutal fight when his opponent gripped him by his flowing locks and used his other hand to bash him repeatedly in the face until Mendoza's clock was a bloodied pulp.

He learned to use his fists at an early age. He was born into a large, very poor family in Aldgate in 1764. His parents were Jewish refugees from the Iberian Peninsula. London's East End might have been a safer alternative for Jews than Madrid or Lisbon but, all the same, antisemitism was rife. Mendoza was apprenticed to a glazier when he was thirteen but lost his job after beating up his employer's son over some slight about his heritage. At sixteen he was working in a tea room and one day he got into yet another argument with an obnoxious porter. He invited the man to step outside.

As luck would have it, as young Mendoza was busy thrashing his much older, much bigger opponent, among the bystanders urging him on was a professional pugilist, Richard Humphries. Impressed by the level of violence offered by the youngster, Humphries offered to teach him the art of self-defence.

Mendoza's first professional fight was against Harry the Coal-heaver, where a forty-round victory won him five guineas. Despite his burgeoning fight career, he kept his day job and continued to get into scraps with customers. According to Mendoza's own rather patchy memoirs, published when he was forty-two, he was an innocent soul who never went out of his way to find trouble, but it is obvious he had a hair-trigger temper and was always up for a good brawl. One day he got into three fights on his way to a boxing match; the first because someone cut him up with a cart, the second when a shopkeeper tried to cheat him and the third because he didn't like the way someone was looking at him. His victims weren't always male: he was once found guilty of beating up a woman because she had short-changed his wife.

Mendoza's early professional bouts brought him to the attention of pugilism's most high-ranking fan, the Prince of Wales. Aristocratic patronage and protection was fundamental for prize-fighting since, technically, the sport was illegal. Through the Prince, a match was arranged with the formidable Samuel Martin, 'the Bath Butcher,' at Barnet racecourse on 17 April 1787. Around five thousand people saw Mendoza bamboozle the Butcher on his way to an easy victory inside twenty-six minutes. Mendoza's apparent invincibility was tested by his former mentor, Richard 'the Gentleman Boxer' Humphries, in a series of three epic, brutal contests between 1788 and 1790. Humphries was assumed to be a 'gentleman' because he was from Anglo-Saxon stock while Mendoza was required to play the part of the 'crafty Jew'. The latter's 'scientific' style was such a novelty that many people assumed he was dodging punches through cowardice: Jews, it was generally supposed, were almost guaranteed to run away from a fair fight.

In the intervening couple of years there had been a falling out between Humphries and his old pupil. Humphries was jealous of the young Mendoza's increasing celebrity and their relationship had soured into one of mutual hatred. They met for the first time as opponents in 1788. Among the ten thousand rain-soaked spectators were the Prince of Wales and his brother, the Duke of York. Humphries, in consideration of his superior size and strength and his reputation as a murderous hitter, was the clear two-to-one favourite. Mendoza surprised almost everyone by having the better of the early exchanges but the ring was slippery and, in the twenty-ninth minute, he sprained his ankle and was unable to continue. Humphries reported to his patron gracelessly, 'Sir, I have done the Jew and am in good health.'

In defeat, Mendoza's fame and reputation soared, a source of growing resentment to Humphries. A contest of trash-talking in the press ensued, whipping up huge enthusiasm for a second bout. Their next encounter was such a massive draw that it was said, apocryphally, to have knocked the storming of the Bastille off the front pages. This time Mendoza prevailed, besting his adversary after more than an hour and fifty-two rounds. The third and final encounter took place in 1790 in Doncaster. This time Mendoza beat Humphries in fifteen rounds, cementing his position as a national hero. Mendoza's brilliant victory also earned him an audience with King George III at Windsor, which made him possibly the first Jew in modern history to have a conversation with an English monarch. Poems and songs were written in Mendoza's praise and portrait painters and engravers invited him to sit for them. The various depictions of the ripped, curly-haired boxer make him look as though he has stepped straight from a Greek urn.

One of his many noble admirers was Lord Camelford, an important patron of the English prize-fighting scene and 'mad as a hatter'. Camelford invited Mendoza to his home and suggested that the two should spar, insisting that the professional prize-fighter shouldn't go easy on him. Mendoza obligingly knocked Camelford straight through the glazed door of a bookcase, slicing the aristocrat's head open. Camelford picked himself up and proposed that they continue the bout, armed with sticks. Again, Mendoza saw him coming and dealt his lordship a violent blow over the ear. The bloodied Camelford insisted they resume the contest with fencing swords and withdrew to fetch some blades. As soon as the coast was clear, Mendoza sensibly made a bolt for the door.

Philip Astley was always on the lookout for novel acts and boxing was perfect for 1790s Dublin. Although it was yet to take off in Ireland on a great scale, English bouts were widely reported in Irish newspapers and most people had heard about 'the fighting Jew' and his famous victory over the great 'English gentleman boxer'. Most Irishmen, of course, were rooting for Mendoza.

Shortly after his third battle with Humphries, Mendoza set off on a triumphant, nine-month tour through the North of England and Scotland. By this time he was the most famous sportsman in Georgian England. In late 1790 Astley wrote to the boxer with an ambitious invitation to appear at his Dublin amphitheatre. Mendoza agreed, pointing out that the Theatre Royal in Covent Garden paid him twenty guineas an evening. In the end, he settled for half his asking rate – sixty guineas for six exhibition bouts featuring himself and his brother. Clearly, Astley was practised in managing egos. In a notice published in the *Belfast Newsletter* the showman even reproduced letters from Mendoza, revealing the boxer's willingness to appear for half his usual fee.

Mendoza made his Dublin debut at Astley's Amphitheatre on 1 February 1792. He was only in the city for a month but managed to get himself into a number of scrapes. Almost as soon as he stepped off the boat he was invited to a pistol duel, after remarking within earshot of a prickly local that Dublin wasn't as big as London.

Mendoza dealt with the affair with characteristic efficiency. He invited his adversary to meet him at a nearby hotel and asked to examine the pistols, then the champion boxer rendered them useless by throwing away the flints and gave the Irishman 'a severe caning'. Mendoza's contract with Astley prohibited him from exhibiting 'the art of self-defence' in public anywhere other than at the amphitheatre but he was not debarred from beating people up in private.

There were several more skirmishes to enliven Mendoza's stay in Dublin. One day he was confronted by a noted local blowhard called Squire Fitzgerald, described as 'a swell of great weight and little prudence'. Fitzgerald was determined to provoke a serious set-to by making offensive remarks about Mendoza's religion. He offered to settle the matter with his fists; Mendoza accepted and proceeded to batter the large Irishman into submission. When Fitzgerald regained consciousness he apologised and hailed Mendoza a credit to his religion and the art of self-defence.

Despite the odd off-stage misadventure, Astley's gamble on bringing Mendoza to Dublin paid off and large crowds turned out to see him in action. He was so popular that rumours of his non-appearance almost sparked a full-scale riot. One evening Astley told Mendoza he was giving him the night off so that he could hold a benefit for his son featuring 'some new entertainments'. When news got around that the famous fighter wasn't going to be on the bill the mood in the amphitheatre turned ugly. The Duke of Leinster, who was in the audience, went backstage and urged Astley to let Mendoza perform as usual, otherwise the house would be demolished.

The day after the near riot of the benefit night, Leinster, who was backstage again, most likely conducting an affair with one of Astley's actresses, witnessed an unusual spat between the showman and the boxer. As the three men were relaxing in Mendoza's changing room, Astley observed, with typical North Staffordshire bluntness, that while he was an admirer of the Jew's boxing skills, a good big 'un would always beat a good little 'un, and if it came to a trial of strength Astley would win. Mendoza took the bait and suggested they might put his theory to the test. Astley agreed and was quickly knocked on his backside. Everyone held their breath as the huge ringmaster lay sprawling on the ground, but Mendoza was quick to repair his employee's injured dignity. 'I assured him if I had hurt him it was not intentionally; and having assisted him to rise, we shook hands, but he never afterwards proposed to renew the contest.' The incident didn't harm their relationship because Astley offered Mendoza the opportunity to repeat his Dublin success by engaging him for the following season. Again, the boxer performed to packed houses which, in no small measure, was thanks to his own skilful self-promotion; at one point, he challenged 'all Ireland' to fight a match for one hundred guineas.

As it turned out, Mendoza's contracts with Astley came at the very peak of the boxer's popularity and success. From this point on his life was overshadowed by debt and scandal. For all his bravura and fancy footwork, Mendoza had no head for finances. He spent his earnings like a drunken sailor and his final years were pitiful and financially ruinous. He was forced to pawn his sparring gloves to secure his release from one of several spells in a debtor's prison. In 1820, one day short of his fifty-seventh birthday, after an absence of more than fourteen years from the ring, destitution forced Mendoza out of retirement to fight Tom Owen. The poorly conditioned pugilist was knocked out by the younger man in under fifteen minutes. He died aged seventy-two in 1836, leaving no money and eleven children.

The best measure of Astley's success in bringing Daniel Mendoza to Dublin was when one of his popular sparring exhibitions went to head-to-head with a true great of the Georgian stage. His local theatrical rival Richard Daly had launched a series of law suits in an attempt to have Astley's closed down. For the time being, he was desperate to do something quickly to staunch the flow of customers heading for the Peter Street amphitheatre to see The Fighting Jew. Daly's secret weapon was Mrs 'Betsy' Billington. She was a major star of the late-eighteenth-century stage and in her heyday the highest paid singer in the world, regarded by some as the greatest English soprano who ever lived. Born Elizabeth Weichsel, she had been a child prodigy, playing piano at a concert in the Haymarket in 1774 at the age of nine, at eleven composing keyboard sonatas. Her life was lived under a spotlight because 'Betsy' Billington was quite a sensation off the stage as well. There was considerable speculation about her sex life, her partners allegedly ranging from provincial actors to aristocracy, most notably the Duke of Sussex and the Prince of Wales. She was about sixteen when she married James Billington, a double-bass player in the Drury Lane orchestra who was giving her singing lessons. They went to Dublin where she made her operatic debut in the part of Eurydice. She was an overnight sensation and within three years *The Times* reported that 'Mrs Billington is already established in the opinion of the public, as the first-rate English singer.'

In 1794 she and her husband left England for Italy following the publication of damaging but largely accurate revelations about her love life, including illegitimacy, incest and sexual abuse: at twelve years old she had accused her godfather, the violinist James Agus, of rape. Shortly after the Billingtons' arrival in Naples, husband James suffered a fatal stroke while in the bed of the composer Francesco Bianchi at the residence of the Bishop of Winchester. According to the official report there was nothing suspicious going on, Billington was merely looking for his hat. He died shortly before the second showing of *Inez di Castro*, an opera written especially for his wife's debut at the Teatro di San Carlo. This was perhaps Betsy Billington's most dramatic stage appearance. Superstitious locals attributed an eruption of nearby Mount Vesuvius to her singing. There were fears for Mrs Billington's safety but a superb performance saved the day and quite possibly her life. The singer stayed on in Italy and, in 1798, she was remarried to a violent, jealous Italian diplomat called Felissent. After a couple of years, she fled back to England to escape her new husband's abuse.

Mrs Billington's return to the London spotlight was risky. Georgian theatregoers were quick to pass judgment on actresses they suspected of immoral behaviour and they had long memories.[106] In Mrs Billington's case the public had rather a lot to get upset about. The publication of James Ridgway's scurrilous *Memoirs of Mrs Billington* was the publishing sensation of 1792. The book was partly based on sixteen letters purporting to be between Billington and her mother, suggesting multiple affairs, illegitimate children, homosexuality on the part of James Billington and widespread incest in the Weichsel family. The composer Joseph Haydn complained on publication day; 'you couldn't get a single copy after three o'clock in the afternoon.' Mrs Billington needn't have worried because, perversely, *Memoirs* made her more bankable than ever. On her return to the stage she found herself in the middle of a bidding war from rival theatres and was able to rake in record fees for her performances.

The managers of London's two leading opera houses, Covent Garden and Drury Lane, were so desperate to secure her services that it was agreed she should sing at both venues, alternating between the two. In one year she earned at least £10,000 – a remarkable sum for a singer at the time, in today's terms around £750,000. Her figure was also a subject of some fascination. The *London Chronicle* was keen to point out: 'In

---

106 When Mrs Johnston returned to the stage at Covent Garden after a two-year absence, keeping her head down after an alleged infidelity, her reappearance was greeted with boos and catcalls. Also at Covent Garden, Mrs Bulkley was hissed when she entered as Portia in *The Merchant of Venice* after it become known that she had taken the son of her long-term lover to her bed. The treatment of divorced women revealed the Georgian public at their most vindictive. When Lady Webster divorced her husband in 1799 and became Lady Holland she was seen in the box at Astley's shortly afterwards and was humiliatingly shunned by her friends. Lord Holland, however, could maintain his social life as though nothing had happened so long as he left his new bride at home.

respect to person, Mrs Billington is rather more embonpoint than when she left England, but her features possess infinite symmetry and beauty, and her whole figure is grand and captivating'. The poet Leigh Hunt, more bluntly, thought her 'a fat beauty'.

Mrs Billington's presence in Dublin at the same time as Daniel Mendoza was due to a falling out with her employees at Covent Garden who wanted to cut her salary from a hundred guineas per night. She was also having an affair at the time with Richard Daly. Mrs Billington was a huge draw in Dublin but, to her lover's mortification, not half as popular as the Fighting Jew sparring with his brother at Astley's Amphitheatre.[107]

The spat between Astley and Daly rumbled on. Astley's patent licence permitted him to stage 'feats of horsemanship, musical pieces, dancing, tumbling, and pantomimes of any nature, provided they be decent and becoming... provided that no regular tragedy, comedy, opera, play, or farce be performed in his amphitheatre, as shall have been exhibited at the theatre royal.' In other words he could do more or less whatever he wanted on condition that he didn't stage any entertainments previously shown by Daly, but he seems to have breached this condition, or sailed close to the wind, often. For instance, he was forced to pay Daly £500 compensation for putting on a performance called *My Grandfather.* Astley in turn complained that Daly had pirated some of his original dramatisations, including *The Siege of Valenciennes.*

The knockout blow for Daly came when his long-running legal battle to have Astley's patent revoked was finally resolved. Twelve English judges found unanimously in Astley's favour. In truth, Daly was already ruined: the public had already voted with their feet for Astley's dazzling new entertainments.

---

107 Betsy Billington retired to London's Soho, where she was celebrated as 'the Poland Street man-trap'.

Astley's showmanship was also noticed by a certain faction intent on whipping up support for their own cause. In the 1700s, Anglo-Irish relations were fraught. King William III paid a brief visit to sort out the Jacobites at the Boyne in 1690 and, in 1821, George IV tottered unsteadily ashore having polished off a goose pie and copious amounts of Irish whisky, but in the century in between, not a single British monarch had dared set foot in Ireland.

Dublin society was organised along religious and class lines. At the top was a small group of the very wealthy, mostly Protestants, who controlled more or less everything and had the law behind them to ensure it stayed that way. At the bottom were vast numbers of very poor Catholics who had no political role and survived on low-paid work, charity, begging or crime. Poverty went hand in hand with sickness. Most of the population weren't living in grand Georgian houses but in hovels, often near one or other of numerous stinking dunghills on the northern or western outskirts among wandering pigs feeding on the ordure and rubbish. The Townsend Street dunghill, adjacent to Trinity College, also contained the dissected remnants of numerous corpses tossed aside by medical students. Typhus was endemic due to grossly inadequate sanitation; as late as 1770 only twenty per cent of households had piped water and many streets had open sewers or cesspits. Dublin was also the sinkhole for Ireland's poor. Every time there was a famine, such as the one in 1740–41 that took the lives of more than a third of the population, the city was filled with the desperate and hungry. There were so many vagrants and beggars on the streets that fights often broke out between the local destitute and the newcomers. Dublin was a dangerous place for reasons other than poor hygiene. Violence was part of everyday life and the streets were riven with tribal warfare. Competing gangs such as the Liberty Boys and the Ormonde Boys fought bloody turf battles, often heavily armed and with many fatalities.

Protestants and Catholics alike resented the English presence in Ireland. Technically, since May 1782 the Irish had had an independent Parliament, but it was almost wholly under the thumb of Westminster with English ministers having the whip-hand, buying seats, offering jobs and handing out bribes. Many Irishmen felt that only force would bring change. In October 1791 Catholics and Protestants came together to form The Society of United Irishmen. Their aim was to abolish religious distinctions and unite against the English. Their leader, Wolfe Tone, a lawyer from County Kildare, took his inspiration from the French revolution, calling it 'the dawn of a new and perfect age'.

Astley, who prided himself more on his loyalty to the Crown than anything else, threw gunpowder on the smouldering fire of Irish nationalism by staging epic spectacles based on successful British military campaigns. He was particularly fond of re-enacting anti-French battle scenes which, to a Dublin audience broadly sympathetic to the revolution, went down like a one-armed juggler. As the 1790s wore on, these spectacles took on an increasingly jingoistic edge, with Irishmen cast as enthusiastic supporters of British forces, including loyalist, tough-talking Irish sergeants subduing rebellious native peoples. In December 1796, the French fleet attempted a landing on the Irish mainland at Bantry Bay. In the months following, the militia terrorised the Irish population with whippings, half-hangings and house-burnings in an attempt to flush out the United Irishmen and their weapons. Astley's response was a new play called 'Cork in an Uproar: or the French Invasion' – a show designed explicitly to ridicule and generally annoy the Irish radicals. Astley must have known that his bill of fare was playing badly with a section of his Dublin audience but he didn't care. The baiting of the United Irishmen continued with another play celebrating Admiral Duncan's defeat of the Dutch at Camperdown; the Dutch were French allies at this point and supporters of Irish nationalism.

A local newspaper attacked Astley for his insensitivity, pointing out that a number of the fallen at Camperdown were also Irish. But Astley had no intention of being sensitive to the Irish nationalist cause, nor was he intimidated, not even when he stepped into the ring and was pelted with missiles. One evening a large open clasp-knife was thrown from the high gallery, narrowly missing his head. If anything, he seemed determined to make himself even more unpopular by ordering his musicians to strike up loyalist anti-Catholic songs twice nightly. His decision to build a large sentry box in the gallery area, containing two soldiers with fixed bayonets pointing at the audience, was a provocation too far.

One of the more brutal practices of the military and government supporters was known as 'pitch-capping'; that is, tarring then setting fire to the head of 'croppies' – men who wore their hair in the cropped French style. There were many reports of people being attacked simply for failing to remove their hats during the playing of loyalist tunes. One of the tunes played nightly at Astley's was called 'Croppies Lie Down', a song composed by a captain in the notorious North Cork militia. With its jeering chorus, 'down, down, ye croppies lie down', it became a rallying call for loyalist rebel-bashing Protestants. In December 1797 a rebel called Hardy, who worked as a printer at a newspaper favouring the United Irishmen called *The Press*, decided to take action against 'the bludgeoner of Peter Street', as Astley was called. One evening, Hardy arrived at Astley's with about thirty Liberty boys and took up position near the house band. As soon as the musicians struck up the Catholic-baiting 'Croppies Lie Down', Hardy gave the signal to attack. His men swarmed into the orchestra pit and smashed all the instruments. Within a couple of minutes the disturbance became a general riot, as audience members tore up seats and broke lamps. Opposing factions spilled outside, extending their battle-lines into the adjoining streets.

On Peter Street the military charged the rioting crowd with fixed bayonets. When they pursued the rioters into nearby Kevin Street a soldier was stabbed to death. Meanwhile, Patty Astley was seen tearing out the silk lining from her velvet cloak to staunch blood from the head of another young soldier.

There were those, including Richard Daly, who suspected all along that Astley was much more than just a supplier of British nationalist propaganda. Daly encouraged rumours that the Englishman was a spy working for the British Government.

In the 1790s, as the conflict with revolutionary France wore on, secret intelligence sources whispered about United Irish links with radical groups in Britain. It was well known that the Prime Minister, William Pitt, was funding a small army of high-placed spies, informers and agent provocateurs in Ireland to sniff out any Jacobin or republican tendencies. There has never been any proof that Astley was involved in this espionage. He was hardly the James Bond type with the suavity of manners to mix comfortably in varied company. But he was the classic spy archetype – a patriot. Astley was supremely loyal to King and country and if he had undertaken to spy on His Majesty's domestic enemies in his spare time, then no one should be in the least bit surprised.

For the next eight years, Irish nationalism ate away at the dodgy supports of Astley's Dublin Amphitheatre, as the United Irishmen did their level best to derail the loyalist circus. With Astley's tumbling clowns throwing themselves about the streets to promote his show, it was often hard to distinguish street theatre from street brawl. The Peter Street enterprise never fully recovered from its mauling and by 1800 the amphitheatre was losing money. The venue had also suffered quite a lot of damage and there was little appetite or available funds to make essential repairs. The Crown's support for Astley waned, too, because the Act of Union established direct rule from London for the dawning century.

In 1802 Astley sold his Dublin circus and it was relaunched by the new owner as a regular theatre. A couple of years later, when the great clown Joseph Grimaldi performed at Peter Street, he found Astley's old stamping ground in a shocking state of disrepair. The rain came through the roof in torrents, drenching the audience below, defying the bundles of rags and tarpaulin sheets rigged up to keep it out. Grimaldi was so saddened by the plight of the famous old venue that he donated his salary to help pay for its renovation.

15

THE CURTAIN CLOSES

Astley's home Hercules Hall, named after his human pyramid act, La
Force d'Hercule. *This shows the building as it was shortly before it was
demolished in 1841. Reproduced by kind permission of the London
Borough of Lambeth, Archives Department.*

The year 1803 was calamitous for the Astley family. Within a few
weeks after the death of his wife Patty, Philip learned of the death
of his sister Sarah. From then on he shared Hercules Hall with his
housekeeper and his three nieces – Sarah's daughters by her third
husband – Sophia, Louisa and Amelia Gill.

Although he had spent most of his adult life in London and Paris, he kept in touch with the town of his birth. His surviving sister Elizabeth was on her second marriage to a Newcastle businessman, John Harding, her first husband James Hall having died when a blunderbuss exploded in his hands in 1798. Elizabeth's family prospered; her grandson James Astley Hall was wealthy from his hat-making business and became mayor of Newcastle. In 1797 Philip made a nostalgic return to the Potteries to try to trace his family roots, placing an advertisement in the *Staffordshire Advertiser* offering a generous reward for information about his great-grandfather Simon Astley.

Although increasingly in ill health and having turned the full-time management of his London amphitheatre over to his son, he hadn't lost his love of show and grand gesture, nor his boyish enthusiasm for fireworks. His great displays to mark the King's birthday were still one of the highlights of the calendar and every year on 4 June huge crowds gathered on the banks of the Thames at Westminster to see his rockets roaring and fizzing with sparks shooting high into the London sky. Philip's 1804 display in honour of the King's sixty-sixth was his last.

In January that year, the King's mania returned. By this time George had such a morbid dread of the Reverend Dr Francis Wallis that it was recognised the doctor's presence might be counterproductive and tip the King permanently over the edge. Dr Samuel Simmons, physician to St. Luke's Hospital for Lunatics, was appointed in his place. Unfortunately, Dr Simmons also favoured a regimen that wouldn't have looked out of place in the Spanish Inquisition and was not appreciably more successful either. It was a tricky situation all round, not least for the Poet Laureate, Henry James Pye, who was still expected to knock out his usual King's Birthday Ode full of the most irreproachable patriotic sentiment.

The King's fireworks display went ahead as usual. Astley's long-serving in-house fireworks expert Johannes Hengler[108] had died, so it was fired by the London pyrotechnicists Messrs. Cabanell and Son who, it was advertised, 'will let [the rockets] off on the Thames this evening at different signals from Astley, Sen., who will be mounted on the Gibraltar Charger, placed on a Barge, in the Front line of the Fireworks'. According to one source there was a serious accident and there were several fatalities. For whatever reason, the fireworks displays were discontinued. From then on, the only public event he sponsored was an annual prize-giving for a wherry-rowing competition, contested by the men who carried cargo and passengers up and down the Thames. The annual race for Astley's Prize Wherry, one of the first ever organised river sports on the Thames, usually took place near Westminster Bridge around 15 June and ran from 1784 until a year or two after the showman's death. The prize-giving was performed on stage at his nearby amphitheatre as part of that evening's entertainments.

The third incarnation of Astley's Amphitheatre under the management of John was a resounding success, but his father, although semi-retired and in his sixty-second year, was never able to remain idle for long and he was itching to expand his empire. Philip was convinced the time was ripe to take his circus into the heart of the capital. His Lambeth headquarters was still compelled by law to close for the winter but across the river in Westminster a royal patent licence would allow him to stage

---

108 Hengler died in 1802 but his widow continued the family fireworks business. In 1845 while living above her ground-floor showroom there was an accident with an oil lamp and the fireworks exploded. Although she managed to make her way to the window, she was too big to climb through it and she became firmly stuck, despite the help of firemen and burned to death. Her grandson, Charles Hengler, opened Hengler's Circus in 1871. He only went into circus management because he was too tall to join the family acrobat team with his brothers, but died a very rich man in 1887 at his home in Hampstead.

winter performances. To acquire this golden ticket he called in a favour from a very influential friend.

Astley's life as a circus mogul was only one aspect of his social ascendancy. He was on increasingly intimate terms with the aristocracy, most notably the King's second youngest son Frederick the Duke of York. Frederick – 'Prince Ned' to his friends – was an odd-looking gentleman even by the standards of the House of Hanover.[109] He was very tall and bald with an enormous gut, which was counterbalanced by a huge backside: people noted that he looked as though he might topple over at any moment from the weight of either. Like his older brother George, he was extravagant beyond the means of a royal prince. In one year, Frederick drank and gambled his way through £40,000. He had a lifelong interest in the theatre, having spent a great deal of his youth chasing actresses. Most of the friendships he cultivated were either in the world of London show business or in the military; Philp Astley qualified on both counts. Frederick was generous with his patronage and the showman was fiercely loyal in return. His latest book, *Astley's System of Equestrian Education*, was dedicated to the Duke of York in suitably ingratiating terms.

When Philip was discharged from the army for the second time in 1794, he left with a letter in his pocket from the Duke recommending him in glowing terms as 'a good and bold soldier'. In 1805, he decided to use his patron's letter to try to infiltrate London's legitimate theatreland. Astley appealed to Queen Charlotte, drawing her attention to his 'forty-two years of study and labour' in the field of equestrianism. The Queen in turn persuaded the new Lord Chamberlain, Lord Dartmouth, to grant Astley a Westminster licence for 'music, dancing, pantomime and equestrian exhibitions'.

---

109 Odder still, Frederick was made a bishop when he was seven months old.

All Philip had to do now of course was build another theatre. After a good deal of travelling around town viewing prospective sites, he chose a spot in Wych Street just off The Strand, roughly where Bush House in Aldwych stands today. Coincidentally, Wych Street was where he and his family lived following his father's release from the Fleet Prison when Philip was nine years old. The land was leased from its owner, Lord Craven, for a term of sixty-one years at a yearly rental of one hundred pounds. It was situated directly behind Drury Lane Theatre and the nearby Strand was one of London's busiest shopping streets, so the location was perfect, but the actual building plot was far from ideal.

It was on the site of the recently demolished Craven House and some adjacent slum tenements – Astley's childhood home was very likely one of them. It was an irregular-shaped piece of ground requiring a great deal of graft and imagination to make it fit for purpose, but he applied himself to overcoming this handicap with his usual grit and resourcefulness. As always, he kept his costs as low as possible by appointing himself builder, architect and surveyor, then assembled some workmen from a nearby tavern called The Compasses.

The new structure was to be called the Olympic Pavilion – 'Olympic' in its original sense of god-like or lofty, 'pavilion' because the roof was conical, just like a tent. Work began in September 1805. Every day, Astley was on site directing operations from his one-horse curricle, specially constructed to accommodate his now very ample stomach. The building was completed by early autumn the following year. At first sight, it was a substantial brick-built structure with a large ring and full stage. On closer inspection it was just as jerry-built as most of his previous efforts. There was hardly any brickwork at all. The frame was improvised from the remains of a captured French warship, the *Ville de Paris* or, as Astley called it, 'the Wheel de Parrey'.[110] If you looked closely enough you could see that the bowsprits of the ship formed the uprights and supports, that the ship's deck formed the stage and floors and the sides for the outside walls. Above, a tin roof kept out the rain. Nevertheless, a newspaper report complemented Astley on 'an excellent and nouvelle piece of workmanship.'

The floor layout of the Olympic Pavilion was roughly similar to that of his amphitheatre on the other side of Westminster Bridge, but because of the limitations of the plot it occupied it wasn't nearly as big or as well-appointed as its predecessor. There was just enough room for one tier of boxes, a pit surrounding the ring and, at the rear, a viewing area which served as a gallery, partitioned off by an iron grating through which the spectators watched like caged animals. There wasn't enough room for an orchestra so the musicians occupied boxes on either side of the stage, fiddling at each other across the house.

The new venue opened on 18 September 1806. To forestall any vexatious allegations of licence infringement, his pre-show publicity boasted; 'Established by authority of the Lord Chamberlain'. The early reviews were encouraging. *The Morning Post* was particularly complimentary to its proprietor:

> When mounted on the beautiful grey, the veteran Astley, apparently in the flower of his age, still conserves the extraordinary management of the horse. What a noble example to the heads of families, civil and military, and to the rising generation in general, is to be witnessed every evening.

Faced with a deluge of competition, Astley decided to appeal to the sensibilities of a more discerning punter. Although his show

---

110 The *Ville de Paris* did not live up to her motto *Fluctuat nec mergitur* (*Tossed by the waves, she does not sink*); she went down in a hurricane in 1782 off Newfoundland with the loss of all hands but one.

at the Olympic Pavilion still featured the usual tightrope walkers and clowns, he indulged his long-held dream of establishing a venue for classical dressage. There were more formal displays of horsemanship and more dramatic, large-scale equestrian theatre. An advert in *The Times* of 1807 promised:

> Haydn's minuet danced by two horses... concluding with a third horse dancing a Pas Seul to the popular air of the Yorkshire Gala: the whole exhibiting a pure example of the noble elements of the Equestrian Arts and Science, so strongly necessary in the field of honour and to victory!

In his eagerness to attract a 'quality' crowd, Astley had forgotten the first rule of show business. His audience found his new entertainments unrelievedly dull. Most people were still struggling to make a living in the shadow of war. They weren't ready for this new highbrow fare; they wanted fun and began to drift away. Still, business at his Lambeth amphitheatre was still very strong and he could afford his Wych Street whim for a few more seasons yet.

Britain was in the mood to celebrate again on 25 October 1809, the occasion of King George III's Golden Jubilee.[111] It also marked the anniversary of Agincourt, a double celebration. All across London, the day was ushered in with the universal ringing of church bells. Local businessmen, in the spirit of ancient hospitality, fed the poor with dinners of roast beef and plum pudding. No mention was made anywhere of the King's ever more perilous health. Exactly a year later, George succumbed to his final bout of madness and was shut away. His spendthrift eldest son was named Prince Regent and celebrated with a banquet

---

111 Opinion was divided as to whether the Jubilee had been celebrated a year too early. 25 October 1809 was the first day of the fiftieth year of the King's reign so he hadn't actually reigned for a full fifty years.

that was so recklessly extravagant that it even made some of his closest friends feel queasy.

Philip was still buying most of his horses from Smithfield market, purchasing up to half a dozen at a time and rarely paying more than five pounds apiece. He didn't care about size, breed or colour; what he always looked for was temperament. He trained them under a simple reward and punishment system. Training a horse to perform tricks requires time, energy and a great deal of patience but, once taught, it is unlikely to forget. For instance, a horse can be taught to count using its strong sense of hearing; the trainer clicks the nails of thumb and finger together, the horse taps the ground with hoof in response, and continues to do it until the last click. Once the horse has learned his tricks, practice is all it takes.

Amazingly, his very first purchase, Little Billy, was still with him after nearly forty years and had performed for all but three of them. The story behind those three missing years was heartrending. The man Philip hired to take care of the little horse was an old groom called Abraham Saunders. He was almost as great a character as his employer, well known to the public as a rider and showman for the best part of seventy-five years. Abraham experienced all the vicissitudes of life as an itinerant showman, occasionally in comfortable circumstances but more often than not in dire poverty. He was born in 1748 to a Jewish father who managed a travelling fairground act. In his teenage years, he performed with his brother Samuel and in the mid-1770s both were taken into the company of 'Astley's Jews', travelling throughout England and Ireland exhibiting at fairs. This ever-changing cast included many who would later mark their names in circus history, including Peter and Andrew Ducrow and the Great Belzoni.

Saunders made enough money to buy his own troop of horses, installing his company at the Royalty Theatre, Whitechapel, only to see it destroyed by fire – the first of many disasters that would dog his career. For a while he worked for the royal stud and was entrusted with transporting the King's valuable Royal Hanoverian Creams, considered the most elite of horses, to Ireland for the King's visit. Abraham also took along his own stud for circus shows during the tour. While the royal horses were shipped safely, Abraham's entire troupe was lost in a storm in the Irish Sea. After a series of bad speculations he was reduced to poverty. One day, Saunders begged Astley to let him borrow Little Billy for a few weeks: he was in a financial hole and was hoping to pay off some of his debts by staging a private exhibition. Astley must have been very fond of the old groom because he generously agreed to loan him his oldest and dearest circus performer. Before Abraham could put his plan into action he was thrown into Fleet Prison and his assets seized – Astley's precious little horse along with them. It was sold at auction to pay the groom's debts. All trace of poor Billy was lost.

Three years later, two of Astley's riders were in Whitechapel when they chanced across a small, shabby-looking brown horse, drawing a cart. This horse looked very much like the Little Billy they remembered. One of the riders, who knew the signals Astley used for his tricks, clicked the nails of forefinger and thumb together. Billy immediately picked up his ears and trotted over to them, greeting the two men as old friends. They tracked down Billy's new owner at a nearby ale house and bought him back 'at a very moderate price'. That evening Billy made an emotional return to his old master. The following Monday, the little horse was back at work, picking tea-kettles off the fire. Eventually, when he became too old for any kind of work and had lost all his teeth, Billy was looked after in comfortable retirement, fed on soaked bread at considerable expense. When he died at the great age of forty-two, universally adored and lamented, his skin was tanned and converted into a stage thunder-drum.

There was no happy retirement, unfortunately, for Abraham Saunders. In his ninetieth year he was brought before magistrates as the owner of an unlicensed penny-gaff theatre in Haggerstone. The old man arrived in a home-made box on wheels, drawn by a Shetland pony and dressed in a bearskin. He died destitute in his Lambeth apartment two years later.[112]

At the end of the 1810-11 season the Olympic Pavilion was refurbished and the stage strengthened so that it could take up to a hundred horses. The bigger the displays, the more complicated the stage machinery became and customers found themselves waiting for ages for scene changes. Their patience tested, audience numbers fell away even more. As a last throw of the dice, Philip tried to turn it into a prize-fighting venue, hiring notable pugilists such as Dutch Sam, but that experiment failed as well. In 1813 Astley took the decision to close with losses of £10,000. But he still had something very valuable. Under the very noses of the two old Patent Theatres at Drury Lane and Covent Garden he had a theatre with a licence for winter performances. 'We'll throw the bone out, Johnny,' he said to his son, 'and let the dogs fight for it: one of them will snap at it.'[113]

An actor called Robert Elliston snapped. He bought the Olympic Pavilion for £2,800 plus an annuity of twenty pounds for the useful lifetime of the licence. Elliston, incidentally, was one of Jane Austen's favourite actors, known as a great lover on stage and a notorious philanderer off it. He re-opened the venue as The Little Drury Lane Theatre, staging burlettas and musical farces, but was shut down just a few weeks later by order of the Lord Chamberlain. The original licence had only been granted

---

112 Saunders son, Matthew, was another circus child prodigy, at age seven a tight-rope dancer and later an equestrian for many seasons at Astley's and elsewhere. He became the fixation of William Beckford, wealthy homosexual recluse of Fonthill Abbey. When Beckford was forced to flee abroad, he tried to persuade Matthew to run away abroad with him. It seems he didn't take up the offer; in 1810 Bow Street runners raided a 'molly house' in Vere Street and Matthew Saunders was one of the men arrested.

113 Jacob DeCastro.

for burlettas and equestrian dramas of the type given by Astley and only during the winter. After several more misadventures in theatre management, Robert Elliston became bankrupt and drank himself to death in 1826, leaving a wife and ten children.

After the collapse of his Dublin amphitheatre, the Olympic Pavilion was Philip Astley's second real taste of professional failure and also his last. In April 1814 the allies signed the Treaty of Fontainebleau, exiling the defeated Napoleon to Elba. Restrictions on travel to France were lifted. Although he was unwell and feeling his seventy-two years, Philip must have felt keenly the need to visit the scene of some of his former triumphs. He went to Paris ostensibly to find a cure for his 'phlegmatic disorder'. Even now, his restless mind was exploring the possibility of a new project, renovating and restoring his old Paris circus building and re-opening it as a tourist attraction for visitors from England. Six months later, on the evening of 20 October, at his home on the Rue du Faubourg du Temple, he took his usual cup of pippin tea, then passed away 'as peaceful as a lamb'.[114] His death certificate reported the cause of his lonely death as gout in the stomach.[115]

The celebrated Philip Astley, whose whole life had been accompanied by the thunder of war and the sound of applause and laughter, had the quietest of funerals, and was buried in the local Père-Lachaise cemetery with little ceremony.

---

114 Jacob DeCastro.

115 A common complaint that carried away many Georgians. 'Gout' was a catch-all to explain acute pain occurring in any area of the body; 'gout in the stomach' was considered fatal and could have been anything from cancer to arsenic poisoning.

16

EVERYTHING WAS DELIGHTFUL, SPLENDID AND SURPRISING

Detail from handbill showing Astley's performers the Monstrous Craws and the Learned Pig. Courtesy of the Wellcome Collection.

Having arrived in Lambeth Marsh on a gift horse and with very little more than his army regimentals and a letter of commendation from his old commanding officer, Philip Astley died a wealthy man. His will excited almost as much curiosity as his handbills. One of the executors, ironically, was Charles Hughes' former treasurer, Vincent de Cleve, nicknamed 'Polly' for his tendency to stick his beak in other people's business. Polly was an odd and solitary man. Believed to be independently wealthy, he kept the books for theatres as a hobby, meanwhile composing music and hoarding bric-a-brac in his second-floor room overlooking Smithfield Market until it looked like 'a conjuror's study'. The old gossip also claimed, although this was never substantiated, that he also took possession of some doggerel Old Astley had written about his wife and son which referred to both in very unflattering terms.

Philip left provisions for all of his family, including his sister Elizabeth and his six nephews and nieces. The most generous settlements went to his closest companions in old age, the Gill sisters, Sophia Elizabeth, Louisa and Amelia Ann. They were made trustees of the estate with an annuity plus the furnishings from Hercules Hall. The whole of his circus business interest and the proceeds from the sale of his extensive estate in France went to his son.

John Conway Philip Astley lived his entire life inside the circus, his long show-business apprenticeship beginning almost as soon as he could walk. At the age of five he was already a competent rider and was an equestrian superstar by the time he was in his late teens. Although he and his father both performed similar feats of horsemanship for most of their careers, it was John who won the most plaudits, spoken of as 'the wonder of the age.' John could dance on the back of a horse as it galloped around the ring 'as confidently as if he had the power to float on air'. By the time he was twenty, he had already reached a level of celebrity and professional status that most performers three times his age would die for. He was also, by universal female consent, quite an eyeful. A lifetime of leaping on and off galloping horses on a daily basis had given him a strong, athletic body, 'One of the finest... we ever remember to have seen', enthused a correspondent. His impact on female audience members was electric. For one lady correspondent, he appeared as 'an angel flying into the seats of Paradise'. Their attention wasn't lost on him either. A reporter advised that during his performances, 'he should be cautioned against admiring the ladies too much, lest he should be thrown off the saddle.'

As well as a fine equestrian performer, under his father's tutelage John Astley also learned all the techniques of showmanship and theatre management. In 1784 he was entrusted with temporary management of the London amphitheatre while Philip toured the country and from then on he took an increasingly leading part in running his father's business in London, while dad was occupied with operations in Paris. By 1799 John was running the Westminster amphitheatre full time.

Where his father was huge, coarse and 'bear-like', John was witty, well-read and urbane. In other respects, he was still his father's son, with a quick temper and a reputation for earthy language. He was also a very capable man-manager and wasn't easily intimidated. One evening his carpenters and stage-hands downed tools over a pay dispute and walked out just before a performance of a pantomime. They adjourned to the local whisky shop, confident of their imminent recall as the play couldn't go on with them. John enlisted the help of a few grooms from his stables and together they worked all the scenery and machinery themselves. He even invited the striking carpenters back in to watch the show. The pantomime went ahead without a hitch and the chastened crew went back to work, disputes over pay never mentioned again.

On the whole, John's employees and business associates found his courteous, mostly gentlemanly behaviour a very welcome change from the bull-in-a-china-shop manner of 'Old Astley'. He also enjoyed a level of social acceptance that his father had never quite been able to achieve. He became a Freemason, founded his own lodge and had his portrait painted by the artist James Saxon.

After his father died it was business as usual at Astley's with a mixture of clowns, tumblers, acrobats and trick-riding, but the venue also became known more and more for swashbuckling horseback melodramas, with swathes of horsemen and soldiers battling across elaborate sets. In 1810 John Reynolds, poet and friend of John Keats, wrote of one of Astley's most successful hippodramas:

> You ought to be in London now to see the Blood Red Knight
> at Astley's Royal Amphitheatre, the last scene a Battle upon real
> horses in Armour, I and my Father expended two shillings upon
> him the other night 'Half Price' – much pleased...

The Blood Red Knight made a clear £18,000 profit – record takings at that time. So long as the war with France continued, this type of epic patriotic display was as popular as ever. In 1812 Astley's celebrated Wellington's Peninsular Campaign with 'The Siege and Capture of Badajoz' and 'The Battle of Salamanca'. They were so successful that Covent Garden, the doyen of legitimate drama and so critical of equestrian drama, mounted the bandwagon and began staging their own, ironically employing Astley's staff and stud. Astley's horses were in great demand just about everywhere. For the new King George IV's coronation, the Duke of Wellington was commissioned to lead the procession on a horse personally trained by John Astley. At one point the horse, mistaking the cheers of the crowd for a cue, launched into its full routine of circus tricks, to the amusement of just about everyone except the Iron Duke.

One notable addition to John's company during this period was the Mancunian clown Robert Bradbury. He was originally an animal trainer and first appeared in London at Sadler's Wells in 1803, performing with a learned pig. Even by the standards of his profession, Bradbury was eccentric. Off-stage he was a dandy, known as the 'Beau Brummell of Clowns'. He travelled the country with a pet bear, one of several eye-catching affectations he kept up to attract publicity for his shows. Mostly he had a reputation for violence. Where Bradbury was concerned, coulrophobia[116] was not an irrational response. He once waded into the audience to beat up a heckler. This latent aggression persisted in his routines, most noticeably in his fondness for

---

116 Fear of clowns.

suicidal stunts. Bradbury leaped from high towers, balanced on
ten-foot poles at the top of unsupported ladders and rested a
sixteen-stone anvil on his chest while three burly blacksmiths
set about it with hammers. He almost ended his career by
falling down one of the stage traps and was lucky to break just
his collar-bone. In truth Bradbury wasn't quite as suicidal as he
pretended to be, as he was always protected on stage by thick
horse-hair pads covertly strapped to his knees, elbows and hips,
and a specially reinforced hat. Bradbury survived to enjoy a long
career as a pantomime artist – an unlikely but memorable Mother
Goose – then left the stage to travel the country as an itinerant
Methodist preacher. He ended his days as a voluntary inmate in a
madhouse in Hoxton.

Having spent his entire life either on stage performing on
horseback or behind the scenes as manager, writer and director, by
early middle age John Astley's appetite for the circus was spent.
He wanted to enjoy himself and, for the most part, that meant
hanging out with a clique of fashionably hard-drinking thespians
including the likes of the young Edward Keane. Increasingly,
the only interest John took in the family business was forced on
him by his bossy wife. Hannah Waldo Smith[117] was one of the
company's leading dancers and equestriennes when John married
her in 1801. Described as very tall and fair, with luxuriant hair
that reached almost the ground, Hannah always had ambitions
to be a dramatic actress, as her late mother had been. Now, as the
wife of a theatre manager, she expected her husband to provide a
showcase for her talents. From now on John Astley was required
to write a string of melodramas with his wife as the heroine.

Where his father had piled up a fortune, John Astley amassed
only debts. He bought himself the sort of country retreat that
had become fashionable among London's well-to-do urban

---

117 She is wrongly identified in some sources as the granddaughter of Adam
Smith, author of *The Wealth of Nations*.

population, an expensive estate near Weybridge in Surrey, where he enjoyed the life of a free-spending gentleman, leaving the business of the ring to his new business partners William Davis and John Parker. They did extremely well out of Astley's Amphitheatre but John blew more than his share of the proceeds on indulgences. By 1820 he was debt-ridden, morose and seemingly determined to drink himself to an early grave.

John survived his father by just seven years. In the summer of 1821 a doctor diagnosed a liver compliant – presumably alcoholic cirrhosis – and sent him abroad to rest up. He went, as his father had done, to Paris. He died in his father's old home on 19 October, on almost the same date, in the same room and on the same bed as 'Old Astley'. John was buried in his father's grave in Père-Lachaise. On his headstone, his wife had the words inscribed: 'The Once Rose of Paris'.

Hannah Astley was left to face debts amounting to £8,000. She tried to pick up where her husband left off but her attempts to run the family concern with his old business partner William Davis were complicated by her late father-in-law's will. Philip directed that if his son died childless, business ownership was to be divided into sixteen shares to be distributed among his surviving relatives, with only two shares allotted to Hannah. William Davis tried to rename the venue Davis's Royal Amphitheatre, but John's widow and the Gill sisters opposed him with costly litigation to keep the Astley brand intact. A compromise was reached in 1822 at Kingston Sessions when a licence was granted under the name of 'Astley and Davis', but the business was still generally known to everyone as Astley's.

Astley's Amphitheatre without either of the Astleys was not the draw it had once been. Davis did his best but he, too, was beginning to feel the financial strain. The enterprise needed another larger-than-life figurehead who could once again capture the public's imagination. In 1824 it found one. Davis was ousted, heralding the start of a great new era for Astley's with the arrival of a new business manager.

Andrew Ducrow was born in the Nag's Head, Southwark High Street in 1793. His father Peter was a Belgian who came to London to work for Astley's Amphitheatre as a strong-man act, 'The Flemish Hercules'. During his act he carried several children, including four-year-old Andrew, on a table held high above his head. Peter Ducrow was a sadistic disciplinarian. He made his son sit under his chair like a miscreant dog. During an exhibition in Bath, Andrew fell and broke his leg and was carried backstage. A few minutes later, the audience was alarmed by the sound of a child screaming: Ducrow was horsewhipping his son for making a mistake.

Andrew Ducrow had a passion for horses and by the time he was twelve he had learned to ride as well as any man. He became a phenomenal horseman, considered by some to have been the greatest of all time. His signature act at the age of nineteen was the 'Flying Wardrobe', a sort of hippo-striptease: dressed in rags and behaving like a drunkard, he cantered around the ring making false falls from the horse, meanwhile gradually removing layers of ripped jackets and torn waistcoats until he revealed himself as the star rider of the show, quickening female pulses with his very racy flesh-coloured bodysuit. Even Queen Victoria was a fan. According to one story, a couple of weeks before her coronation, Ducrow saved her life when her horse bolted in Hyde Park.[118]

Andrew Ducrow was as driven and as ambitious as Old Astley and had a volcanic temper – a contemporary described Ducrow as 'indelicate, even revolting'. He was a perfectionist and a control freak, inflicting brutal punishments on performers who didn't meet his own high standards, but the results were spectacular.

---

118 Probably apocryphal. A very similar tale was told about Philip Astley's heroism around King George III on Westminster Bridge.

For the best part of thirty years Ducrow's lavish equestrian spectacles made Astley's the most popular attraction in London. Most famous of all was his Mezappa and the Wild Horse, loosely based on the legend of a Ukrainian folk hero and made famous by the eponymous poem penned by Lord Byron. It had all the elements of a classic Astley's hippodrama and then some: it was noisy, colourful and featured a cast of several hundred performers and dozens of horses, the immensely popular Ducrow himself as the star rider. Fame went to his head. After a trip to Paris he insisted on being addressed at all times as 'Monsieur Ducrow'. He once took his company to Sheffield but ruined the prospect of a successful season with his supremely arrogant and overbearing manner. The city's Master Cutler visited his circus at the head of a cortège of up to fifty carriages, containing the principal manufacturers and their families. When he sent his card to Ducrow hoping for a personal reception, Ducrow replied through one of his subordinates that he only waited on crowned heads, 'not a set of dirty knife-grinders'.

It seems Andrew Ducrow was more fragile than he liked to let on. He and his family lived next door to the amphitheatre, separated only by a thin wooden partition and surrounded by circus artefacts, including Old Astley's cherished chandelier; his present from the Duke of York. In the early hours of 8 June 1841, Ducrow and his family were awoken by smoke. The report in *Freeman's Journal* takes up the story:

Astley's Amphitheatre, the scene of the glories of old Philip Astley, and of the more recent triumphs of Ducrow, is now a heap of ruins. Shortly after four o'clock this morning (Tuesday) a tremendous fire broke out at the back of the Theatre, and in less than three hours the whole of the premises, with the exception of the front towards the Westminster Bridge road, was totally destroyed. The fire is supposed to have had its origin in the stable facing Stangate Street, and to have arisen from some defect in the gas pipes but on this subject it is impossible at present to obtain any accurate information... Three of Mr Ducrow's valuable horses have perished in the flames, and an unfortunate donkey, which was in the stables at the time, has also fallen a sacrifice. We are sorry to add, that this calamitous fire has not been unattended with loss of human life. One of Mr Ducrow's female servants was suffocated in the flames and the body, dreadfully burned, was this morning dug out of the ruins.

It transpired that a cannon used in the previous night's performance had ignited the old wooden building. Almost the entire stud of fifty horses also perished with a total loss estimated at £30,000. Ducrow and his family narrowly escaped with their lives, but there was a tragic and unexpected postscript. The shock of this near-death experience proved too much for the circus owner and he had a mental breakdown. Unable to move or speak, he was removed to an asylum in Peckham, where he died a little over six months after the fire, a couple of weeks after the centenary of Philip Astley's birth, on 27 January 1842. It was assumed that insurmountable financial losses were the cause of Ducrow's distress but he left property valued at around £60,000 – nearly £6 million today. His family gave him a spectacular send-off and he was buried amid the hype and trappings of a film star in an exotic Egyptian-style mausoleum in Kensal Green Cemetery, West London. Ducrow was remembered as one of the greatest performers of his generation and clearly he thought so, too. The inscription on his self-designed mausoleum reads: 'This tomb was erected by genius for the reception of its own remains.'

Astley's Amphitheatre would hang on to the name of its charismatic founder for many more years and went on to further triumphs. A subsequent owner, William Cooke, had the idea of applying equestrian drama to Shakespeare's historical plays. Accordingly, for the first time ever, the hunchback King Richard III was seen on the stage surrounded by his staff on horseback. Encouraged by this success, Astley's applied the same technique to *Henry IV* and *Macbeth*. 'I will not assert that Shakespeare's plays thus converted into equestrian pieces satisfied all artistic conditions,' noted a critic, 'but when I look at the moral effect, I cannot but applaud the experiment.'

The fourth Astley's, under a new owner William Batty, was one of the best-equipped theatres in the country. Batty made his name on the touring circuit and one of his performers was a talented young black equestrian and rope-vaulter called William Darby, going by the stage name Pablo Fanque. Fanque went on to become the first black circus proprietor. The Beatles' song lyrics for 'Being for the Benefit of Mr Kite' are taken verbatim from a Pablo Fanque circus poster from 1843: Mr Kite was one of his performers. Fanque's own circus suffered terrible tragedy in 1848 when a gallery collapsed, killing his wife, who was working in the box office below.

In time the horses were replaced by more sensational acts, but many lamented the changing of the guard and thought some of the old magic was missing. A writer in *Once a Week* lamented in December 1862:

> If there was one place of entertainment – an institution it may be termed – more sacred to Londoners in particular, and provincialists in general, one more presumably probable to have withstood the changes of time and fashion, less likely to have succumbed to a novel and not very classical style of dramatic entertainment, that place most certainly was Astley's. For, though the remodelled theatre in Westminster Bridge Road is still associated with the name of its founder, yet an Astley's without horses is as yet simply a misnomer, a shadow without a substance.

But night after night, Astley's was packed, London's enthusiasm for the old venue unabated. For the city's poorest, each evening the grinding horrors of poverty and daily toil were temporarily suspended. In 1864 Charles Dickens, on one of his evening strolls to cool 'a boiling head', presented himself at the box-office and was told 'standing room only'. A clerk, recognising him, offered him the proprietor's box. The novelist preferred to walk away.

The final owner of Astley's Lambeth amphitheatre was 'Lord' George Sanger, who achieved a childhood ambition when he bought it from Batty's widow for £11,000. George ran the Westminster venue as Sanger's Amphitheatre for twenty-two years. His production of *Gulliver's Travels*, possibly the biggest show ever attempted by any circus manager before or since, featured a cast of 700 men, women and children plus thirteen elephants, nine camels and fifty-two horses along with a sprinkling of ostriches, emus, pelicans, deer, kangaroos, buffaloes, Brahmin bulls and lions.

By the end of the 1880s the old building was badly in need of repairs and it is days were numbered. On 4 March 1893 Sanger closed the doors for the last time and the amphitheatre was demolished.

In his lifetime Philip Astley inspired many imitators. In 1800 England had eight independent circuses; when he died there were twenty-one, nine in London alone. Within forty years of his death, what had started out in a field with a couple of nags bought at five pounds apiece at Smithfield market had grown into an international phenomenon. In 1787 the Englishman James Price sailed to Sweden and constructed Scandinavia's first circus in a field outside Stockholm. In 1805 the Latvian equestrian, Christoph de Bach, set up the first permanent circus in Vienna. In 1827 one of Astley's top riders, Jacques Tournaire, built Russia's first circus in St. Petersburg. Another French equestrian, Louis Soulier, took the circus to Constantinople and as far east as Japan. The young, tragic John Bill Ricketts built twelve circus buildings across America before the Atlantic took him.

Neither Philip Astley nor his son John reassumed control of the Amphitheatre Anglais in Paris. When Philip died, the vacant building in the Faubourg du Temple was acquired and renovated by his old employee, Antonio Franconi, and after extensive renovations reopened on 8 February 1817. Together with his sons, Laurent and Minette, Franconi established a Parisian circus dynasty of great fame and repute.

On 14 March 1826, a wayward firework landed in the drapery and Astley's beloved Paris circus was destroyed by fire. Antonio Franconi died just over ten years later at the great age of ninety-nine, still bearing a lion's teeth marks in his arm.

There was literally nowhere the circus was unwelcome. The Taylor's Ride to Brentford was the comedy act of the nineteenth century, a shamelessly recycled classic that never grew old. In America, under Barnum, Ringling and others, the big top generated a fascination that might have astonished Astley himself.

From the perspective of our age it is hard to grasp just how huge the circus once was. Before TV and cinema it was the world's most popular spectator event and, as we glorify footballers and actors today, the public once worshipped performers of the ring.

Philip Astley didn't invent clowns, or acrobats, or strongmen, or any of the other acts we associate with the circus. He was a horse-breaker without equal and a supremely talented equestrian, but he didn't begin the trend for trick-riding; that was already long established. He wasn't even the first person to ride around in a circle. Islington had a circular ride with seating long before Astley appeared on the scene and riding school instructors had been doing it for years. Circus historians point out that he probably wasn't the first to combine horsemanship with other variety acts. He didn't even invent the term 'circus' – that was Charles Dibdin's idea.

If Philip Astley originated so little, how does he deserve the title 'father of the modern circus'? His legacy rests not so much on what he invented himself as what he did with a performing culture that already existed, pushing its possibilities further than any of his rivals. And unlike all his bitter rivals, he endured. Without his drive, his ambition, his constant quest for growth, the circus wouldn't be what it is now. And of course there are many things he can call his own. He was the first man to put a clown in the ring and combine comedy with horsemanship. His Taylor's Ride routine is arguably the progenitor of all slapstick comedy. He gave the circus colour, sound, shape and smell. Some of the small details of his original circus have survived to an astonishing degree: the red, blue and gold of the British cavalry, the ringmaster's military coat and black riding boots, the music of military brass bands, the smell of sawdust, first used to cover the floor of his original amphitheatre near Westminster Bridge. Most of all, he gave the circus a beating heart, the forty-two-feet diameter ring, still the same in circuses all around the world. This was the crucible into which he put all of the different elements to create something new, in the process defining the modern circus as we know it.

The showmanship that brought in the public and built up his success was entirely his, too. He had a genius for understanding what the public wanted to see – how to 'catch John Bull'. In a highly class-conscious age, his shows broke down barriers and democratised entertainment. His adverts on the front page of *The Times* boasted that his shows attracted the 'Nobility and Gentry' and anyone else who could afford the basic sixpence for standing room. His rivals and imitators also contributed to the development of the early circus but it was Astley who triumphed in the end because of his skills as an impresario and by sheer force of character. A hundred years before P. T. Barnum, he set the bar in his profession, trailblazing advertising and promotional techniques including posters, publicity stunts and pre-show parades. But he never adopted the cheating practices of Barnum and others who followed. He was essentially an honest man who believed in giving his audience good value and his shows were always of the highest quality that he could possibly manage.

The English circus clown fraternity once observed an annual custom of laying a wreath on the grave of the greatest circus clown of all, Joseph 'Joey' Grimaldi. They still honour his memory today by meeting once a year for a memorial service for the man who is regarded as the founder of their art. There has never been anything like it to honour the memory of Philip Astley, but there was a time when his was one of the most famous graves in what is now the most famous cemetery in the world, the French capital's neo-Gothic Père-Lachaise. For over a century Astley's grave was a site of circus pilgrimage, but then people forgot all about the dead showman and his final resting place fell into neglect. At the time of writing the location of his grave is lost. Somewhere amidst the bones of Balzac, Chopin, Colette, Molière, Ernst, and Oscar Wilde, Astley still lies anonymous and neglected.[119] But then, circus folk never worried too much about leaving monuments behind them. They played, then they packed their bags and moved on. Their art was ephemeral, a here-today, gone-tomorrow affair and that is part of its charm.

Twenty years after the death of its founder, Charles Dickens described his own fond memories of Astley's Amphitheatre in *The Old Curiosity Shop*:

Dear, dear, what a place it looked, that Astley's; with all the paint, gilding, and looking-glass; the vague smell of horses suggestive of coming wonders; the curtain that hid such gorgeous mysteries; the

---

119 According to a guide book written in 1824, Philip Astley's grave was near to and possibly even adjacent to that of the composer Monsigny. It became 'lost' sometime in the 1930s or 1940s and no-one had thought to record the location.

clean white sawdust down in the circus; the company coming in and taking their places; the fiddlers looking carelessly up at them while they tuned their instruments, as if they didn't want the play to begin, and knew it all beforehand! What a glow was that, which burst upon them all, when that long, clear, brilliant row of lights came slowly up; and what the feverish excitement when the little bell rang and the music began in good earnest, with strong parts for the drums, and sweet effects for the triangles!

… Then the play itself! the horses which little Jacob believed from the first to be alive, and the ladies and gentlemen of whose reality he could be by no means persuaded, having never seen or heard anything at all like them – the firing, which made Barbara wink – the forlorn lady, who made her cry – the tyrant, who made her tremble – the man who sang the song with the lady's-maid and danced the chorus, who made her laugh – the pony who reared up on his hind-legs when he saw the murderer, and wouldn't hear of walking on all fours again until he was taken into custody – the clown who ventured on such familiarities with the military man in boots – the lady who jumped over the nine-and-twenty ribbons and came down safe upon the horse's back – everything was delightful, splendid, and surprising!

Not a bad advertisement. Big Philip would have loved it.

EPILOGUE

In 2017, as far as Astley's legacy is concerned, things were looking up. The circus was big news again, thanks to the success of the Hugh Jackman-led film *The Greatest Showman*. The film, like the circus impresario P. T. Barnum on whose life it is based, dupes its viewers, glossing over the showman's cruelty and racism.[120] 2018 was the year we observed the 250th anniversary of Philip Astley's first show. Circuses across the world celebrated the event and there were tributes and collaborations dedicated to the 'father of the circus' from Brazil to Monte Carlo. In Lambeth, a blue plaque was unveiled at the spot where he staked out his first ring on a muddy field at Halfpenny Hatch, now the site of a pub and an electrical substation near to Waterloo Underground. On the South Bank, a flagstone was laid in the garden of St. Thomas Hospital on the exact site of the entrance to the first circus amphitheatre.

---

120 Barnum was four years old when Philip Astley died. He was a bankrupt shop worker when he purchased a blind, almost completely paralysed 80-year-old black woman named Joice Heth from a failed showman. He reinvented her as the 160-year-old 'Nanny' of George Washington. On finding that Heth had a weakness for alcohol, Barnum got her drunk so that he could remove all her teeth to make her look older. His exploitation of Heth was the springboard to fame and wealth. She lived barely a year, but long enough to recoup Barnum's investment many times over. He made more money from her death, charging the public 50 cents each to attend her public autopsy. The profits allowed him to set up his infamous Barnum's American Museum, which became the cornerstone of his circus empire.

Astley's home town of Newcastle-under-Lyme was ablaze with celebrations. There were circus skills workshops, museum and street exhibitions, film showings, school poetry competitions, subway murals, a stage play, a summer *Astleyfest* with circus performances, horse shows and military displays, an Astley ale, a town-centre shopping mall named after him; you almost couldn't move without bumping into an Astley-themed event. There is now the UK's first permanent monument to Astley, a fourteen-foot high set of sculptures on the road into town, illustrating the original ringmaster flanked by two horses. There is a hoped-for life-size statue of Philip Astley on horseback in the town centre, beneath the Guildhall tower clock donated by his great-nephew, James Astley Hall. Inexplicably, a statue of Philip Astley cast in bronze resin for the 250th anniversary of his birth in 1992 remains largely hidden from view in a local school for the performing arts.

For two hundred and fifty years, however, the circus was strangely reluctant to capitalise on its founding father. P. T. Barnum is remembered for his showmanship but the giant on whose shoulders he stood was a well-kept secret known only to the circus fraternity. Even Philip Astley's birthplace was bewilderingly slow to reclaim its most illustrious son. On the streets of Newcastle-under-Lyme, until very recently his name would elicit a shrug or a blank look. If it hadn't been for the doggedness of two professional performers who live in Newcastle it probably would have stayed that way.

Ask any circophile about their first exposure to the circus and they will be able to recall it in detail. For Fred Yoxall it was when he was four years old and he was sent on an errand to his local butcher's. He was perplexed to see a picture of an elephant in the window. He thought they were selling elephant meat. He raced home to tell his mother who explained that it was a poster for the visiting Chapman's circus. Fred was taken to see it and was captivated; from then on regular trips to Blackpool Tower Circus were the highlight of his year. Later, in school, he was amazed to read that the first circus was created by someone born just a few miles down the road from where Fred lived. That was the beginning of a lifetime's obsession, a journey that, for his family, would span decades and result in more frustration than they ever could have imagined possible.

Like Philip Astley, Fred developed a thirst for travel and adventure, what Barnum called life beyond 'the ordinary trade', and resolved to make the circus his life. From his home town, Sandbach, the young boy would abscond to the nearby winter headquarters of Gandey's Circus in Brereton where he would listen to the old showmen's tales. In the circus, everyone's willing to give you their time and pass on a new skill and in old Bob Gandey he couldn't have wished for a better mentor. By the time national service called, Fred was already putting on his own small shows. When he left the army he was taken on by Gandey's and, as The Great Yoxani, he swung on the trapeze, clowned, had a dog and monkey act and, later, performed magic tricks. In those early days, like his hero Astley, Fred too had a safety net, a 'proper' job. His mother didn't like the direction her son was heading and insisted he take up an apprenticeship; he chose cabinet making. She didn't know, no-one knew, that Fred was secretly following in Philip Astley's footsteps.

He decided to concentrate on magic and illusion and struck out on his own. He met 18-year old farmer's daughter Connie and it was love at first sight, especially when he realised she was just the right size to fit in his magic boxes. In 1961 he married the girl he made disappear twice nightly and they became a family act, touring as The Great Yoxanis. In 1962 there was a name and nationality change when their agent persuaded them that they might break into the big time as Van Buren and Greta, 'Holland's greatest magicians'. Together, they created a spectacular show including their signature performance, the Vanishing Motorcycle and Rider, the only magic act in the world performed while completely surrounded by the audience. Fred and Connie travelled the world, creating bewitching, baffling illusions working in circus, theatre, cabaret and on television until their retirement in 1997.

If there is one thing you probably already knew about the history of the circus it is that it was a family affair, and so it was with the Van Burens. Fred and Connie's son Andrew was born in Newcastle-under-Lyme, although he jokes that he was actually born inside a circus trunk while his parents trotted the globe, perfecting their legendary vanishing motorbike act. Steeped in the circus arts as a child, he was sent to sleep each night by the hum of the circus generator. Today Andrew Van Buren is an internationally renowned trick-cyclist, juggler, escapologist, magician and illusionist. Like his parents, he is among the lucky few to have achieved worldwide fame and relative fortune through his craft. Fittingly, the boy from North Staffordshire is also the UK's pre-eminent plate spinner. You may know him from his TV appearances on the likes of *The Generation Game* and *Ant & Dec's Saturday Night Takeaway*, but the rewards of the live stage performance are still his biggest thrill.

Thanks to his parents, Andrew learned to love the circus, and everything there was to know about his father's hero. Andrew, too, wondered why Philip Astley's achievements were largely lost to history. The Van Burens made it their personal mission to try to restore his name and legacy. In 1981 Newcastle-under-Lyme council invited Fred to give them some advice on organising their town carnival. He suggested a Philip Astley and circus theme. Fred's proposal met a unanimous response: 'Who?' Even in his birthplace, Astley's name meant nothing. Reluctantly, they took up Fred's idea and the 1982 carnival was the first ever Astley-themed event. It was a short-lived success, then civic enthusiasm for Astley just as quickly evaporated.

In 1992 they tried again. For the 250th anniversary of Astley's birth, at considerable personal expense, Fred and

Andrew commissioned a bronze resin life-size statue of the ringmaster, hoping to find a permanent public site for it, then cajoled the local authority into running a series of circus-inspired events through the summer. It was a huge triumph, but not for the Van Burens. Fred and Andrew were cut out of the picture, their links to the anniversary celebrations erased. Tragically, as far as they were concerned, the people who took the credit for the event cared nothing for Astley's legacy. They were left with a statue that no-one wanted and his name already fading from public memory. Out of pocket, betrayed and exhausted, the Van Burens walked away from Philip Astley. In 1993 his homeless statue was placed in a shipping container at Gandey's Circus winter quarters and locked away, presumably for good.

In 2009, during a break from international tours with his partner Allyson, Andrew had a crazy idea. In nine years' time it would be the 250th anniversary of Astley's first equestrian show at Halfpenny Hatch. He decided to gamble on one last attempt to persuade his hometown to recognise their own 'father of the circus'. He realised just how much of an uphill struggle he was facing when the local newspaper ran an article about circus history and somehow failed to mention Astley's name. Andrew kept the show on track, tirelessly shouting his hero's achievements from the rooftops, badgering anyone who might listen for support. Fred worried for his son's health, concerned that he was trying to keep too many plates spinning, but it was third time lucky. A better-informed Newcastle took Van Buren's project, and Philip Astley, to their hearts. Local organisations joined in to form The Philip Astley Project and they spread the word creating collaborations and celebrations around the world.

I met Andrew and Fred in their workshop and private museum of circus and showbiz memorabilia. Fred's mother would have been delighted to know that her son's carpentry apprenticeship was not wasted. I am surrounded by fabulous, mysterious stage props hand-made by Fred. There are models of fairground attractions exquisitely crafted from recycled scraps, hundreds of posters and show bills, a library of showbiz memoirs, magician's and juggler's paraphernalia of every conceivable shape and size. This, they are keen to tell me, is just a fraction of their collection.

Fred, eighty-six years old and as keen as ever to put on a show, gives me a private performance. As Andrew pulls some levers, Fred steps into a beautiful wooden 'time machine' and vanishes, then reappears, just three feet in front of my nose. I let the side down by asking how it is done. 'It is magic,' Andrew deadpans. Fred is encyclopaedic in his knowledge of British variety from the 1930s onwards. He worked among, and is still friends with, some of the biggest names in British stage and TV. The walls of his home are crammed with photos of the Van Burens with showbiz royalty and actual royalty. Andrew is still searching for old Astley memorabilia and suspects there is more out there in private hands: he has even heard someone has a pair of big Philip's riding boots. He fears that more Astley artefacts have been deliberately destroyed. Retired showground people, it seems, guard their intellectual property so suspiciously that they would rather trash their old equipment than let it fall into rival hands. Andrew says he once saw a bonfire made from priceless circus posters.

I see now how they made Astley's rebirth happen, because it is impossible not be infected by their enthusiasm. It had been a gruelling and expensive journey (eventually there was support from the Heritage Lottery Fund, but at the start it was all bankrolled by Andrew) but he admits that the 250th anniversary year of 2018 was bigger and better than he could have imagined. A personal highlight was when he met Prince Albert and Princess Stephanie and together they unveiled a plaque to Philip Astley in Monte Carlo. I am surprised to learn that the Principality's annual international festival is to the circus world what the Oscars are to the film industry and is broadcast almost everywhere except the UK.

Andrew points out: 'Of course the real anniversary is 2020, because that's 250 years from when Astley put a clown in his ring alongside his equestrian show and it became a proper circus.' He hopes local civic leaders have learned their lesson and Astley won't be just as quickly forgotten. At the moment it is looking good, but politicians come and go. Plans for the life-size equestrian statue are on hold.

Today, Newcastle's high street struggles, just like most other English market town centres, to survive the ravages of digital commerce and retail park superstores. As much as anything, Andrew is motivated by his determination to help his local community reinvent itself as a tourist attraction. His dreams for the future include a local centre of excellence for circus arts and a circus museum and more, making Astley's home town an ambassadorial home for circus, learning and enlightenment. Andrew says that Philip Astley could be Newcastle's Shakespeare.

Meanwhile, he has another more immediate mission, to locate and mark Philip and John Astley's final resting place in Paris. 'We're fairly sure we know the exact spot, we just need to prove it'. As I leave he says; 'That blockbuster film, it should have been about Astley, not Barnum, shouldn't it?' That really would be the greatest show on earth.

APPENDIX I

Books written by Philip Astley:

Astley's Method of Riding, a Preventative of Accidents on Horseback (1773)
The Modern Riding-master (1774)
Natural Magic, or Physical Amusements Revealed (1785)
A Description and Historical Account of the Places now the Theatre of War in the Low Countries (1794)
Remarks on the Profession and Duty of a Soldier (1794)
A System of Equestrian Education (1801)
Astley's Projects in his Management of the Horse (1804)

APPENDIX II

One of the earliest surviving advertisements for an Astley's performance, from 1772:

Horsemanship and New Feats of Activity, This and every evening at six, Mr and Mrs Astley, Mrs Griffiths, Costmethopila, and a young Gentleman, will exhibit several extraordinary feats on one, two, three, and four horses, at the foot of Westminster Bridge.

These feats of activity are in number upwards of fifty; to which is added the new French piece, the different characters by Mr Astley, Griffiths, Costmethopila, &c. Each will be dressed and mounted on droll horses.

Between the acts of horsemanship, a young gentleman will exhibit several pleasing heavy balances, particularly this night, with a young Lady nine years old, never performed before in Europe; after which Mr Astley will carry her on his head in a manner different from all others. Mrs Astley will likewise perform with two horses in the same manner as she did before their Majesties of England and France, being the only one of her sex that ever had that honour. The doors to be opened at five, and begin at six o'clock. A commodious gallery, 120 feet long, is fitted up in an elegant manner. Admittance there as usual.

N.B. Mr Astley will display the broad-sword, also ride on a single horse, with one foot on the saddle, the other on his head, and every other feat which can be exhibited by any other. With an addition of twenty extraordinary feats, such as riding on full speed, with his head on a common pint pot, at the rate of twelve miles an hour, &c.

To specify the particulars of Mr Astley's performance would fill this side of paper, therefore please ask for a bill at the door, and see that the number of fifty feats are performed, Mr Astley having placed them in acts as the performance is exhibited. The amazing little Military Horse, which fires a pistol at the word of command, will this night exhibit upwards of twenty feats in a manner far superior to any other, and meets with the greatest applause.

Another handbill printed fourteen years later. By 1786, Philip's son John is the star attraction:

This evening, Young Astley will display His astonishing equestrian exercises, In three parts, on several Horses, among which are his still vaulting. An Exercise never attempted by any Performer whatever; the great Agility, strength, and Dexterity, exhibited in this Exercise, has been the Admiration of the principal Nobility of this and Other-Countries. Exercises on Two Horses, Among which are various curious Attitudes, dancing, ballancing, and flying over the Garter and Stick, at the same Instant jumping at least twelve Feet perpendicular from the Ground, and sixteen Feet horizontally. Extraordinary Exertions on a single Horse, Consisting of a new Hornpipe; a comic Attitude; a Peasant Dance, &c. &c. - The Equestrian Exercises of Young Astley, are peculiar to himself, and his Abilities so well known, that they need no Encomiums; the Minuet danced by two Horses, the Entry of Horses, and the Evolutions by the whole Troop; which will conclude with the Representation of light Troops dispersed, as in real Action, will also be presented every Evening this Week. In the Intervals of the Equestrian Exercises, an Entertainment of Singing and Dancing, called, The Double Jealousy; Or, A Trip to Dover. Singers, Mr Connell, Mr Johannot, Mr Birkitt, Mrs Nathan, Mrs Hilliard, and Miss Platel. The Royal and only troop of female Rope-Dancers, in the world, Will perform their surprising Exercises. The Venetian Exercises of Strength, By nine capital performers. Also, a Musical Entertainment, of Singing and Dancing, called, The Poor Cobler. Singers, Mr Decastro, Mr Fox, Mr Carlo, Mr Miller, Mrs Nathan, and Mrs Woodman. The Whole to conclude with a Supurb Entertainment, called, Neptune's Friendship; Or, Harlequin crowned in the Temple of the Sun. The Music, Dances, Dresses, Decorations, &c. entirely new. Doors to be opened at Half past Five, and to begin at Half past Six precisely. Box 3s. - Pit 2s. - Gall. 1s. - Side Gall. 6d. N. B. Entertainments at Astley's will be varied every Week. Places for the Boxes to be taken of Mr Smith, at the amphitheatre Ladies and Gentlemen instructed to ride.

APPENDIX III

From *Sketches by Boz* by Charles Dickens, 1836:

There is no place which recalls so strongly our recollections of childhood as Astley's. It was not a 'Royal Amphitheatre' in those days, nor had Ducrow arisen to shed the light of classic taste and portable gas over the sawdust of the circus; but the whole character of the place was the same, the pieces were the same, the clown's jokes were the same, the riding-masters were equally grand, the comic performers equally witty, the tragedians equally hoarse, and the 'highly-trained chargers' equally spirited. Astley's has altered for the better – we have changed for the worse. Our histrionic taste is gone, and with shame we confess, that we are far more delighted and amused with the audience, than with the pageantry we once so highly appreciated.

We like to watch a regular Astley's party in the Easter or Midsummer holidays – pa and ma, and nine or ten children, varying from five foot six to two foot eleven: from fourteen years of age to four. We had just taken our seat in one of the boxes, in the centre of the house, the other night, when the next was occupied by just such a party as we should have attempted to describe, had we depicted our BEAU IDEAL of a group of Astley's visitors... The play began, and the interest of the little boys knew no bounds. Pa was clearly interested too, although he very unsuccessfully endeavoured to look as if he wasn't. As for ma, she was perfectly overcome by the drollery of the principal comedian, and laughed till every one of the immense bows on her ample cap trembled, at which the governess peeped out from behind the pillar again, and whenever she could catch ma's eye, put her handkerchief to her mouth, and appeared, as in duty bound, to be in convulsions of laughter also. Then when the man in the splendid armour vowed to rescue the lady or perish in the attempt, the little boys applauded vehemently, especially one little fellow who was apparently on a visit to the family, and had been carrying on a child's flirtation, the whole evening, with a small coquette of twelve years old, who looked like a model of her mamma on a reduced scale; and who, in common with the other little girls (who generally speaking have even more coquettishness about them than much older ones), looked very properly shocked, when the knight's squire kissed the princess's confidential chambermaid.

When the scenes in the circle commenced, the children were more delighted than ever; and the wish to see what was going forward, completely conquering pa's dignity, he stood up in the box, and applauded as loudly as any of them...

We defy anyone who has been to Astley's two or three times, and is consequently capable of appreciating the perseverance with which precisely the same jokes are repeated night after night, and season after season, not to be amused with one part of the performances at least - we mean the scenes in the circle. For ourself, we know that when the hoop, composed of jets of gas, is let down, the curtain drawn up for the convenience of the half-price on their ejectment from the ring, the orange-peel cleared away, and the sawdust shaken, with mathematical precision, into a complete circle, we feel as much enlivened as the youngest child present; and actually join in the laugh which follows the clown's shrill shout of 'Here we are!' just for old acquaintance' sake. Nor can we quite divest ourself of our old feeling of reverence for the riding-master, who follows the clown with a long whip in his hand, and bows to the audience with graceful dignity. He is none of your second-rate riding-masters in nankeen dressing-gowns, with brown frogs, but the regular gentleman-attendant on the principal riders, who always wears a military uniform with a table-cloth inside the breast of the coat, in which costume he forcibly reminds one of a fowl trussed for roasting. He is - but why should we attempt to describe that of which no description can convey an adequate idea? Everybody knows the man, and everybody remembers his polished boots, his graceful demeanour, stiff, as some misjudging persons have in their jealousy considered it, and the splendid head of black hair, parted high on the forehead, to impart to the countenance an appearance of deep thought and poetic melancholy. His soft and pleasing voice, too, is in perfect unison with his noble bearing, as he humours the clown by indulging in a little badinage; and the striking recollection of his own dignity, with which he exclaims, 'Now, sir, if you please, inquire for Miss Woolford, sir,' can never be forgotten. The graceful air, too, with which he introduces Miss Woolford into the arena, and, after assisting her to the saddle, follows her fairy courser round the circle, can never fail to create a deep impression in the bosom of every female servant present.

When Miss Woolford, and the horse, and the orchestra, all stop together to take breath, he urbanely takes part in some such dialogue as the following (commenced by the clown): 'I say, sir!' - 'Well, sir?' (it is always conducted in the politest manner.) – 'Did you ever happen to hear I was in the army, sir?' – 'No, sir.' – 'Oh, yes, sir – I can go through my exercise, sir.' – 'Indeed, sir!' – 'Shall I do it now, sir?' – 'If you please, sir; come, sir – make haste' (a cut with the long whip, and 'Ha' done now – I don't like it,' from the clown). Here the clown throws himself on the ground, and goes through a variety of gymnastic convulsions, doubling himself up, and untying himself again, and making himself look very like a man in the most hopeless extreme of human agony, to the vociferous delight of the gallery, until he is interrupted by a second cut from the long whip, and a request to see 'what Miss Woolford's stopping for?' On which, to the inexpressible mirth of the gallery, he exclaims, 'Now, Miss Woolford, what can I come for to go, for to fetch, for to bring, for to carry, for to do, for you, ma'am?' On the lady's announcing with a sweet smile that she wants the two flags, they are, with sundry grimaces, procured and handed up; the clown facetiously observing after the performance of the latter ceremony - 'He, he, oh! I say, sir, Miss Woolford knows me; she smiled at me.' Another cut from the whip, a burst from the orchestra, a start from the horse, and round goes Miss Woolford again on her graceful performance, to the delight of every member of the audience, young or old. The next pause affords an opportunity for similar witticisms, the only additional fun being that of the clown making ludicrous grimaces at the riding-master every time his back is turned; and finally quitting the circle by jumping over his head, having previously directed his attention another way.

Did any of our readers ever notice the class of people, who hang about the stage-doors of our minor theatres in the daytime? You will rarely pass one of these entrances without seeing a group of three or four men conversing on the pavement, with an indescribable public-house-parlour swagger, and a kind of conscious air, peculiar to people of this description. They always seem to think they are exhibiting; the lamps are ever before them. That young fellow in the faded brown coat, and very full light green trousers, pulls down the wristbands of his check shirt, as ostentatiously as if it were of the finest linen, and cocks the white hat of the summer- before-last as knowingly over his right eye, as if it were a purchase of yesterday. Look at the dirty white Berlin gloves, and the cheap silk handkerchief stuck in the bosom of his threadbare coat. Is it possible to see him for an instant, and not come to the conclusion that he is the walking gentleman who wears a blue surtout, clean collar, and white trousers, for half an hour, and then shrinks into his worn-out scanty clothes: who has to boast night after night of his splendid fortune, with the painful consciousness of a pound a-week and his boots to find; to talk of his father's mansion in the country, with a dreary recollection of his own two-pair back, in the New Cut; and to be envied and flattered as the favoured lover of a rich heiress, remembering all the while that the ex-dancer at home is in the family way, and out of an engagement?

Next to him, perhaps, you will see a thin pale man, with a very long face, in a suit of shining black, thoughtfully knocking that part of his boot which once had a heel, with an ash stick. He is the man who does the heavy business, such as prosy fathers, virtuous servants, curates, landlords, and so forth.

By the way, talking of fathers, we should very much like to see some piece in which all the dramatis personae were orphans. Fathers are invariably great nuisances on the stage, and always have to give the hero or heroine a long explanation of what was done before the curtain rose, usually commencing with 'It is now nineteen years, my dear child, since your blessed mother (here the old villain's voice falters) confided you to my charge. You were then an infant,' &c., &c. Or else they have to discover, all of a sudden, that somebody whom they have been in constant communication with, during three long acts, without the slightest suspicion, is their own child: in which case they exclaim, 'Ah! what do I see? This bracelet! That smile! These documents! Those eyes! Can I believe my senses? - It must be! – Yes – it is, it is my child!' – 'My father!' exclaims the child; and they fall into each other's arms, and look over each other's shoulders, and the audience give three rounds of applause.

To return from this digression, we were about to say, that these are the sort of people whom you see talking, and attitudinising, outside the stage-doors of our minor theatres. At Astley's they are always more numerous than at any other place. There is generally a groom or two, sitting on the window-sill, and two or three dirty shabby-genteel men in checked neckerchiefs, and sallow linen, lounging about, and carrying, perhaps, under one arm, a pair of stage shoes badly wrapped up in a piece of old newspaper.

Some years ago we used to stand looking, open-mouthed, at these men, with a feeling of mysterious curiosity, the very recollection of which provokes a smile at the moment we are writing. We could not believe that the beings of light and elegance, in milk-white tunics, salmon-coloured legs, and blue scarfs, who flitted on sleek cream-coloured horses before our eyes at night, with all the aid of lights, music, and artificial flowers, could be the pale, dissipated-looking creatures we beheld by day.

We can hardly believe it now. Of the lower class of actors we have seen something, and it requires no great exercise of imagination to identify the walking gentleman with the 'dirty swell,' the comic singer with the public-house chairman, or the leading tragedian with drunkenness and distress; but these other men are mysterious beings, never seen out of the ring, never beheld but in the costume of gods and sylphs. With the exception of Ducrow, who can scarcely be classed among them, who ever knew a rider at Astley's, or saw him but on horseback? Can our friend in the military uniform ever appear in threadbare attire, or descend to the comparatively un-wadded costume of every-day life? Impossible! We cannot – we will not – believe it.

William Makepiece Thackeray also wrote about Astley's in his novel *The Newcomes: Memoirs of a Most Respectable Family*, published in 1856:

Who was it that took the children to Astley's but Uncle Newcome? I saw him there in the midst of a cluster of these little people, all children together. He laughed, delighted at Mr Merriman's jokes in the ring. He beheld the *Battle of Waterloo* with breathless interest, and was amazed - yes, amazed, by Jove, sir! – at the prodigious likeness of the principal actor to the Emperor Napoleon... The little girls, Sir Brian's daughters, holding each by a finger of his hands, and younger Masters Alfred and Edward clapping and hurraing by his side; while Mr Clive and Miss Ethel sat in the back of the box enjoying the scene... It did one good to hear the colonel's honest laugh at the clown's jokes, and to see the tenderness and simplicity with which he watched over this happy brood of young ones.

APPENDIX IV

Astley's Amphitheatre at Westminster Bridge, more or less as it stood towards the end of his life, is described in Allen's *History of Surrey*, published in 1830:

The front of the theatre, which is plain and of brick, stuccoed, stands laterally with the houses in Bridge Road, the access to the back part of the premises being in Stangate Street. There is a plain wooden portico, the depth of which corresponds with the width of the pavement. In front of this portico is the royal arms. Within the pediment in front of the building is 'Astley's' in raised letters, and in the front of the portico, in a similar style, 'Royal Amphitheatre.' Beneath this portico are the entrances to the boxes and pit; the gallery entrance is lower down the road, and separated from the front of the theatre by several houses. The boxes are approached by a plain staircase, at the head of which is a handsome lobby. The form of the auditory is elliptical and is lighted by a very large cut-glass lustre and chandeliers with bell-lamps; gas is the medium of illumination used all over the premises. There is one continued row or tier of boxes round the auditory, above the central part of which is the gallery; and there is a half tier of upper boxes on each side, with slips over them. The floor of the ride within the auditory is earth and sawdust, where a ring or circle, forty-four feet in diameter, is bounded by a boarded enclosure about four feet in height, the curve of which next the stage forms the outline of the orchestra, and the remainder that of the pit, behind which is an extensive lobby and a box for refreshments. The proscenium is large and movable – for the convenience of widening and heightening the stage, which is, perhaps, the largest and most convenient in London – and is terminated by immense platforms, or floors, rising above each other, and extending the whole width of the stage. These are exceedingly massive and strong. The horsemen gallop and skirmish over them, and they will admit a carriage, equal in size and weight to a mail coach, to be driven across them. They are, notwithstanding, so constructed as to be placed and removed in a short space of time by manual labour and mechanism.

PICTURE CREDITS

SELECT BIBLIOGRAPHY

Ackroyd, Peter (1996), *Blake*

Allen, Thomas (1827), *The History and Antiquities of the Parish of Lambeth*

Angelo, Henry (2010), *Reminiscences of Henry Angelo*

Arundell, Dennis (1978), *The Story of Sadler's Wells 1683-1977*

Bemrose, Paul (1992), *Circus Genius; Tribute to Philip Astley*

Broadbent, R. J. (1908), *Annals of the Liverpool Stage from the Earliest Period to the Present Time*

Cannon, Richard (1836), *Historical Record of the Fifteenth, Or the King's Regiment of Light Dragoons*

Cross, Anthony (2007), *By the Banks of the Neva*

DeCastro, Jacob (1824), *The Memoirs of J. DeCastro, Comedian*

Dibdin, Charles (1956), *Professional & Literary Memoirs of Charles Dibdin the Younger*

Disher, Maurice Willson (1937), *Greatest Show on Earth*

Frost, Thomas (1875), *The Old Showmen and the Old London Fairs*

Gibberd, Graham (1992), *On Lambeth Marsh: The South Bank and Waterloo*

Green, John C. (2011), *Theatre in Dublin, 1745-1820*

Highfill Philip H. and Burnim, Kalman A. (2006), *A Biographical Dictionary of Actors, Actresses, Musicians, Dancers, Managers & Other Stage Personnel in London, 1660-1800*

Holmes, Richard (2001), *Redcoat: The British Soldier in the Age of Horse and Musket*

Kennedy, Dennis (2010), *The Oxford Companion to Theatre and Performance*

Kotar, S. L. and Gessler, J.E. (2011), *The Rise of the American Circus, 1716 - 1899*

Kwint, Marius (1994), *Astley's Amphitheatre and the Early Circus in England, 1768-1830*

Mattfeld, Dr Monica (2013), *Undaunted All He Views: The Gibraltar Charger, Astley's Amphitheatre and Masculine Performance*

Mayes, Stanley (2008), *The Great Belzoni*

Mendoza, Daniel (1792), *The Art of Boxing*

Moody, Jane (2000), *Illegitimate Theatre in London, 1770–1840*

Murray, Marian (1956), *Circus! From Rome to Ringling*

Ó Grada, Diarmud (2015), *Georgian Dublin: The Forces That Shaped the City*

Raymond, George (2018), *Memoirs of Robert William Elliston*

Savory, Sir Reginald (2009), *His Britannic Majesty's Army in Germany during the Seven Years War*

Saxon, A. H. (1978), *The Life and Art of Andrew Ducrow and the Romantic Age of the English Circus*

Simms, R. (1894), *Bibliotheca Staffordiensis*

Simon, Linda (2014), *The Greatest Shows On Earth: A History of the Circus*

Speaight, George (1981), *History of the Circus*

Stoddart, Helen (2000), *Rings of Desire: Circus History and Representation*

Stott, Andrew McConnell (2010), *The Pantomime Life of Joseph Grimaldi: Laughter, Madness and the Story of Britain's Greatest Comedian*

Swindells, Julia and Taylor, David Francis (2018), *The Oxford Handbook of the Georgian Theatre 1737–1832*

Thornbury, Walter (1878), *Old and New London, Volume 6*

Van Buren, Andrew (2010), *The Van Buren Story* (DVD)

INDEX

performance in the ring 57–58;
opens at Westminster Bridge
66–67; and King George III
72, 104, 142, 232; as author
13, 79, 135–136, 234; at
Fontainebleau 72–73; in
France 73, 79, 89, 116–125,
185–187; and magic tricks
13, 82–83, 135–136; and
licensing laws 85, 88, 107–109,
146–147, 233–234; in
Bridewell prison 88–89; dances
named after him 90; fixes
size of circus ring 92; wild
animals 93–96; retires from
trick-riding 98; in Austria 104;
and Charles Hughes 75–76,
105–106, 129, 183; on tour
62, 89, 112–114, 128, 134;
building work 10, 126–127,
147, 181–182, 190–191,
209; Versailles 116–119;
malapropisms 118, 153 ;
and Amphitheatre Anglais
119, 122–125; and human
'freaks' 138; and hippodrama
127–129, 193, 244–245;
and floating bath 130; and
balloons 131–135; and William
Blake 148–150; accent 153;
treatment of animals 161;
relations with employees
155–160, 162–163; thrift 91,
163; sense of humour 154,
157; and music 160; alleged
illiteracy 154; generosity 157,
177, 239; patriotism 42, 71,
116, 155, 183, 229; in Dublin
89, 169–170, 208–230; and
fireworks 142, 169–170, 188,
232; re-enlists for army 175;

injuries and ill health 68, 70,
98, 130, 170; and fires 180,
188; house arrest and escape
187; and death of Patty 187;
work ethic 12, 181, 191; and
Daniel Mendoza 220–222; and
Irish nationalism 226–229;
spying 229; and Olympic
Pavilion 235–237, 240; death
241; will 242–243, 247; legacy
252–258, 260–263
Astley, Sarah 24, 232
Astley's Amphitheatre (London)
96–98, 103, 109, 133, 150,
174, 180, 183, 189, 233,
247–252 (Dublin) 210, 220,
225
Astley's Jews 162
Astley's Prize Wherry 233
Astley's Riding School 56, 60,
62, 68, 75, 93, 108
America 17–18, 22, 29, 114,
116, 200–205
Augusta, Princess 91
Austen, Jane 13, 100, 184

Bagnigge Wells 20
ballooning 131–135
Bates, Jacob 17–18
Barnum, PT 159, 205, 25–255,
258–259, 263
Bartholomew Fair 51
Bastille, storming of 140,
171–174, 219
Bath 80, 95, 113, 248
bathing machines 130
Batty, William 251
Bedlam 48–49, 167
Belzoni, Giovanni 192, 238
benefit performances 106, 134,
157, 181, 191, 221, 251

Also available from Amberley Publishing

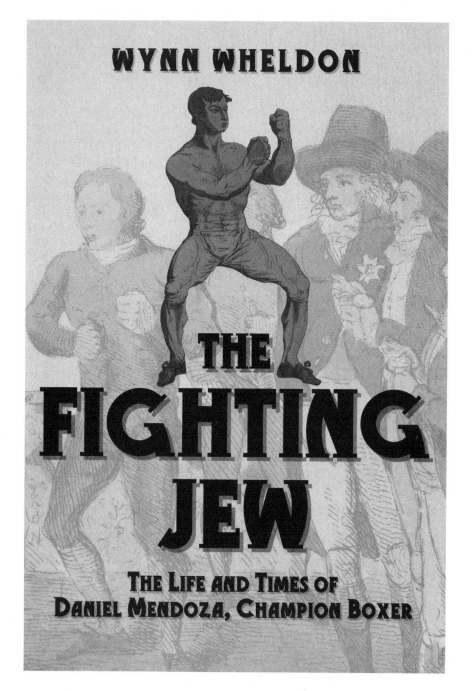

WYNN WHELDON

THE
FIGHTING
JEW

THE LIFE AND TIMES OF
DANIEL MENDOZA, CHAMPION BOXER

Available from all good bookshops or to order direct
Please call **01453-847-800**
www.amberley-books.com